# ADOLESCENCE, DISCRIMINATION, AND THE LAW

# Adolescence, Discrimination, and the Law

*Addressing Dramatic Shifts in Equality Jurisprudence*

Roger J. R. Levesque

NEW YORK UNIVERSITY PRESS
*New York and London*

NEW YORK UNIVERSITY PRESS
New York and London
www.nyupress.org

References to Internet websites (URLs) were accurate at the time of writing. Neither the author nor New York University Press is responsible for URLs that may have expired or changed since the manuscript was prepared.

Library of Congress Cataloging-in-Publication Data
Levesque, Roger J. R.
Adolescence, discrimination, and the law : addressing dramatic shifts in equality jurisprudence / Roger J. R. Levesque.
pages cm  Includes bibliographical references and index.
ISBN 978-1-4798-1558-6 (cl : alk. paper)
1. Adolescence—Social aspects—United States. 2. Age discrimination—United States. 3. Teenagers--United States—Civil rights. 4. Criminal justice, Administration of—United States. I. Title.
HQ796.L3475   2015
305.2350973—dc23    2014045878

New York University Press books are printed on acid-free paper, and their binding materials are chosen for strength and durability. We strive to use environmentally responsible suppliers and materials to the greatest extent possible in publishing our books.

Manufactured in the United States of America

10 9 8 7 6 5 4 3 2 1

Also available as an ebook

*For*

*Mom and Dad*

*Your sacrifices, support, and guidance will always be appreciated.*

# CONTENTS

# ACKNOWLEDGMENTS

This book would not have been possible without the encouragement and guidance of Jennifer Hammer, senior editor at New York University Press. Several years ago, she suggested that there was a need for a thoughtful book that addressed adolescents' rights in relation to discrimination. I was very intrigued by the topic, but it took me a long time to get a manuscript to her. Once I did, though, she quickly transformed it by obtaining incredibly helpful and insightful external reviews and even providing her own thorough edits of multiple drafts. I could not have been more pleased with her stewardship. I always was impressed by her care, dedication, and high standards. Working with her constantly reminded me of how wonderful it is to work with a press that really develops books and plays a critical role in both the creation and dissemination of knowledge.

I also would like to thank two professors, Alan Tomkins and Gary Melton, both of whom supported me while I was a postdoctoral fellow at the University of Nebraska's Psychology and Law Program about twenty years ago. At that time, Alan introduced me to empirical research on discrimination and the way it could influence legal systems. I was fascinated by that research and always wanted to write about it. About two years ago, Gary helped create a sense of urgency as he invited me to give a talk on youth's civil rights at one of his conferences in South Carolina. That invitation prompted me to think through more clearly what the legal system could do, and how it could benefit from our understanding of adolescence and the nature of discrimination. I cannot thank Alan and Gary enough for always finding ways to encourage me and support the work I do.

I also would like to acknowledge my students and colleagues at Indiana University and elsewhere. I benefited tremendously from discussing adolescents' rights with undergraduate students who were introduced to the study of law for the first time. They helped me focus on key issues and think through why they were important. I also learned much from law students who had entirely different views of the legal system and what it could accomplish. I am particularly grateful to Julie Spain, Maurer Law class of 2014, for reading and commenting on the first few chapters. Cher Paul also helped tremendously as she read the entire text, provided edits that tightened the language, helped reformat references, and checked citations. I also would like to thank Bruce Sales, my colleague, who always is available to think through issues and keep my spirits up by reassuring me of the importance of what we do and how we do it.

My family deserves much credit as well. When I started the first drafts of this book, my family was half the size that it is now. My wife, Helen, and I now have six children: Lydia, Emma, William, Thomas, Henry, and Marc. As any parent who writes for a living knows, our work places immeasurable burdens on our families. I, however, benefited from much more than the time they gave me to work. I found no stronger motivation than thinking about the social issues that they face and will continue to face as the legal system determines how people treat one another.

# Introduction

Society places great hope in youth. They are seen as pivotal for addressing society's ills, as they will be responsible for its future. For this reason, there is deep concern about the values that we as a society instill in our youth. The task of preparing them to live in a diverse society plays a crucial role in the nation's commitment to ensuring equality and fostering justice.

The legal system figures prominently in these efforts. The legal system addresses issues of equality and helps to instill key values, as it has the power to regulate all socializing institutions. No institution, just like no person, can escape the law's reach. With regard to efforts to end discrimination, the legal system's most comprehensive and revolutionary efforts have focused on institutions devoted to the socialization of youth. Regrettably, however, societal and legal ideals often go unrealized. The legal system often fails in its control of the institutions that serve as the sites that inculcate values. Public schools offer an important example of these challenges.

Public schools serve as the center of the legal system's efforts to end discrimination, but these efforts arguably have not produced their intended outcomes. For example, the U.S. Supreme Court's most famous case addressing discrimination, *Brown v. Board of Education* (1954), centered on school segregation. It did so not only on the rationale that the law had played a role in segregating students on the basis of race but also on the belief that desegregation was needed given the way schools shaped people's hearts and minds and so heavily influenced their eventual place in society. On the basis of those rationales, *Brown* formally ended segregation based on race. Yet, rampant disparities in the racial compositions of public schools continue. Schools are even more "segregated" now than they were before *Brown* (Clotfelter 2004). More than 70% of all African American and Latino students in the United States

1

now attend largely minority schools (Frankenberg, Lee, & Orfield 2003). And segregation typically returns when courts end oversight of desegregation efforts (see Reardon et al. 2012). This continued and increasing segregation raises questions about how much progress has been made toward properly addressing discrimination. As it has developed, the legal system has become an increasingly ineffective tool with which to address racial and ethnic disparities among schools.

Schools also have been charged with instilling values that foster the ability to live effectively in a diverse society. But again, schools have failed to do as hoped. Schools have developed programs to address diversity, embrace multicultural understandings, and reduce group tensions. These programs seek to encourage dispositions supportive of equality. In addition, education itself—the major project of schools—continues to be relied on to enhance economic and other outcomes associated with social success and access to social opportunities. Yet societal discrimination continues, as do differential access to higher education, economic security, residential options, and a myriad of other social opportunities and resources (and much research identifies schools as the root of these outcomes; see Mickelson, Bottia, & Lambert 2013). The legal system, which guides the work of schools, ineffectively shapes schools' efforts to instill values that counter societal forces that lead to differential outcomes.

Moreover, schools have been tasked with addressing discrimination by socializing youth in contexts free from discrimination. Yet, again, schools routinely fail to provide effective environments. The legal system assumes that unprejudiced and equitable school environments serve as breeding grounds for the development of attitudes and dispositions favoring equality. That assumption rings true. But the legal system has trouble producing such environments. Positive outcomes cannot emerge when adolescents experience rampant differential treatment while in school, either from school staff or from each other. Some of that treatment results from school policies themselves, and sometimes it occurs despite them. Formally integrated schools can become functionally segregated through the implementation of academic tracks, ability grouping, special education, zero-tolerance initiatives, alternative schooling, and high-stakes testing (Walsemann & Bell 2010). Integrated schools and classrooms may experience higher levels of racial and ethnic tension, and hence produce fewer positive interracial relationships than environments with relatively small minority populations (see, e.g., Vervoort, Scholte, & Overbeek 2010). And students continue to experience "microaggressions" as a result of such factors as their race, ethnicity, sexual orientation, gender, religious commitments, and socioeconomic status (see, e.g., Huynh 2012). The legal system's efforts to address youths' day-to-day experiences have yet to produce broad hoped-for changes.

The experience of public schools illuminates the challenges facing the legal system. By regulating public schools, the legal system controls the socialization of youth. Yet, despite its overt commitment to equality, the legal system remains unable to overcome circumstances that challenge youth's development of the values associated with a more just society. That inability continues mainly because youth continue to experience prejudice, differential treatment, and unequal outcomes as they develop in an institution meant to foster the opposite.

Unequal treatment and its associated failures are not, of course, restricted to public schools. Youth experience discrimination in other key socializing institutions, including those purportedly dedicated to equality and presumed to be instilling values supportive of equal treatment. The criminal justice system reveals pervasive differential treatment of minority youth (Levesque 2006). Minority youth also are at increased risk for more intrusive interventions from child welfare and juvenile justice systems, and are at risk for receiving disproportionately ineffective health services (Levesque 2014a). A strong case could be made that the benefits of legal developments protecting youth from unjust interactions with the government unevenly go to those already privileged, typically middle-class white students. But even assumed-to-be-privileged middle-class white youth may suffer from discrimination. The legal status of all youth renders them dependent on others who can subject them to differential treatment. When allocating resources, for example, families can differentially treat their children on the basis of such factors as gender, birth order, intelligence, weight, illegitimacy, sexual orientation, religious beliefs, and physical attractiveness (Levesque 2008). In a variety of ways, youth routinely experience being treated differently from others due only to the fact that they are deemed different and unworthy of equal treatment.

Remarkably, the legal system condones much unequal treatment even though it owes each individual equal protection. This is so for a number of reasons. The legal system does not deem all inequalities and disparities to be discrimination worth addressing. Whether the law will allow differential treatment turns on a variety of factors, such as the government's relative involvement, the target of the differential treatment, the extent of the differential treatment, the rationale for the differential treatment, the availability of alternatives for addressing the disparity, the nature of the involved rights, and the social context. But the major reason why the legal system allows differential treatment is that it seeks to remain neutral when addressing claims of discrimination. In a real sense, much of the differential treatment we may witness or experience is becoming defined as not being the legal system's business.

This focus on neutrality to address claims of discrimination—on the need for the legal system to simply remove itself from supporting one group over another—follows the Supreme Court's increasing acceptance of an "anticlassification" approach to implementing the Constitution's mandate of equal protection. This approach aims to ensure that the legal system neither privileges nor disfavors individuals who could be classified into particular groups. It essentially seeks to be blind to group status. The Court even adopts the anticlassification approach to address claims involving race. For example, it acts in a "color-blind" fashion by treating people of different races the same way. It does not take any account of racial stigmatization, subjugation, or other disadvantage that contributes to inequality in a particular situation. Instead, neutrality serves as the Court's vehicle for increasing equality.

The Supreme Court's favored approach attracts controversy, but no one doubts the Court's commitment or the dramatic change from earlier approaches that it entails. The legal system's increasing allegiance to formal equality, which resists making accommodations in order to achieve equal treatment for some, is viewed by many as anathema to the civil rights movement. Others counter that the social experiment of ensuring equality through laws, championed by the civil rights movement, fostered important progress but also rampant failures. They argue that change was long overdue. Yet others argue that current directions may diverge from the civil rights mandate of the 1960s and '70s but that the increasingly dominant approach of neutrality actually retains the most legitimate claim to civil rights and its fullest commitment to equality for all. Even members of the Supreme Court itself express these varying views (see *Parents Involved in Community Schools v. Seattle School District No. 1*, 2007).

In any event, the legal system seems to have stalled in its efforts to foster aggressive reform to ameliorate the plight of those traditionally deemed disadvantaged and subordinated. Buoyed by recent Supreme Court jurisprudence, the legal system increasingly removes itself from addressing inequality. It must do so because the Court's understanding of the Constitution sets the parameters for all legal developments. Following these parameters, the Court has developed a legal system that remains neutral to the classifications of groups heretofore deemed to be in need of special recognition, care, and protection. We seem to have reached an end to the pursuit of equality as we knew it.

This book approaches equality jurisprudence from a different angle. Rather than focus solely on whether to remain neutral to claims of discrimination, equality jurisprudence also must focus on the values that the legal system seeks to instill. Opposing the Court's commitment to neutrality is not only an exercise in futility but also unnecessary, especially because that approach can prove useful. Equality jurisprudence simply needs to broaden its reach. It needs to concern itself with the inculcation of values supporting equality and shape socializing institutions accordingly.

The impetus for this different approach to contemporary equality jurisprudence comes from three sources. The first source involves the difference between goals and the practical realities leading to their realization. The legal system may champion ideals of neutrality in the goals it sets itself for treating individuals. But the legal system cannot remain neutral in the values it supports and imparts. Neutrality toward groups may be possible in doctrinal formulations, but not necessarily in practice. Even seeking to remain neutral requires adopting the value of neutrality over other values. The values that shape notions of equality and the experience of inequality provide no exception to the impossibility of neutrality. The legal system routinely takes sides in disputes, including those involving claims of inequality.

The legal system's now-resolute commitment to maintaining neutrality in order to foster equality makes it important to consider how the ideal of neutrality may falter in practice. Examples from adolescents' everyday experiences again illustrate well the gap between formal law and the realities that come from neutral stances. Minority students seeking more effective schools experience a sense of discrimination when required to return to underperforming schools because their districts no longer can consider a student's race when making school assignments. Students in integrated schools feel discriminated against when they cannot wear Confederate flag–styled belt buckles to demonstrate pride in their heritage or are barred from sporting Malcolm X t-shirts because they might disquiet students and administrators. Religiously conservative students feel discriminated against for not being able to express their views about homosexuality, while gay youth feel discriminated against by their school's failure to protect them from disparaging remarks about their sexuality. These examples all come from real-life cases, and all result from efforts to treat members from different groups the same way as those from other groups. Scholarly and empirical articles and newspaper accounts report similar results based on youth's views, expressions, and experiences relating to numerous other markers of identity, such as their immigration status, weight, attractiveness, disabilities, socioeconomic status, physical prowess, and gender (see Levesque 2014a). Formally treating groups the same way when they have different needs does not readily lead to a sense of equality for those who must live with the imposed value.

The second source that spurs a broader approach to equality jurisprudence stems from a simple observation about empirical research. Even as the legal system now stalls in its efforts to confront gaps in the ideals and realities of equality, empirical research has made important strides in showing how to achieve greater equality. The developmental sciences offer considerable hope for reducing prejudice, increasing tolerance, and addressing inappropriately unequal treatment. Indeed, much of the recent research has strong roots in theoretical underpinnings first developed during the court battles involving *Brown* (see Allport 1954; Williams 1947). They have the ability to connect closely to practical attempts to implement appropriate interventions and procedures for combating conflict and reducing both prejudice and the discrimination that can accompany it. The now-vast literature on the meaning, causes, expression, and reduction of prejudice is teeming with ideas, so much so that this area of study has few rivals in size, breadth, and vitality.

Regrettably, the legal system has yet to take more fully into account the insights and understandings revealed by empirical research, particularly developmental science. Some empirical findings have found their way into court opinions, but beyond focusing on the narrow legal disputes at hand, the legal system has yet to determine how to translate a fuller empirical understanding into effective policies. The general failure to embrace empirical findings more fully may derive from the reality that efforts to reduce prejudice and increase tolerance and equality face dismaying challenges. But a central reason for those challenges is that the ways known to reduce prejudice and disparate treatment have gone without the legal system's adequate support. Potential ways to offer robust support have been largely ignored. They simply have not been part of contemporary equality jurisprudence.

The third source that led to seeking a broader equality jurisprudence comes from dramatic developments reshaping the law's inculcative powers. Just as the legal system has moved away from aggressive reforms to address inequalities, so it has moved toward supporting the values it deems fitting. The legal system can favor its messages over others'. It even can enact programs that just happen to favor one religious group's views, programs, and messages over those of another group. This is an incredible development given traditional views that the state should avoid supporting religious groups, that a wall must separate church and state (Levesque 2014b). This power transfers to other domains devoted to inculcating values. The government can shape the values instilled by the media, community groups, and families, just as it shapes those of its own systems—those of child welfare, criminal justice, juvenile justice, welfare, and education. That the legal system can influence all of these systems' efforts to inculcate preferred values and influence societal change emerges as one of the most important developments in modern legal history. Yet it remains unheralded and ignored by equality jurisprudence. Indeed, it has been ignored even though it addresses the central challenge of fostering equality: how to instill preferred values.

That equality jurisprudence has played down the inculcative function of law is not surprising. This area of law still has no cohesive core and essentially no champions. It perhaps lacks advocates because much of it derives from contexts that permitted what some view as blatant discrimination, such as in situations that supported only conservative sexuality education programs (*Bowen v. Kendrick*, 1988), used public funds to support schools that could avoid civil rights protections (*Zelman v.*

*Simmons-Harris*, 2002), allowed community groups to discriminate (*Boy Scouts of America v. Dale*, 2000), and permitted families to raise children outside of mainstream social influences (*Wisconsin v. Yoder*, 1972). These now-leading cases, all of which involved the inculcation of youth and their socializing institutions, may have supported inequality. But they also created the foundation for the opposite. They consistently affirmed the government's power to shape socializing institutions. They supported the government's power to pursue its own preferred values, support those of private groups, or counter those that it does not favor with its own vast resources. A close look at doctrine in this area reveals impressive developments that can be fashioned into workable policies that support the inculcation of values conducive to increased equality. The legal system may require the neutral treatment of groups, but it still permits governments to embark on efforts that instill preferred values toward groups.

The above three observations lead to the central point of this book. Rather than accept the Supreme Court's confidence that a neutral stance best leads to equality, this book champions the opposite: legal systems need to recognize that they regulate the systems that influence the development of values and that they can foster values conducive to increased equality. The Constitution may demand neutrality to ensure formal equality, but the legal system still permits the development of laws that take stances on difficult issues that go to the core of individuals' values and their sense of self. The pages that follow provide the basis for thinking through changes in the way the legal system approaches discrimination and the way it can face the key challenges that lie ahead. The analysis draws from empirical understandings of ways to foster equality and charts ways to foster youth's development of values that reduce invidious discrimination and its harms. It champions enlisting the socializing and inculcative powers of the law to shape institutions so that they can instill values consistent with ideals of equality.

## Chapters Ahead

Chapter 1 begins our discussion by examining the general parameters of contemporary equality jurisprudence, which is the manner by which the legal system addresses discrimination and seeks to ensure equality of treatment. The discussion centers on the foundations of equality jurisprudence by examining its fundamental tension: the need to treat everyone the same way as well as the need to treat some differently so that they can be in positions to be treated equally to others. Stated differently, contemporary equality jurisprudence seeks to discern whether to treat people differently so that they actually are treated the same way in terms of, for example, the ability to take advantage of similar opportunities—and if so, when such differential treatment is appropriate. After exploring that tension, the discussion highlights current directions in equality jurisprudence by describing the central holdings and rationales of key cases addressing inequality. That discussion necessarily focuses on cases of racial inequality, as that area of law has been central to the jurisprudence dealing with equality. That discussion concludes that current jurisprudential trends move toward formally treating everyone the same way, toward an "anticlassification" approach that seeks to rid the system of efforts to protect individuals by classifying them into protected groups. The chapter ends with an examination of the inherent limitations of that approach. To do so, it necessarily also considers the limitations of an alternative model that seeks to offer added protections to individuals from subjugated groups, aptly known as the antisubordination approach. These limitations lead us to look at alternative ways to approach inequality.

Chapters 2 through 5 craft the argument for refocusing equality jurisprudence. They do so by looking at empirical research to gain a better understanding of discrimination and to think through how the legal system can benefit from that understanding. Chapter 2 provides an overview of the empirical understanding of the nature and extent of prejudice and discrimination, their developmental roots, and their potential alleviation. The analysis centers on the implications that arise from recognizing that youth shape their environments and respond to multiple social forces as they develop judgments about others and determine whether to act on those judgments. Although research findings have long underscored the importance of pathological aspects of prejudice and actions relating to them, this area of study now emphasizes even more how prejudice and discrimination emerge as expected outcomes of normal social categorization, social identity, and group processes. Building on these findings, the discussion explores how influential social sources can be structured in ways that increase the likelihood of fostering dispositions, relationships, and institutions marked by tolerance, inclusion, and a sense of equity. These areas of research lay the foundation for thinking through the legal and policy analyses presented in the remaining chapters.

Chapter 3 begins to develop a refocused equality jurisprudence. The chapter provides a foundation for the next chapter as it addresses the government's broad role in inculcating values and in shaping people's dispositions. The analyses gain significance given the prevailing view that the government must resist such intrusions. Although admittedly framed to limit the government's role in our lives, the legal system actually evinces important contrary impulses. These contrary impulses must become key components of equality jurisprudence. They provide the rationales for the legal system's power to harness developmental science's insights and foster the structuring of institutions in ways that alleviate prejudice, discrimination, and inequity.

After chapter 3's broad introduction to the government's role in shaping the inculcation of values, chapter 4 moves the analysis to actual sites where inculcation occurs and addresses the question of how to capitalize on them. The chapter begins by focusing on families and schools. It then moves on to other institutions critical to shaping adolescent development, such as religious groups, justice systems, health organizations, media, and community groups. At this point, the focus narrows to determining and respecting the rights of adolescents. That focus emerges from the recognition of the need to balance societal interests with those of adolescents' right to exercise their fundamental freedom to develop their own thoughts and dispositions regarding how they will treat others. Throughout, the analysis reveals much that remains unregulated and ignored. These gaps gain particular significance in that analyses of discrimination law have not sought to explore key socializing institutions' ability to inculcate values even though these institutions remain central to addressing the root causes of prejudice and discrimination.

Chapter 5 builds on the notion that a close look at laws regulating the various sites of inculcation reveals multiple ways in which social institutions can serve as an impetus and guide for change, furthering the ideals of equality jurisprudence. It examines how the legal system can balance the immense freedom retained by socializing institutions and private individuals with the need to foster civic development that embraces a sense of equality, tolerance, and just opportunities, which brings us closer to the ideal hallmarks of modern civil society. It articulates broad principles grounded in empirical evidence, such as the need to clarify the values of different socializing systems, the need to provide guidance in determining responsibilities and obligations, and the need to focus on local implementation that can support structural change. While doing so, it provides concrete examples to demonstrate how the legal system can fail and how it can succeed in shaping the values that alleviate invidious discrimination.

The conclusion revisits the book's central arguments and highlights their implications. It champions the need to take seriously what the Supreme Court recognized so well in *Brown*. The legal system necessarily plays a deeply inculcative role in our lives. Legally, that understanding has contributed to two important developments. One resulted in what we recognize as antidiscrimination law. The other resulted in something that still does not even have a name and remains virtually ignored in efforts to address equality. That unnamed and unheralded development involves the manner in which the legal system actually can favor some values over others. The conclusion underscores the need for embracing these developments to create a more effective equality jurisprudence.

This book's broad scope brings with it notable limitations and strengths. This text cannot cover all legal cases and empirical findings dealing with the very wide breadth of topics relating to this area of law. It particularly cannot do so given its central argument that the laws addressing discrimination need to take a much broader view of equality than the current narrow focus on the Constitution's equal protection of laws mandates. Taking a broader look means selecting examples of trends and principles, rather than providing analyses steeped in string citations and spreading across multiple jurisdictions. Yet another key limitation relates to the recognition that no magic bullets exist for the problems plaguing this area of jurisprudence, public policy, and society. Instead of providing simple solutions, this text develops broad principles and suggests ways of implementing them. Thus, the book expands our knowledge in important ways while remaining mindful of the law's limitations, particularly of deep-rooted controversies.

This book details and responds to dramatic shifts in the legal system's understanding of equality. Rather than stopping at demonstrating how the increasingly dominant legal approaches to equality pervasively fail to address the roots of prejudice and discrimination, the analysis moves forward by using the current empirical understanding of prejudice and discrimination as a springboard to expand jurisprudence relating to equality. That expansion provides a foundation for crafting law and policy reforms. Those reforms emerge not only in response to limitations of existing approaches but also with knowledge of broader issues that underlie those limitations and of how to counter them. In the end, this book argues for a shift in current thinking relating to laws addressing equality, a shift necessitated by dramatic developments in the legal formulations relating to equality and spurred by cutting-edge developmental science relating to discrimination and its alleviation. A close analysis of this complex area of law leaves this simple message: effectively addressing inequality requires a legal system that is doubling down, not backing down.

# 1

## Shifts in Equality Jurisprudence

The law's efforts to address the discriminatory treatment of individuals raise thorny issues and countless complexities. But all of the law's efforts necessarily rest on the United States Constitution and the Supreme Court's jurisprudence relating to it. The Constitution's significance emerges for two fundamental reasons. First, constitutional law sets the floor that guides the local, state, and federal governments' development of laws. Regardless of the desires of those who seek to address social issues, the Supreme Court remains the final arbiter of the appropriateness of legal mandates as well as their application, and the Supreme Court fundamentally bases its decisions on interpretations of the Constitution. Second, constitutional law articulates the evolving standards of the prevailing moral consciousness relating to particular topics. Sometimes the Court merely reflects consensus, at other times it spurs consensus forward, and at other times it leaves room for differences to exist until such time as society achieves increased consensus. The Court, guided by the Constitution, serves as the premier site for addressing the most challenging societal issues.

The Court may offer powerful statements reflecting or spurring consensus, but it rarely speaks with only one voice. Even in the rare instances of unanimity, the Court's decisions remain open to multiple interpretations and nuanced applications. This is unsurprising. Cases that find their way to the Court tend to raise complex and multiple issues—two characteristics that also mark the Court's opinions on many legal disputes. Indeed, although only an opinion joined by a majority of the justices states binding law, the Court's decisions frequently contain vigorous dissenting opinions that often help guide the development of law as much as the opinions that rule that particular moment. Together, those multiple opinions and interpretations encapsulate broader discourses and pinpoint issues that can direct the understanding of entire areas of social disputes and shape responses to them.

The Court's deliberateness ensures its significance. Its opinions are important not only for legal technicians but also for those seeking to understand how society can, does, and should approach social issues, especially divisive ones. The Court's different statements, which often offer a sense of finality muted by a sense of flexibility and reasoned compromise, are the types needed to forge constitutional principles that can compel the allegiance of the people whose lives it would constrain. The significance of these different statements means that our discussion necessarily starts by examining the general parameters of jurisprudence relating to the manner in which the Supreme Court addresses discrimination and seeks to ensure equality of treatment and opportunity.

This chapter examines the foundations of contemporary equality jurisprudence by unraveling the fundamental tension that it addresses: the need to treat everyone alike as well as the need to treat some differently so that they can be in positions to be treated equally to others. The discussion highlights current directions in equality jurisprudence by describing the central holdings and rationales of key cases addressing difference. The discussion concludes that current jurisprudential trends move toward formally treating everyone the same way. The chapter ends with an examination of the inherent limitations of that approach, as well as the limitations of its alternative, which permits differentiated treatment in order to address the needs of groups historically excluded from appropriate legal recognition. That examination leads to one fundamental conclusion: equality jurisprudence must take another approach if it wishes to take a more assertive role in addressing inequality and its harms.

## Foundations of Equality Jurisprudence

In the United States, jurisprudence addressing discrimination inevitably looks to the central meaning of the Fourteenth Amendment to the U.S. Constitution and, equally importantly, the Supreme Court's interpretation of that meaning. The Fourteenth Amendment contains the Equal Protection Clause, which provides that "no State shall . . . deny to any person within its jurisdiction the equal protection of the laws." This clause is one of the most intensely litigated and one of the most often subjected to vigorous debates. Although the language may appear straightforward, it can be understood as containing conflicting ideals. Those seeking to treat individuals alike may find themselves at odds with those seeking to provide equal protection to differently situated individuals by treating them differently. This is just one example of how meaningful ideals may conflict. These ideals take different forms, and at different times the legal system tends to prioritize one goal over another. A close look at legal developments in equal protection doctrine since the post–civil rights era reveals a struggle between these two ideals. The nature of that struggle serves as the needed foundation for understanding current jurisprudence in this area as well as for formulating its potential development.

Commentators use many labels to describe the sometimes conflicting ideals according to which legal systems approach difference, but the approach originally conceptualized by Owen Fiss (1976) has gained broad acceptance. Fiss conceptualized the ideals as following either of two principles. The first, the anticlassification principle, which he also unfortunately called the "antidiscrimination principle," involves treating everyone alike. The second principle, known as the "antisubordination principle," focuses on treating some groups differently so that they can achieve greater equality with others. The two principles reveal the core struggle of discrimination law: treating like cases the same, treating different cases differently, and struggling to find out whether they are the same or different.

The conceptualization has become central to law addressing discrimination, but it must be used with care. For example, analyses of Supreme Court jurisprudence sometimes construe these conflicting principles as battles between conservative justices who tend to adopt anticlassification principles and progressive justices who tend to abide by antisubordination principles (Colker 1986). That construction may be real. However, not all justices can be categorized so readily. Even Supreme Court decisions may not be categorized so readily, given that they often contain multiple opinions. In addition, the resolution of legal disputes may involve components of both principles. The ideals produce polar opposite conclusions in some instances. Despite the possibility that the principles may not be used distinctly in some situations, they still operate in practices that shift over time in response to social contestation, social struggle, and the facts of particular cases (see Balkin & Siegel 2003).

But, although the two guiding principles provide useful heuristic tools, they offer incomplete guides. They are nuanced by those who subscribe to them, and their applications can vary depending on the particular demands of disputes. Although some of these important realities and nuances tend to get lost in efforts to explain these ideals and their related legal doctrine, they remain important in that they may point us toward areas of agreement and potential directions for reform. These conceptualizations also provide useful heuristic devices that highlight important approaches to equality that have real implications. Bearing in mind the limitations of polarizing conceptualizations, then, we explore briefly the nature and consequences of these ideals as they lay the foundation for further analyses of efforts to address inappropriate discrimination and denials of equal opportunity and treatment.

## The Anticlassification Equality Impulse

Concern about treating people similarly sometimes lends itself to enforcing formally neutral rules as a way to resist classifying individuals, and so developed the "anticlassification" approach to ensuring equality. The anticlassification model has its roots in the notion of a "color-blind Constitution." Under this view, classifications are inherently problematic and should not be tolerated except in very few particularly compelling instances. Treating individuals differently because they fall within a particular classification is deemed particularly troublesome because it fails to respect their individuality and an individual's right to self-determination. The focus on individuality and on not infringing on self-determination translates into resisting treating individuals differently even if these individuals may have experienced discrimination on the basis of their unchosen characteristics, such as race, ethnicity, sexual orientation, or gender. That resistance stems from a desire to avoid the harm that the state inflicts on individuals when it categorizes them on the basis of group characteristics. An anticlassification approach asserts that a harmful stigma attaches to the state's expression that individuals matter only to the extent that they belong to a group identifiable by a specific characteristic such as race. Bold state interventions that take into account group characteristics, the anticlassification approach purports, entrench these harms rather than end them. Group-based interventions are said to demean individual dignity and worth as individuals are judged by their group status instead of by their own merit, essential qualities, and unique personalities.

Thus, color-blind judicial interpretations and policies view with equal skepticism racial classifications aimed at preserving and perpetuating racial subordination and those aimed at remedying past discrimination. To secure equal treatment, the approach envisions limiting the government's role to its responsibility to protect the rights of all individuals to pursue their self-determined goals and objectives. Status hierarchies may exist among groups, but the best way to dismantle them is to prohibit all classifications. Hence, the approach evinces concern about "reverse discrimination" when addressing affirmative action. It views special considerations that privilege certain groups as inherently problematic in that they treat individuals in such groups as inherently inferior and unable to be like those in other groups. This focus on resisting classification to ensure equality is now foundational to understanding jurisprudence in this area, making it important to further specify its typical uses and contours.

A helpful starting point in explaining the anticlassification approach is to highlight the Court's move from focusing on suspect classes to focusing on suspect classifications. For example, the Court once referred to African Americans as a suspect class, a group that would receive close consideration when laws regulated them differently from others. In a sense, like other classes that were recognized as highly protected (such as those based on religious beliefs, gender, and national origin), they were deemed highly suspect. Although nonlegal analyses unfortunately (and wrongly) later would view the classification as treating the groups themselves as suspect (e.g., viewing some racial groups with suspicion), the actual focus of the suspicion centered on the legal system, which might treat the groups unequally. Rather than using the phrase "suspect class," the Court now refers to race as a "suspect classification" (*San Antonio Independent School District v. Rodriguez*, 1973, 7; *Adarand Constructors v. Peña*, 1995, 216–17; *Grutter v. Bollinger*, 2003, 326). Legal decisions following the anticlassification approach fundamentally concern themselves with resisting classifications based on membership in a specific group, and they operate on the assumption that groups essentially should not matter for the purposes of offering legal protections.

The shift from suspect class to suspect classifications is significant and illustrative. The new language better encapsulates the analytical work that goes into legal analyses relating to differential treatment. But, it also does much more. By articulating equal protection problems in terms of suspect classifications rather than classes of people, the Court shifts the relevant inquiry from one that looks at groups of people to one that looks purely at the legal system's use of classifications. By emphasizing the classification itself rather than whether a law or policy advantages or disadvantages an individual within it, the Court evinces a shift toward supporting formal equality in that it considerably plays down who is in the class and emphasizes, instead, the extent and appropriateness of using a classification based on a certain category such as race, gender, and ability. Thus, under this approach, the Court can deem a particular law, on its face, to be treating individuals equally, which is what is meant by formal equality. The approach removes the need to look into the details of how individuals are treated within categories; it simply seeks to determine whether the legal system treats them the same way, essentially regardless of any particular individual circumstances.

Several examples nicely illustrate the significant implications of adopting approaches that focus on formal equality. *Plessy v. Ferguson* (1896) provides the archetypical example of formal equality analysis. *Plessy* involved accommodations in railroad cars that separated Blacks and Whites. The Court found such accommodations permissible, and used them to announce the constitutional rule that permitted separate but equal accommodations for Blacks and Whites. The Court reasoned that the treatment received by both races is equal when they are parallel. In this case, the law was parallel because it prohibited Whites from using Black accommodations, just as it prohibited Blacks from using White accommodations. The Court articulated no role for itself in removing the problems that emerged from the separation that treats the different classifications equally. Most notably, the Court avoided embracing a role that would involve it in addressing any "badge of inferiority" that might derive from the separate treatment, and it noted that, if they exist, perceptions of inferiority arise from constructions imposed by African Americans themselves. This approach articulates a view of equal protection that requires equality only on its face; it excludes considerations of historical and social context that would recognize the existence of inequality and suggest that Black and White individuals are not similarly situated. As Justice John Marshall Harlan's influential language put it in dissent, "In view of the Constitution, in the eye of the law, there is in this country no superior, dominant, ruling class of citizens. There is no caste here. Our Constitution is color-blind, and neither knows nor tolerates classes among citizens" (*Plessy v. Ferguson*, 1896, 559). The law of the land, following the approach endorsed in *Plessy*, does not treat groups of citizens differently, regardless of who is in those groups.

The focus on formal equality continues to resonate and finds expression, among other places, in the context of affirmative action. Those who take an approach focused on formal equality find that affirmative action for racial or other minorities, which permits differential treatment based on race or other classification, violates the equal protection rights of other groups, such as Whites. *Regents of the University of California v. Bakke* (1978) illustrates well that position. That landmark case asked the Court to consider the scope of factors that medical schools could consider when determining admission to their programs. The Court found the only permissible factor that would support considering an individual's race to be the purpose of improving the learning environment through diversity, and even then race must have been one of several admission criteria. (The Court would continue to follow this principle over twenty-five years later, in *Grutter v. Bollinger*, 2003.) The focus on diversity constituted important evidence that the school had considered other factors when developing its admissions program. Notably, the affirmative action program originally was designed to ensure admissions of traditionally discriminated-against minorities so as to (1) reduce the historic deficit of traditionally disfavored minorities in medical schools and the medical profession, (2) counter the effects of societal discrimination, (3) increase the number of physicians who will practice in communities currently underserved, and (4) obtain the educational benefits that flow from an ethnically diverse student body. Although the decision was an important one, it was split, with Justice Powell casting the deciding vote. Powell rejected the use of race to fill specific percentages (quotas) as facially invalid. Equally importantly, the Court permitted diversity as a rationale to support differential treatment based on race as long as considerations of race were only one factor in admissions decisions and the reason for diversity was not to remedy past discrimination. Pursuing a diverse student body was permissible because of its perceived benefits, not because it was needed to address a group's disadvantage or redress broad societal discrimination. On those grounds, Justice Powell joined four other justices who contended that any racial quota system supported by the government violated equal rights principles, including the Civil Rights Act of 1964.

Justice Powell's explanation for not supporting racial quotas in *Bakke* illustrates the anticlassification approach's resistance to considering histories of subjugation. He noted that almost every ethnic group has suffered at least some discrimination at some point. The United States, he argued, "has become a Nation of minorities, in which even the so-called 'majority' is composed of various minority groups, most of whom can lay claim to a history of prior discrimination" (*Regents of the University of California v. Bakke*, 1978, 292, 295). He saw no principled basis on which to prioritize their competing claims to remedial justice. "The kind of variable sociological and political analysis necessary . . . simply does not lie within the judicial competence" (297). Powell concluded that "[p]referring members of any one group for no reason other than race or ethnic origin is discrimination for its own sake" and that such preference would "hinder rather than further attainment of genuine diversity" (315). He further explained this position succinctly when finding that "equal protection cannot mean one thing when applied to one individual and something else when applied to a person of another color" (289–90). Under this vision, which the Court would follow in several other opinions, treating people equally means treating them the same way. To the extent that some groups are situated differently in the first instance, the best way to address such inequality and achieve true equality is to assume that equality already exists. The vision allows little room for treating individuals differently to achieve similar ends.

## The Antisubordination Equality Impulse

If formally treating people the same way to achieve equal ends exemplifies the anticlassification approach, then the antisubordination approach stands for treating people differently to reach more equal ends. That position emerges from the recognitions that society treats certain broadly defined groups of individuals differently and that not all groups of people are situated similarly. The antisubordination principle, however, does much more than recognize that some groups (and individuals in them) are situated differently; the approach seeks to accommodate that difference. The fundamental challenge facing this approach, then, involves not only accommodating but also determining the nature and significance of the initial difference worth addressing.

If groups were simply and obviously situated differently, then addressing those differences leading to inequality could be done by simply scrutinizing the differences and accommodating them. However, since inequality can result from multiple sources, the puzzle that emerges is agreeing on those sources and their relevance. Common sense may dictate that the first step to addressing a problem properly requires understanding that it exists and ferreting out its source. But this is where the anticlassification and antisubordination impulses fundamentally diverge. Antisubordination approaches look back to how a group has been treated in the past to gain insight into how members of that group should be treated in the future in order for equality to be achieved. This is unlike the anticlassification approaches that generally focus on current treatment and on immediate equal treatment. The antisubordination approach raises quite complex issues as it requires a more searching look at differences: it requires a look backward and forward, whereas the anticlassification approach urges neither.

The nature of biological sex and sex discrimination provides a useful and illustrative example of the types of complexities that arise from focusing on the extent to which individuals belong to differently situated groups. When a court addresses an issue that affects the sexes the same way, the court requires equal treatment that considers the two sexes to be "like" each other. Conversely, when a court finds that the matter under dispute relates to differences between the sexes, the court requires different treatment that considers the two sexes to be "unlike" each other. Neither the anticlassification nor the antisubordination model is unproblematic when the alleged distinction is based solely on an actual biological difference between the sexes, as they are to be treated according to the biological distinction. When a biological difference applies to all members of a particular sex and is based on science rather than stereotypes or prejudices, then everyone should be treated according to that difference. Situations exist in which the clear physical differences in anatomy may require differential treatment, but determining when a situation demands this different treatment or what this different treatment should be is more problematic. These difficulties emerge, for example, in situations that treat the sexes differently when the reason for the differential treatment has to do with broad group differences like some forms of physical strength and endurance. One of the more dramatic and controversial examples of these differences has emerged in discussions of the legitimacy of excluding women from some forms of military combat situations. Regrettably, discrimination rarely is based on actual biological differences. Many alleged biological affirmations of difference between the sexes turn out to be based on stereotypes regarding a sex's biological capabilities or tendencies. Entire groups of opportunities and protections may be denied to the individuals of a certain sex merely because of a court's own assumptions regarding the differences between men and women. Decision making based on those assumptions runs the risk of misunderstanding the social importance of such distinctions, particularly how one group may have been disadvantaged systematically and subordinated to another. Distinguishing between biological and socially conceptualized differences, and responding to them, raises thorny issues.

Even if socially created differences are recognized, they do not clearly dictate what the appropriate responses may be. But the antisubordination approach champions the notion that recognizing difference rooted in prejudice and disadvantage may require efforts to achieve equal protection that allow classification-specific means of overcoming obstacles, such as taking affirmative action to remedy the vestiges of past inequities. This approach to achieving equality contends that the formal equality framework both disregards important social contexts and, by doing so, legitimizes discrimination. Thus, and in the context of race, judicial interpretations of the Constitution that adopt antisubordination approaches do not seek to be color-blind; they seek to be color-conscious. They seek to treat groups of people differently and in a manner that addresses their historical subjugation. This position adopts the view that constitutional and moral imperatives require structural remedies to end status hierarchies. Among the most obvious and controversial examples of the remedies include affirmative action programs that give preferential treatment to individuals from subjugated groups or mandate the development of programs that provide similar or even parallel opportunities (such as Title IX programs requiring equity in girls' and boys' sports). The antisubordination impulse does not ignore the costs of such remedies but rather deems them to be necessary sacrifices to be borne by a polity that seeks to create a more just social order. Antisubordination thus conceptualizes a different relationship between the Constitution and such status hierarchies. It suggests that the Fourteenth Amendment acknowledges the existence of such hierarchies and mandates an end to them. It is not, in other words, blind to difference.

Being conscious of problematic differences for the purposes of addressing antisubordination means more than recognizing difference and the need to respond to it; it fundamentally means considering the context in which discrimination takes place, addressing that context, and considering the nature of the legal rules that hamper remediation. The antisubordination impulse views formal anticlassification rules for dealing with discrimination as creating barriers to achieving genuine equality because the law will be applied to the oppressed group's disadvantage. The classic examples of the law's subjugation provides a strong case in point: laws can make it difficult even to bring legal actions to address discrimination, or can set the standard for obtaining relief so high that few can reach it. The antisubordination framework perceives formal equality not merely as ineffectual but also as actually detrimental for members of disadvantaged classifications. From an antisubordination perspective, then, reaching equality requires looking beyond formal equality: truer equality of treatment emerges from uncovering instances and societal standards (including formal rules) that create subordination, and addressing that subordination so that the disadvantaged group will be able to overcome obstacles that create disfavored treatment. At its core, it means treating the context in which people find themselves in a manner that increases the chances that people who may have been unequal eventually end up equal. It means more than focusing on equality in opportunity; it means moving toward policies and practices that take a realistic look at the circumstances of disadvantaged individuals and attempt to ensure that these individuals can actually avail themselves of those opportunities. It means that laws must follow the principle that laws should not aggravate or perpetuate the subordinated status of a specially disadvantaged group.

Legally, the archetypical understanding of antisubordination also comes from *Plessy v. Ferguson* (1896), and it also comes from Justice Harlan. Justice Harlan argued that the majority's opinion in *Plessy* was grounded on an obvious but ignored fallacy. He argued that "everyone knows that the statute in question had its origin in the purpose, not so much to exclude White persons from railroad cars occupied by Blacks, as to exclude colored people from coaches occupied by or assigned to White persons" (557). Justice Harlan exemplified the antisubordination perspective as he highlighted what was both commonly known and accepted. This perspective approaches equal protection by seeking to understand what equality means in a particular case, which in this instance involved the racist underpinnings of the issues at stake. Under this view, ensuring equal protection requires moving beyond classifications and delving into the reasons for their existence. Ignoring those underpinnings means that inappropriate discrimination cannot be addressed and will continue. This position insists that the Constitution opposes the maintenance of racial caste, group subordination, or second-class citizenship; it understands that opposition as permitting classifications and not being color-blind.

Another leading case that demonstrated the anticlassification view, *Regents of the University of California v. Bakke* (1978), also provides an antisubordination view of laws and reveals the type of legal responses needed to achieve equality. In this case, the antisubordination view suggests that equating discrimination against Whites in the context of affirmative action with the historical discrimination against minorities is equivalent to ignoring the past. In Justice Marshall's opinion (400), he noted that "[t]he experience of Negroes in America has been different in kind, not just in degree, from that of other ethnic groups. It is not merely the history of slavery alone but also that of a whole people marked as inferior by the law." Given that history and subordinating experience, Marshall rejected the notion that African Americans could not be afforded greater protection under the Fourteenth Amendment when it was necessary to remedy the effects of past discrimination. The antisubordination approach embraces the notion that the meanings and history behind classifications matter—that meaning derives from specific contexts, and that those meanings matter.

From an antisubordination perspective, *Plessy* and *Bakke* support the view that color-blindness is blind, and that it is inappropriately so. Part of that blindness manifests itself in the failure to acknowledge historical truths and the failure to embark on efforts to redress past wrongs. It rejects the notion that equal protection means providing the same protection to all of the nation's "minorities." The antisubordination approach takes a historical view of equal protection that emphasizes the provenance of the equal protection mandate adopted to address and counter racist norms positing Black inferiority, recognizing that not all minorities are situated similarly. This history means that current situations can be deemed unequal and the inevitable consequences of centuries of unequal treatment. Simply put, the antisubordination principle urges scrutiny of governmental and other social actions that, given their history, context, source, and effect, seem most likely not only to perpetuate subordination but also to reflect a tradition of hostility toward a historically subjugated group or a pattern of blindness or indifference to that group's interests.

## The Significance of Different Equality Impulses

Although each impulse lays claim to being the most faithful to the law's mandate to ensure equality, the two approaches reveal striking differences. Unlike an anticlassification perspective, an antisubordination perspective takes the classification as the beginning of the analysis, rather than the end. An antisubordination approach focuses on going backward to identify harms rather than centering on the present and playing down historical forces that led to current situations. An antisubordination analysis rests on whether the classification exists to exclude or include the group that has been subordinated and the need for special accommodations to ensure equality. And such concerns essentially remain inconsequential and even anathema to those adopting an anticlassification approach. The anticlassification focus on the present rests on the belief that refusing to classify individuals now will best ensure greater equality both in the immediate future and in the long term. The antisubordination perspective searches the past to understand how groups should be treated differently now to ensure greater equality later and recognizes a need to continue support until equality has been reached in fact. The anticlassification view evinces the concern that treating one group preferably results in harming innocents whose interests could be disadvantaged in the process, whereas the antisubordination view emphasizes the need to focus on the innocents who have been, and continue to be, disadvantaged. The legal system clearly can take very different approaches to determining whether different groups receive equal treatment and opportunities.

Adhering to either of the dueling perspectives' identification of difference results in quite different consequences for the way the legal system treats groups. At the heart of debates between anticlassification and antisubordination rest different conceptions of harm, of that harm's significance, and of the state's interest in crafting a remedy. Adopting a particular approach requires making a decision about which method better advances the interests of members of disadvantaged classifications as well as the interests of society as a whole, including those who are advantaged. Embracing a particular stance means taking a stand on whether the focus will be on the short term or the long term, as well as whether to focus narrowly on overtly discriminatory actions, such as invidious discrimination and direct state actions, or broadly on subtle discriminations, such as those that result from informally and indirectly produced patterns. It also means, fundamentally, whether the legal system's conception of equality entails a commitment to individuals or to groups. The different methods also determine whether the legal system will seek guidance from the social sciences, as taking a narrow view of equality and difference essentially vitiates the need for social science evidence. Both approaches to equality jurisprudence may embrace equality, but the meaning and effect of that embrace markedly differ, with important consequences for the legal system's role in ensuring equality of treatment and opportunity.

## Current Directions in Equality Jurisprudence

Tensions between the anticlassification and antisubordination principles undoubtedly remain strong, but the Supreme Court currently finds anticlassification principles more persuasive. The dominant legal approach to equality adopts formal equality as the default rule, permitting classification-specific approaches to equal protection problems in very narrow sets of circumstances. The ascendency of this view derives directly from *Brown v. Board of Education* (1954). That foundation may appear odd given that the case is popularly known as having inaugurated the modern civil rights movement. But the issues raised by the case have been the subject of considerable litigation and analysis, all of which have resulted in important twists and turns in antidiscrimination doctrine. We thus begin with *Brown* and quickly move to the Court's current view of it, for doing so gives us the clearest image of what equality now means under law.

*Brown* is famously known for putting an end to the notion of "separate but equal" as permissible under the U.S. Constitution. No one disputes what the case sought to end. But there were actually two *Brown* cases. In *Brown I*, Chief Justice Earl Warren announced for a unanimous Court that "in the field of public education the doctrine of 'separate but equal' has no place" (*Brown v. Board of Education*, 1954, 495). The Court reserved its pronouncement on how to reach integration, again in a unanimous opinion, for *Brown II* (*Brown v. Board of Education*, 1955). *Brown I* and *Brown II* conventionally became lumped together as *Brown*. Both cases resulted in surprisingly short decisions. Given their importance in law and the manner in which they infused public consciousness, one would have expected that the justices would have written a lot more than they did. But, the brevity was intentional. The Court purposefully limited itself to gain unanimity, as it is well known that the chief justice set out to write short, nonrhetorical, unemotional, and nonaccusatory opinions that would antagonize opponents of racial equality less (see Graber 2008). That approach may have been necessary to ensure the immediate legitimacy of the Court's ruling, but it also had the effect of contributing to *Brown*'s problematic status, and arguably to its ultimate demise.

Both opinions were problematic. Even when it was decided, *Brown I*'s legal foundation was criticized widely as weak, even by the most famed legal commentators who championed integration (see Wechsler 1959; Black 1960). To exacerbate matters, the nonlegal sources of support also were problematic, although quite intuitively appealing. *Brown I* was premised on controversial social psychological findings that, even if they were equal in terms of resources, racially segregated schools were not equal because racial separation among school children generated feelings of inferiority as to their status in their communities. Yet, the strongest criticism of *Brown I* arguably would involve what it failed to address. Even if the case had had a more secure legal and empirical footing, it also failed because it did not address ways to achieve integration. *Brown II* sought to provide remedies but, like the case before it, *Brown II* also sought to offer a compromise. *Brown II* became legendary for the manner in which it sought compromise by ordering the admission of students "to public schools on a racially nondiscriminatory basis with all deliberate speed" (*Brown II*, 301). The case focused on how quickly children were to be assigned in a nondiscriminatory manner to their schools, and its mandate was far from an assertion to move quickly. Importantly, the Court left school authorities with the discretion to determine the precise parameters of what was meant by a racially nondiscriminatory school system and gave them the responsibility to address such systems. The Court emphasized that implementing the constitutional principles would require varied solutions to varied local school conditions but should be guided by traditional, equitable principles characterized by practical flexibility and reconciliation of public and private needs. The articulated local remedies included the need to address problems relating to the condition of the school physical plant, the school transportation system, personnel, and revision of school districts and attendance areas in order to achieve "a system of determining admission to the public schools on a nonracial basis . . . and to effectuate a transition to a racially nondiscriminatory school system" (*Brown II*, 301). Thus, both *Brown I* and *Brown II* evince a lack of strong commitment to either the anticlassification or the antisubordination approach, in that they can be read as focusing on nondiscrimination in admissions as well as on the creation of nondiscriminatory school systems, and in that they require the elimination of obstacles to ensure admission to public schools on a nondiscriminatory basis, which need not be read as a focus on ensuring equality of outcomes once a student is admitted.

The lack of a more forceful statement may have been important to gain support from colleagues on the Court as well as the broader society, but the statement left much to interpretation and, as might be expected, contributed to a focus on minimizing efforts. This occurred for several reasons, but one is especially important to highlight. Concurrent with the Court's major focus on the central harm of segregation—the inflicted psychological harms that come from a sense of inferiority—the Court ignored the way segregation could contribute to a sense of superiority among Whites. The Court's views of segregation causing a one-way harm set the legal system on a narrow path regarding remedies, a path that would not address the falsely created psychological sense of superiority for one group or the benefits that would come to that group. By focusing on one group, the Court left open the types of remedies that would have an effect on the other. This failure was symptomatic of the Court's unwillingness to articulate a decisive and broad approach to nondiscrimination.

Few may dispute that *Brown* served as an initial foundation for addressing racial inequality, but how to build on that foundation still remains contested. That is, *Brown I* and *Brown II* may have put an end to the dispute that segregation based on race needed to stop, and it may have required governments to take steps to end barriers to educational integration, but commentators, jurists, scholars, and legal practitioners did not (and still do not) agree on how to reach that end. Their disagreements about equality tend to follow along the lines of the classification and subordination principles. Given that *Brown* lacked a firm legal foundation, proponents of anticlassification as well as of antisubordination now claim to be *Brown*'s legitimate heirs. This is not surprising given that *Brown* contained language that condemned two different practices: the practice of classifying citizens by race as well as the practice that enforced subordination or that inflicted harm on the basis of racial status. *Brown I* (1954, 493) argued, for example, that "[t]o separate [Negro children] from others of similar age and qualifications solely because of their race generates a feeling of inferiority as to their status in the community that may affect their hearts and minds in a way unlikely ever to be undone." It could be argued that *Brown* clearly focused on the negative effects of segregation, but it also could be argued that it focused on the legal system's separation of individuals solely on the basis of race. Particularly if we focus on *Brown* itself (rather than historical events leading to *Brown*), both views appear reasonably tenable.

## The Rise of Antisubordination Impulses

*Brown* left plenty of room for not being followed earnestly. And indeed, nearly a decade passed without much reform. The lack of movement away from segregation after *Brown* was even more dramatic given the failure of progress over the century since the Equal Protection Clause was ratified to end differential treatment based on race. As a result (and from the middle to late 1960s), *Brown*'s directive actually was given considerable substance by both statutory developments and Court decisions. Recognizing the lack of progress, the federal government intervened aggressively to end resistance.

The Civil Rights Act of 1964 (2003) played a decisive role. The act, which was designed to enforce the Fourteenth Amendment, fostered *Brown*'s concern for greater equality of treatment in three major ways. First, despite *Brown*'s announcement of basic rights, it did not create circumstances that could lead to respect for those rights. Notably, opponents of segregated school systems could challenge schools, but they would need to do so at great personal and economic cost to themselves. As a result, plaintiffs actually were difficult to find, as were attorneys willing to represent litigants. To exacerbate matters, once litigated, the implementation of desegregation was a costly process: schools needed to be overseen to ensure that they followed judicial mandates. The Civil Rights Act authorized the U.S. Department of Justice to pursue legal actions against segregated school systems. Rather than rely on individual plaintiffs and private attorneys, the federal government intervened directly. Second, the act fostered greater equality by linking federal funds to desegregation efforts as well as by threatening litigation against states that failed to comply. Third, and equally important, federal aid to public education increased dramatically, and much of that increase was to provide assistance to schools with disproportionate numbers of economically disadvantaged children. This ended up earmarking large portions of these funds to poverty-stricken schools in the deep South, where desegregation had been most resisted. To receive those funds, schools needed to follow federal guidelines that determined what constituted a nondiscriminatory school system, an approach that provided a powerful incentive to desegregate. Although Congress took a decade to enact a legislative response to *Brown*, the ultimate result was dramatic and impressive.

Federal involvement also took the form of a series of important cases, from the late 1960s to the early 1970s, that imposed affirmative duties on school districts to remove the vestiges of segregation in educational systems. Again, it took nearly a decade for the Court to support reforms, but when it did, its rulings truly showed impatience with half-hearted efforts to end segregation. The Court evinced an eagerness to speed up integration by permitting the plaintiffs challenging the misconduct of school boards that denied minority students equal protection to bring their cases directly to federal courts rather than waiting to exhaust administrative remedies under state law (*McNeese v. Board of Education*, 1963). The Court invalidated a school desegregation plan that permitted students to transfer on request from a school where they would be in the racial minority back to their former segregated schools where their race was in the majority; the Court found the transfer plan unconstitutional because the policy relied solely on the students' race and the racial composition of their assigned schools, criteria for the transfers that tended to perpetuate segregation (*Goss v. Board of Education*, 1963). The Court struck down a board's refusal to keep the public schools open after a court order to desegregate; it required the board to reopen schools (*Griffin v. County School Board of Prince Edward County*, 1964). The Court found unacceptable efforts to delay integration by desegregating only one grade per year and leaving Black high school students, who were assigned to a segregated school, unable to take courses offered only in the White high school (*Rogers v. Paul*, 1965).

The Court also struck down freedom-of-choice plans. One such case combined elementary and high schools in two formerly segregated school districts on the grounds that the plan that permitted enrollment in either school was inadequate for conversion to a unitary school district, given that no White children had enrolled in the Black school (*Raney v. Board of Education*, 1968). The Court also invalidated a transfer plan in which, after three years, one junior high school continued to have all Black students because no White students living in its attendance zone chose to remain in it, and, at the same time, only seven Black students had enrolled in the formerly all-White junior high schools (*Monroe v. Board of Commissioners*, 1968). In yet another case, the Court ordered the school board to eliminate a plan that gave students (and their parents) the freedom to choose their own school assignments; the Court saw this as necessary to redress segregation, given that almost no White student chose to attend the school with Black students, and vice versa (*Green v. County School Board of New Kent County*, 1968). These cases gain significance in that the schools variously had argued that they had complied with *Brown's* desegregation mandate unless the Fourteenth Amendment could be read as requiring compulsory integration. The Court found that *Brown* did mandate integration in places where segregation had been imposed by law. It imposed an affirmative duty to take the necessary proactive steps to convert to a unitary system that eliminated racial imbalance in every facet of school operations. The cases stood for a firm finding that schools that were not integrated could not satisfy *Brown's* mandate by simply enacting nondiscriminatory student assignment policies; schools that had been segregated by law needed to integrate. More directly stated, the cases stand for the propositions that the state can and must use racial classifications to remedy past illegitimate uses of classifications and that the use of classifications to remedy past illegalities does not amount to an equal protection violation.

The above line of cases would continue into the 1970s, as the country continued to take expansive antisubordination approaches to dealing with segregation. *Swann v. Charlotte-Mecklenburg Board of Education* (1971) emerged as especially illustrative as it was a quite sweeping case that recognized the need to address links between residential and educational segregation. In *Swann*, the Court found that racially segregated schools led to segregated housing, as families lived near the schools that accepted their children. The Court found the situation untenable and took the opportunity to provide lists of needed corrective actions, such as the need to eliminate invidious discrimination with respect to such matters as extracurricular activities, support for personnel, building maintenance, and equipment. To pursue these objectives, the Court approved the busing of students beyond their neighborhood schools. The Court found busing to be an appropriate remedy for addressing racial imbalance in schools, even when the imbalance resulted from the selection of students based on geographic proximity to the school rather than from deliberate assignment based on race. The Court imposed the remedy to ensure that the schools would be integrated "properly" and that all students would receive equal educational opportunities regardless of their race. Even after *Swann*, the Supreme Court stood firm in its adoption of an antisubordination approach, such as when it prohibited cities that had been part of segregated county school systems from withdrawing from the county and establishing separate school systems

(*Wright v. Council of the City of Emporia*, 1972; *United States v. Scotland Neck City Board of Education*, 1972). The Court evinced considerable impatience as it sought to have schools move more aggressively to dismantle state-enforced dual school systems based on race and promote integrated public schools.

The above statutory and jurisprudential developments revealed the federal government's and the Supreme Court's willingness to take *Brown*'s directive seriously. Both constitutional interpretations and statutory law required affirmative steps to be taken in dismantling racial segregation in education, which lowered barriers to educational opportunities for minority youth. These were significant developments in that the initial opinions of *Brown I* and *Brown II* had been met with resistance, the lower federal courts had responded, and the Supreme Court had marched in lockstep with its view that the legal system needed to afford educational opportunities regardless of race. The impact of these new developments was immediate and dramatic—and short-lived.

## The Shift toward Anticlassification Impulses

The *Brown* cases may have spurred important reforms, but the legal foundation supporting them shifted as the legal system sought to define the types of remedies needed to ensure that it no longer dictated school assignments on the basis of race and, instead, established equal opportunities regardless of race. Courts evaluating legislative mandates could have taken a broad or narrow approach to addressing these issues, once they were committed to addressing them. Courts also could have adopted either approach, once they had addressed the remnants of a legal system that explicitly classified individuals on the basis of race in order to subjugate them. The courts chose the narrow route.

Arguably one of the most dramatic cases that limited the expanse of remedies to combat racial imbalances among schools related to disparate educational opportunities was *Keyes v. School District No. 1* (1973). *Brown* had created an affirmative duty for school districts segregated pursuant to a state statute to effectuate a transfer to a racially nondiscriminatory school system. In *Keyes*, the Court addressed a novel situation: unlike in prior cases it had addressed, the Court confronted a desegregation case from a state that had not segregated its students by statutory mandate. It was this case in which the Court ruled that only *de jure*, not *de facto*, segregation violated the Constitution. The Court required a showing of intentional state action directed specifically at segregating schools, not a mere showing of imbalances in racial concentrations of students. In so ruling, the Court dramatically backed away from supporting desegregation based on the concern for improving educational opportunities for minority youth, as racially segregated schools now could exist and not be part of the broader societal desegregation movement. *Brown* had stressed that segregation had a detrimental effect on "colored" children, and that the impact was greater when it had the sanction of law. *Keyes* interpreted this language to mean that the effect of segregation as a factual matter was still harmful, but only the harm caused by discriminatory governmental intent would trigger an equal protection violation. The case illustrates the Court's movement toward a color-blind approach to interpreting the Constitution in school contexts. And the approach would spread to other contexts that eventually would stand for the now-uncontroversial position that the Constitution prohibits the state from enacting policies motivated by discriminatory intent. The approach lets individuals follow their own desires and self-determining actions, and equally importantly, the legal system itself can permit disparities so long as they result from actions motivated by nondiscriminatory considerations. Eventually, and as we will see below, disparities in the lack of opportunities would be viewed as unfortunate byproducts of racially neutral actions.

*Keyes*'s movement toward a color-blind approach to addressing inequality would be furthered by a quick succession of cases that buttressed its trend. Notably, in *Milliken v. Bradley* (1974), the Court addressed an interdistrict school desegregation remedy. The plan involved the busing of public school students across district lines among fifty-three school districts in metropolitan Detroit. The Court found that state and city public school officials operated a *de jure* segregated school system, but the Court also found that, absent a finding that a violation in one school district produces a significant segregating effect in another, the schools lacked justification for imposing a cross-district remedy. The ruling clarified the distinction between *de jure* and *de facto* segregation, confirming that segregation was allowed when not considered the school district's explicit policy. In particular, the Court held that the school systems were not responsible for desegregation across district lines, absent evidence that the school deliberately engaged in a policy of segregation. *Milliken* severely limited *Swann's* reach, as *Swann* had given the hope that much could be accomplished through busing students from one school to the next. This ruling became particularly significant given that, for example, it meant that the legal system could not deem suburban schools to be influencing urban schools because they were not in the same district, and so large swaths of urban school districts would remain segregated as not enough White students remained in their districts.

The Court also supported limitations on state court initiatives to foster integration. For example, in 1980, California had enacted Proposition 1, which was an amendment to its constitution's equal protection provision that prohibited state courts from ordering mandatory pupil assignments through transportation unless ordered to do so by federal courts. The Court held that voters could enact the provision because the state had no obligation to have a higher standard than the one established by the federal Constitution (*Crawford v. Board of Education of the City of Los Angeles*, 1982). In another important case, the Court supported a trial court's refusal to effect a change in a desegregation order once a school board had achieved unitary status. In this instance, the Court refused to require further action because it interpreted the government as not having a role in causing the new disparities in school assignments. The Court viewed the changes in its previously neutral system of assigning students as resulting from changes in residential patterns due to people's relocating within the school system rather than as resulting from the actions of educational officials (*Pasadena City Board of Education v. Spangler*, 1976). With cases like these, the Court started to shift power to local courts and communities that could control school officials.

The Court also retreated from a more aggressive approach to removing racial imbalances in schools and educational opportunities when it took a limited view of the remedies available for uncovered imbalances. In the leading case of *Wygant v. Jackson Board of Education* (1986), the Court rejected a school board's policy of protecting minority employees by laying off nonminority teachers first, even though the nonminority employees had seniority. The Court rejected the argument that providing role models for minority public school students constituted a compelling state interest. The Court reasoned that "societal discrimination, without more, is too amorphous a basis for imposing a racially classified remedy" because a "court could uphold remedies that are ageless in their reach into the past, and timeless in their ability to affect the future" (276). The Court conceptualized a need to identify a specific injury by a clearly identified actor, which meant that a vaguely articulated societal discrimination could not rise to the level of a constitutional violation. Also importantly, the Court further reasoned that the injury suffered by the affected nonminorities could not justify the benefits to minorities. The burden on innocent parties who would lose their employment was too much to bear. These lines of cases indicated an increased need for specificity in articulating harms and remedies; they further indicated how remedial burdens should not be borne by innocent individuals but rather generally diffused across society.

By the late 1990s, the tide that *Brown* had raised had begun to recede as Supreme Court cases narrowed the scope of the constitutional guarantee of equal protection in education. Notably, a series of opinions decreased school districts' burdens relating to desegregation. For example, *Board of Education v. Dowell* (1991) held that a federal court desegregation order should end once a "unitary" system could be established, even if it resulted in a resegregation of schools. The Court reasoned that the lower court should address whether the school had complied in good faith with the desegregation decree and whether the vestiges of past discrimination had been eliminated to the extent practicable. The Court came to that conclusion on the belief that desegregation orders were not meant to operate in perpetuity. Also importantly, *Freeman v. Pitts* (1992) held that a formerly segregated school district may be declared partially "unitary" and released from federal oversight as long as the district meets part of its desegregation order. And in *Missouri v. Jenkins* (1995), the Court overturned massive educational improvements that had been ordered by a lower court to address desegregation by making the urban schools more attractive to suburban students from other districts and thereby increasing student achievement, which was below the national average. The Court found, for example, that the desegregation remedy ordering an increase in salaries for instructional and noninstructional staff went beyond the state's authority. The Court ruled that the remedy had exceeded the scope of the violation, with the previous violation being intra- rather than interdistrict. The Court reasoned that numerous external factors beyond the control of school officials were affecting the minority students' achievement, and that those external factors should not factor into the imposed remedial duty. The Court repeated its principle that the nature and scope of remedies for *de jure* segregation should be determined by the violation. In a concurring opinion that received wide attention, Justice Clarence Thomas explained what makes state-enforced integration harmful: assuming that African Americans could achieve a quality education only through integration implies that they are inferior. The counterargument to this position, one no longer subscribed to by the courts, views the injury as systemic rather than particular to state action. That position held that segregation, regardless of its cause, emerges from a systemic labeling device derived from a larger system that defines some schools as inferior and their pupils as inferior persons. The Court decisively moved toward an anticlassification view that sought to eliminate the use of race as a factor in state actions rather than adopt an antisubordination perspective that views the injury as requiring the courts to address multiple factors that define groups of children as inferior.

The above cases marked a significant shift from the views of the constitutional violation and needed remedies articulated in earlier cases; they also signaled a reticence to identify and address racial inequality that did not clearly flow from specific instances of school segregation that existed directly because of a legal mandate. Even formerly segregated districts seeking to maintain racially integrative policies after achieving "unitary status" would be stymied by existing judicial models of redress. These developments eventually allowed school districts to remain segregated, and they also reveal a strong hesitancy to focus on the historical social contexts surrounding persistent racial segregation and inequality in public education. Indeed, legally, racially imbalanced schools are not even defined as segregated when the factors causing the imbalance are not attributable directly to the state.

The movement away from focusing on the historical contexts of inequality and segregation highlights the importance of the selected approach to achieving equality. By moving toward an anticlassification approach, the school cases reveal the Court's decision to narrow what the government can do to address racial imbalances and unequal opportunities. It is not the case that the Court is indifferent to inequality. The Court simply views the legal system as having important limitations in efforts to address it. The Court permits pervasive segregation so long as the legal system did not have a direct part in creating it. If the legal system did not directly create it, then the legal system must remove itself from interfering in a way that would make distinctions based on race.

## The Fanning and Dominance of Anticlassification Impulses

The Court did not limit its retreat from using antisubordination remedies to redress pervasive racial inequities to elementary and secondary education. In the 1970s and '80s, the Court issued several groundbreaking opinions marking a retreat from addressing structural, or systemic, racial inequities. These cases rejected the use of race-conscious remedies designed to ameliorate "societal discrimination" that would address widespread evidence of discrimination in an industry and/or across the nation. Eventually, these approaches to addressing inequalities in opportunities would reinforce disputes relating to primary and secondary education and lead to what would become viewed as the inevitable adoption of anticlassification approaches that reject race-conscious remedies unless they relate directly to abolishing a state's improper use of classifications based on race.

Race-conscious plans fell into disfavor by the end of the 1970s. The leading case that would highlight the shift was *Regents of University of California v. Bakke* (1978). The Bakke case did more than reject the University of California–Davis School of Medicine's plan, which set aside a specific number of admission slots for minority applicants, resulting in the automatic exclusion of others based only on race. The Court's decision to limit affirmative (antisubordination) efforts made *Bakke* notable because it marked the beginning of efforts to limit the reach of Title VI of the Civil Rights Act by ruling that the standard for a Title VI violation ought to be the same as for an equal protection challenge. Later cases would confirm the limited circumstances in which *Bakke* permitted affirmative action. Notably, they would confirm that *Bakke* forbade only intentional discrimination (*Guardians Association v. Civil Service Commission of New York City*, 1983; *Alexander v. Sandoval*, 2001). In many ways, *Bakke* served as a dramatic beginning to the end of antisubordination impulses.

*City of Richmond v. J.A. Croson Co.* (1989) contributed to much of the transformation initiated by *Bakke*. In *Croson*, the Court held that the city of Richmond's minority set-aside program, which awarded municipal contracts by giving preference to minority business enterprises, was unconstitutional because of the city's failure to establish a compelling interest to treat the races differently. For the first time, affirmative action was judged as a "highly suspect tool" (493). The Supreme Court ruled that an "amorphous claim that there has been past discrimination in a particular industry cannot justify the use of an unyielding racial quota" (499). The *Croson* Court's language highlights the approach that eventually would dominate this area of law:

> We, therefore, hold that the city has failed to demonstrate a compelling interest in apportioning public contracting opportunities on the basis of race. To accept Richmond's claim that past societal discrimination alone can serve as the basis for rigid racial preferences would be to open the door to competing claims for "remedial relief" for every disadvantaged group. The dream of a Nation of equal citizens in a society where race is irrelevant to personal opportunity and achievement would be lost in a mosaic of shifting preferences based on inherently unmeasurable claims of past wrongs. Courts would be asked to evaluate the extent of the prejudice and consequent harm suffered by various minority groups. Those whose societal injury is thought to exceed some arbitrary level of tolerability then would be entitled to preferential classification. We think such a result would be contrary to both the letter and the spirit of a constitutional provision whose central command is equality. (505–6)

As *Croson* reveals, the Court would not only turn away from considering past societal discrimination but also invoke a judicial standard that would make it quite difficult ever to use.

Cases like *Croson* limited constitutional remedies to a narrow band of injustices. As Justice Powell expressed in *Bakke* (1978, 307), the Constitution requires redress for identifiable state-sponsored discrimination in education, but not for the more nebulous forms of societal discrimination: "in the school cases, the States were required by court order to redress the wrongs worked by specific instances of racial discrimination. That goal was far more focused than the remedying of the effects of 'societal discrimination," an amorphous concept of injury that may be ageless in its reach into the past." The Court rejected a race-conscious remedy in favor of a race-neutral approach; importantly, the race-conscious remedy that was designed to alleviate "societal discrimination" was rejected even after the Court reviewed detailed findings of racial discrimination in the contracting industry. The Court rejected past societal discrimination as an insufficiently compelling basis to justify race-conscious remedies under the standard that the effects of societal discrimination are "inherently unmeasurable." This approach was unsurprising in that it built on the principle that the Court had followed in *Wygant*, which has become the seminal case for the "strong-basis-in-evidence" standard for affirmative action programs. A public employer such as a school board needs to ensure, before embarking on an affirmative action program, that convincing evidence supports the need for remedial action. The state must establish a showing that, rather than general societal discrimination, prior state-endorsed discrimination continues to manifest itself. Without more, the situation remains too amorphous a basis for imposing a legal remedy resting on a racial classification.

In this line of cases, *Croson* was significant because the Court adopted a heightened review of affirmative action measures. In legal parlance, the Court adopted a "strict scrutiny" standard. That standard means that courts must examine very closely a state's action to ensure that it acts to further a compelling state interest (here, addressing discrimination) and that it does so in the most narrow way so as not to infringe unnecessarily on individuals' rights. In this context of equality jurisprudence, strict scrutiny serves to smoke out illegitimate uses of race by closely examining whether a legislative body is pursuing a goal important enough to warrant the use of what the Court has deemed a highly suspect tool. The standard also ensures that the means chosen to address the compelling interest "fit" the compelling goal so closely that there is little or no possibility that illegitimate racial prejudice or stereotype serves as the motive for the classification. The heightened review of classifications, in essence, seeks to ensure that the classifications are both legitimate and necessary to further the compelling state interest of achieving equality. The Court applied the standard in multiple important cases, and the use of that standard again reveals how the Court concerns itself with the burden the classifications can place on innocent parties. Several cases would draw on this standard to evaluate and put a halt to affirmative action for the simple reason that strict scrutiny analysis places an immense burden on the state to justify remedial measures. Most notably, *Adarand Constructors v. Peña* (1995) rejected federal affirmative action measures because of their failure to survive strict scrutiny, and *Shaw v. Reno* (1993) held that redistricting based on race warranted a standard of strict scrutiny. Those cases were essentially an application of the Court's position in *City of Richmond v. J.A. Croson Co.* (1989).

The movement away from supporting color-conscious remedies also finds expression in instances where the Court does allow for some race-conscious policies. Most notably, the Court has done so in the context of higher education, where it avoids supporting the view that courts have a direct role in attenuating broad societal discrimination. In the now-leading case in this area, *Grutter v. Bollinger* (2003), the Court upheld the constitutionality of a race-conscious admissions policy in a public university. The Court found permissible the University of Michigan Law School's admissions policy, which used race as one of many factors considered in the selection of students because such considerations further "a compelling interest in obtaining the educational benefits that flow from a diverse student body" (307). The Court, however, found the more formulaic approach of the University of Michigan's undergraduate admissions program, which used a point system that rates students and awards additional points to minorities, unconstitutional and in need of modification. The undergraduate program had failed to provide the "individualized consideration" of applicants deemed necessary in previous Supreme Court decisions on affirmative action. The Court would hold firm to this approach. At the next opportunity it had to revisit these issues, in *Fisher v. University of Texas* (2013), the Court declined to rule on Texas's race-conscious plan by, instead, returning the dispute back to the lower courts to ensure that they effectively had addressed whether the state had appropriately furthered a compelling state interest.

Although momentous, *Grutter* had important limitations. The Court did not recognize a constitutional duty to eliminate the various forms of structural racial inequality that cannot be easily cabined into the traditional definitions of state-mandated racial discrimination and segregation that existed at the time of *Brown*. The Court articulated a narrow view of constitutional protections, which neither acknowledges nor reveals an understanding of the myriad historical, social, spatial, political, and economic factors contributing to the continued racial inequities in education or other spheres. Unless applications to elementary and secondary public education would broaden significantly *Grutter*'s holding, it provided little room for public schools to use racial classifications to promote integrated education. The Court revealed no intention to expand *Grutter*'s reach when it was given the opportunity to do so. The Court limits the use of color-conscious approaches to addressing inequality to professional and graduate training, and even in that context the Court permits only a narrow set of possibilities.

The narrow set of possibilities was narrowed even more for primary and secondary school levels in the case that exemplifies the Court's approach to addressing unequal access in public schooling. That case, *Parents Involved in Community Schools v. Seattle School District No. 1* (2007), did more than repeat the claim articulated in cases that rejected calls for more active race-conscious approaches to ending segregation and addressing the negative effects of segregated education. In *Parents Involved*, the Court ruled impermissible state-sponsored efforts to redress segregation based on race unless essentially required to do so by a court finding that the state intentionally and directly had discriminated against the group that was excluded from specific schools. Such a position may be seen as flying in the face of *Brown*, which some viewed as using race-conscious plans to ensure equal access. But the leading opinion in this case, authored by Chief Justice Roberts, holds a different view and asserts that it remains true to *Brown*'s mandate. *Parents Involved* may or may not be a reversal of *Brown*, but its outcome portends to be quite different for articulating the government's role in shaping affirmative efforts to end the separation of racial and other groups from each other.

*Parents Involved* considered whether, to prevent *de facto* segregation, local school districts could voluntarily adopt race-conscious student assignment plans in pursuit of racially integrated schools. The plans in question had sought to ensure that the student population in each school reflected the racial demographics of the school district. The Supreme Court struck down the plans and, as a result, may be deemed to be asserting an end to *Brown*'s role in fostering race-conscious policies. By curtailing efforts to prevent *de facto* segregation, the Court did not leave much to address except instances that had been mandated by the courts. In these instances, the general legal resolution of *de jure* segregation already had drawn to a close. Supreme Court decisions already had accelerated the federal courts' drive to end existing desegregation orders, and those still subject to court orders continue to face virtually no enforcement activity (see Parker 1999). *Parents Involved* confirmed that *de facto* segregation did not present an issue as a matter of law. As Chief Justice Roberts put it, "Before *Brown*, schoolchildren were told where they could and could not go to school based on the color of their skin. The school districts in these cases have not carried the heavy burden of demonstrating that we should allow this once again—even for very different reasons" (*Parents Involved*, 2007, 747).

*Parents Involved* was resolved through a complex plurality of opinions (unlike *Brown*, which had been unanimous). Chief Justice Roberts, who provided the Court's opinion that rules this area of law, articulated an anticlassification interpretation of *Brown*, a view that equal protection invalidates all distinctions—malicious or benign—based on race. He quoted directly from a brief submitted by NAACP attorneys and their arguments before the Supreme Court: "The Fourteenth Amendment prevents states from according differential treatment to American children on the basis of their color or race," and "no State has any authority under the equal-protection clause of the Fourteenth Amendment to use race as a factor in affording education opportunities among its citizens" (*Parents Involved*, 747). Justice Thomas similarly drew on the briefs and oral arguments of the NAACP attorneys in *Brown* to support his anticlassification interpretation, noting that this "view was the rallying cry for the lawyers who litigated *Brown*," as he observed that the attorneys had argued, "that the Constitution is color blind is our dedicated belief," and "the Fourteenth Amendment precludes a state from imposing distinctions or classifications based upon race and color alone" (772). Both justices asserted that the Fourteenth Amendment categorically prohibits the government from engaging in racial classification. Although past decisions may have supported the claim that some classifications are benign and that their burdens are tolerable when spread broadly, those cases' judicial posture portended a quick end to their line of reasoning. The upshot was a move toward prohibiting classifications based on race.

Justice Breyer's dissent advanced an antisubordination claim, arguing that segregation "perpetuated a caste system rooted in the institutions of slavery and 80 years of legalized subordination" (*Parents Involved*, 867). Defending the use of race-conscious criteria by local school boards to achieve integration, Justice Breyer noted that "dozens of" post-*Brown* cases saw the Court requiring school boards to utilize "race-conscious practices, such as mandatory busing and race-based restrictions on voluntary transfers" in order to "comply with *Brown*'s constitutional holding" (804). Justice Breyer further observed that, in these cases, "the Court left much of the determination of how to achieve integration to the judgment of local communities" (804). He affirmed that "the lesson of history is not that efforts to continue racial segregation are constitutionally indistinguishable from efforts to achieve racial integration" (864). He emphasized the need for contextual sensitivity in distinguishing types of racial classification. Justice Breyer also highlighted the importance of context in "acknowledging that local school boards better understand their own communities and have a better knowledge of what in practice will best meet the educational needs of their pupils" (849). He further emphasized the widely held belief that judges are ill-suited to act as school administrators and that the law often leaves legislatures, city councils, school boards, and voters with a broad range of choice, thereby giving different communities the opportunity to try different solutions to common problems and to gravitate toward those that prove most successful or seem to them best suited to their individual needs. In addition, Justice Breyer made considerable use of social science findings to support the importance of remedial efforts. Research indicated that demographic trends augured "a return to school systems that are in fact (though not in law) resegregated" (806) and that integrated schooling suggested multiple positive "educational benefits" and "civic effects" (839–41). Without doubt, his version of what should happen in this case will stand as much as an example of the antisubordination view as Justice Roberts's version will stand as an example of the anticlassification model.

Legal developments since *Brown* reveal that the default rule in equality jurisprudence requires formal equality. The cases leading to that default rule may contain opinions that persuasively urge the Court to take an antisubordination perspective, but the Court is moving in another direction. The dominant rule does permit classification-specific approaches to equal protection problems, but it does so only in a very narrow set of circumstances. These developments are of considerable significance in that they go to the heart of the central meaning of the Fourteenth Amendment of the U.S. Constitution and how our legal system will seek to ensure equality. Generally speaking, equal protection challenges have shifted from focusing on the damages that arise from racial isolation due to the psychological environment it creates to embracing the principle that all should be treated as individuals. The shift to an anticlassification Constitution meant that the Court focuses more on the propriety of official behavior than on the lived experience of inequality and the costs exacted from the disadvantaged. Given the significance of these two approaches, it is important to understand their limitations, to which we now turn.

## Limitations of Current Approaches to Equality Jurisprudence

Both impulses found in the history of equality jurisprudence present clear implications for how society will assist individuals and groups that have suffered important harms and, indeed, for determining whether their experiences even can be construed as the type of harm worthy of consideration. Without doubt, current trends in equality jurisprudence indicate a rising commitment to anticlassification impulses. This commitment does not come without cost, as the approach has notable limitations. These limitations are important to consider, as they reflect a broad and profound shift within antidiscrimination law away from accommodating differences and toward ensuring formal equality. The limitations of this shift do not necessarily mean that courts should return to antisubordination approaches. Antisubordination impulses also evince important limitations. This section examines the limitations of both dominant impulses to addressing inequality.

### Limitations of the Anticlassification Approach

The ascendency of the anticlassification approach has not rid it of its limitations. Those limitations fundamentally relate to the approach's views of the types of inequalities that deserve formal redress. The approach resists taking into account some of the key factors causing some groups of individuals to be differently situated, and it can fail to address the reality that some of the norms that the anticlassification approach would apply across the board may be biased norms. The failure to address this reality can render irrelevant important differences and the social practices supporting those differences. By rendering these differences irrelevant, the legal system fails to see many problems as in need of remedy. It is difficult to play down the broad ramifications that emerge from limitations in the legal system's perceptions of harm and needed redress.

A fundamental limitation of the anticlassification approach to perceptions of harm relates to its requirement of state action. Under this view, the problem with unequal treatment is not inequality itself but the state enforcement of inequality. This type of differential treatment is *de jure*, as it arises by virtue of intentional acts of the state. As a result, this approach focuses on particular governmental actions that contribute to unequal treatment. For example, the Court notably requires that evidence exists of particular segregating acts by a school district before a federal judge may order relief against the school district. For example, in *Keyes v. School District No. 1* (1973), the Court required evidence that the racial imbalance in the schools was brought about by discriminatory actions of state authorities in order for it to warrant a legal remedy. The Court requires the state to have acted intentionally and to have had direct and causal involvement in the segregation before the legal system would hold the state responsible. This approach makes sense, as the language of the Constitution focuses on equal protection in the way laws apply to individuals, regardless of their particular group status; if it is the legal system that discriminates, then the legal system must be held accountable and must take a different course of action justified by the circumstances. But the distinction between public (state) and private actors raises important concerns.

The central limitation of the focus on state action is that actions that lead to differential treatment may not be caused directly by the state, but may still be related to state action. Discriminatory actions that are not caused directly by the state involve situations deemed *de facto*—situations that happen on their own or by private actions, not directly involving the state. This approach finds its roots in the well-established equitable principles that require a remedy's scope not to extend beyond the scope of the injury. However, the Court's narrow definition of what constitutes an injury makes this approach problematic. The narrow focus on state action provides the courts with a limited range of situations in which they may act aggressively and more expansively to address disparities in the way groups experience social life and receive some of society's benefits.

Contrary to the narrow view of state action, *de facto* actions are not necessarily outside of state actions. Even *de facto* segregated public schools, for example, have not occurred in the absence of official state action; schools are creatures of the state. An argument for viewing *de facto* segregated public schools as the result of governmental actions that discriminated is that segregation needs only minimal maintenance once the state has institutionalized it as a labeling device. Once established and entrenched, segregating systems essentially make impossible efforts to diminish the passive or neutral tolerance of private segregation.

The argument asserts that present neutrality and passivity simply continue past discriminatory actions. For example, schools may be desegregated formally, but disparate treatment can continue within schools. In addition, in some instances, the legal system still allows state actors to use race in allocating public resources (for example, through voucher systems), so long as private citizens, rather than state officials, supply or use the racial criteria. In such cases the state is not deemed to be the actor; private citizens are deemed to be doing the discriminating, as they are the ones using public funds. By supporting these types of efforts, the anticlassification approach enforces formal civil equality in a way that preserves various elements of social inequality. The anticlassification approach simply does not address well the various spheres of social life, particularly distinctions between private actors and those acting on behalf of the state.

Another key limitation of the anticlassification approach's view of harm involves the extent to which it focuses more on the categorization itself than on what the categorization expresses. The construction of harm in *Brown* highlights the importance of this distinction. In *Brown I* (1954, 494), the Court recognizes that segregation violates the Equal Protection Clause of the Fourteenth Amendment because to separate Black children from others solely because of their race would harmfully breed feelings of inferiority. The *Brown* Court also agreed that a sense of inferiority engendered by segregated schools tends to hinder the education and mental development of Black children. The Court focused on the effect of school segregation, specifically on the negative effects that segregation has on the educational opportunity of Blacks. Focusing less on the separation than on the results of separation in relation to opportunities has the effect of focusing on segregation as the sole source of feelings of inferiority rather than on the larger institution of which segregated schooling was a part. Focusing only on segregation and, therefore, only on the classification, ignores the larger institutional framework. This is important in that even if racially segregated schools had possessed equal resources and facilities, it was the policy that expressed a belief in Black inferiority that was inappropriate and that was deemed to lead to a sense of inferiority and lack of equal opportunities for social, educational, and mental development. The Court disapproved of "separate but equal" schools on the basis of the harm caused by the law's categorization of Blacks as inferior to Whites.

Yet another key limitation of the anticlassification principle relates to the failure to apply it consistently. Notably, the approach equally would protect superordinate and subordinate groups from the harm of classification based on group membership. In the case that led to the development of its analytic approach to protecting minority groups, *United States v. Carolene Products Corporation* (1938), the Court suggested that it would apply judicial scrutiny to laws burdening discrete and insular minorities, necessarily implying that courts review laws burdening nondiscrete or noninsular majorities differently. The Court has both rejected and accepted this view. In *Adarand Constructors v. Peña* (1995, 226–27), for example, the Court rejected this view by applying strict scrutiny to affirmative action and embracing a principle of "consistency of treatment irrespective of the race of the burdened or benefitted group." It did so while also insisting that a court applying strict scrutiny would have sufficient knowledge of racial status in the United States to distinguish between "'remedial preferences [and] invidious discrimination' . . . or, more colorfully, 'between a "No Trespassing" sign and a welcome mat'" (229). As seen in *Grutter*'s permitting the use of race in law school admissions decisions, the Court still permits affirmative action and remedial benefits to members of racially subordinate groups that it may not give to members of racially superordinate groups. These may be narrow contexts, but they challenge the principle of consistency. Permitting remedies in some contexts raises important issues about the necessary distributive or dignitary harm that must exist before a classification can be challenged.

In addition to the potential lack of overt consistency, the application of the anticlassification approach lacks consistency in subtle ways. For example, the anticlassification view of equality and constitutional interpretation pays little or no attention to dynamic and fluid conceptions of race. That lack of recognition runs the risk of making race a biological irrelevancy and ignoring shifting social practices. An individual's race has meaning, and that meaning shifts over time and in different contexts. Recognizing that race, like ethnicity, reflects socially contingent practices makes it difficult to equate the notion of formalism with neutrality. The English-immersion efforts intended to rid communities of other languages serve as a clear example. The legal system may justify these mandates in the name of nation building or economic mobility, but these policies disadvantage racial and ethnic groups that speak other languages in that they do not neutrally allocate burdens and benefits among groups that command very different linguistic resources. Benefits may accrue for some, but the effects on families, individuals, and communities probably vary considerably, as languages serve as critical cultural tools influencing definitions of achievement and success. The extent to which groups find themselves arrayed along a racial and ethnic hierarchy with very different histories, traditions, and resources casts doubt on the assertion that color-blindness operates in a neutral manner.

The anticlassification approach also has the same key limitation found in other legally formalistic approaches. Legal formalism holds to the tenet that laws constitute sets of principles and rules that exist independently of other social and political institutions. In the context of equality jurisprudence, it means that embracing an anticlassification approach includes assuming that equality does exist and that instances of discrimination are the actions of individuals and institutions that have been abstracted out of actual society. It assumes that existing discrimination results from discrete behavior that can be identified and neutralized. This approach views the legal system as a whole as functioning properly; it views discrimination as a malfunction stemming from misguided conduct of some actors that simply needs correction. The anticlassification impulse assumes that the legal system functions in a nondiscriminatory manner when it avoids distinguishing among protected classifications. The extent to which the legal system does not function in a nondiscriminatory manner reveals the extent of the flaws inherent in anticlassification approaches to inequality.

The anticlassification approach, then, evinces important limitations. It plays down the way institutions can privilege ostensibly neutral practices because they can serve other dominant interests. Even if the norms are not biased, their use may reflect past violations of formal equality, and they may ignore past oppression. The anticlassification approach does not encourage the tailoring of social policies to current social realities. The focus on approaching current realities in a neutral manner also means that social policies fail to reflect current realities and do not help facilitate the broad inclusion of previously disadvantaged or subordinated groups into important social institutions in a manner that more readily would foster equality. The approach resists using classifications even when some short-term use of them could mean that they would not be needed in the future; it assumes that not using classifications now best assures their speedy and ultimate demise.

## Limitations of the Antisubordination Approach

Numerous factors can account for the plummeting popularity of the antisubordination approach to equality and discrimination. Fundamentally, just as the anticlassification approach adopts principles that either may be inherently biased or may have biasing effects, so does the antisubordination approach. The focus on social meaning, particularly on subordination, inherently raises contested matters. For example, making claims that one group subordinates another raises concerns about bias and the evidence that supports the claim. Just as neutral positions could be deemed to be resulting in biased outcomes, positions seeking not to be neutral leave themselves open to charges of bias from the get-go, which leads to biased outcomes. In addition to the concerns about the antisubordination approach to recognizing harms, concerns exist about the potential breadth of available remedies. Because the harms that the antisubordination approach deems important to address are potentially contentious, concerns about remedies become exacerbated. These twin limitations pose considerable challenges.

The antisubordination principle remains problematic in that its practical reach remains open to debate. Interpretive judgments about social meaning and status, for example, are needed to determine which practices or institutional arrangements might contribute to the subordination of a certain group of people. And even if the factors contributing to subordination could be readily identified, divining the extent to which they do so poses additional challenges. Critical issues relate to, for example, determining how much subordination warrants government intervention and what causes the subordination, with even the possibility that groups cause the subordination of each other in different ways. Similarly, whether a practice violates an antisubordination principle depends on factual and historical contexts, particularly on the social mores that prevail at a given moment in history. As noted above, categories are no longer easily constructed; conceptions of race change, complicating the analysis. Race may be a concern, but conceptions of race are increasingly more fluid as issues of race become conflated with ethnicity, gender, and nationality. Also contestable are value judgments about appropriate responses, such as the extent to which distributive arrangements are unjust, and how responses to them should be integrated with other societal goals. The anticlassification approach seeks to avoid wading into these issues as it appropriates the notion of the laws' need to remain neutral, which, as we have seen, has its own limitations. The antisubordination impulse embraces the complexities and the concerns surrounding those complexities. It takes a stand rather than remaining neutral. In short, the actual nature of the antisubordination approach and its practical reach open themselves up to debate.

The antisubordination approach problematizes such cherished values as individual responsibility, competence, qualifications, merit, and even equality. Notably, rather than viewing these characteristics as purely those of individuals, it views them as related to groups and contexts in which individuals and groups find themselves. Although the values placed on these characteristics may be problematic and not easily determined, their conceptions often are held deeply, and as a result, individuals resist approaches that would question them. This resistance reveals the contested nature of the values that the antisubordination approach addresses. For example, the anticlassification approach presupposes an objective view of merit, whereas the antisubordination view approaches merit as context-driven. It is true that it may be inappropriate to conflate the failure to be equal with the failure to take advantage of equal opportunities, such as the anticlassification approach charges: some simply are not equal to others because of a lack of ability, personal failures, and failure to take advantage of new eras of nondiscrimination. Yet the presumed failures may simply be manifestations of the legal system's failures to take into account how perceived societal benefits are not available to all groups of individuals—how some benefits have already gone to particular groups and how individuals in other groups have not been able to obtain those benefits regardless of efforts to do so. Both the anticlassification approach and the antisubordination approach require some definition of merit, and yet determining what constitutes merit will probably always involve some subjectivity. The challenges against subjectivity are difficult to overcome. Recognizing that these matters are not objective opens up many debates that are altogether avoided by other approaches claiming objectivity. Between these two approaches, one way need not be seen as more fair or just than another, but the approach that challenges ingrained notions of individuality readily becomes viewed as more problematic.

Just as efforts to determine what can be deemed an appropriate harm are problematic, so are efforts to identify adequate remedies. Antisubordination approaches adopt broad remedies—remedies that have a direct impact on some individuals who may not have played a direct role in creating the harm. Such circumstances arise because the antisubordination approach focuses on groups to determine the treatment of individuals, whereas the anticlassification approach centers instead on individuals. For example, if a quota is deemed necessary for receiving a particular public service, such as access to university admissions or to employment, those who were not directly involved in discrimination also pay the price for the remedy. This is the case involving what some construe as "reverse discrimination." Under antisubordination approaches, positions of advantage potentially become illegitimate and lost; individuals who may otherwise have power and advantage lose it for the sake of a remedy. This is quite different from the anticlassification approach, which requires direct causation and individual responsibility; the rights that people already have are deemed legitimate and not subject to challenges unless individuals fail to use them as they should.

The antisubordination approach, then, allows for focusing on groups and seeks to advantage one group to remedy past harms to that group. This means that members of other groups may enjoy more limited rights than they otherwise would have had. A focus on individuals who discriminate means that those who do not are innocent; under the antisubordination approach, the "innocents" do not exist because a larger group of individuals is held responsible and essentially deemed culpable for the negative consequences of the differential treatment that needs to be remedied. The remedy must be had even at the cost of some who were not necessarily directly involved. In its efforts to remedy the effects of past discrimination, the antisubordination approach engages even with those who were not involved in direct, active, and invidious discrimination. Doing so runs the risk, at a minimum, of creating situations in which some individuals feel unfairly disadvantaged or robbed of opportunities due to situations not of their making (a parallel to what might be experienced by individuals in the already subjugated group). This type of interaction demonstrates the approach's inevitable conflict with cultural values that espouse the virtue of individualizing responsibility, blame, and merit.

The antisubordination approach focuses on creating an immediate change. Even as this position has intuitive appeal, it also has potentially significant limitations. Similar to the anticlassification approach, the antisubordination approach encourages social change and the creation of a society in which classifications no longer would be grounds for treating people differently. But the antisubordination impulse seeks immediate change to ensure later equality, whereas the anticlassification impulse seeks to treat individuals the same way immediately to ensure greater equality later. This raises two important concerns for those seeking differential treatment in the near future rather than assuming that equality exists now. First, focusing on difference emphasizes people's differences from one another, and this may encourage people to identify themselves and others in terms of group membership and factions rather than as individuals with common interests and as human beings. Second, it remains unclear how long protections will be needed for those deemed powerless to protect themselves from continued discrimination. This second concern has become a hot topic in legal decisions. The antisubordination approach leaves much to be determined, which leads some to view it as too inherently problematic. It remains especially problematic in light of the anticlassification approach's attempts to prevent society from entrenching classifications and thus allowing them to become more important than they should be, or allowing them to be misused. Comparing the antisubordination approach to an approach that concerns itself with the long-term implications of using classifications as a basis for different treatment, rather than with the result in a particular case, makes clear the ways in which antisubordination may misalign with cultural values that embrace notions of individuality and concern for long-term fixes, especially when members of a privileged group would suffer immediate negative consequences.

## Conclusion: The Commitment to Formal Equality

The tensions between the dueling equality impulses, at their core, focus on the central meaning of the Fourteenth Amendment of the U.S. Constitution and on how our legal system should seek to ensure equality. Generally, legal claims alleging discrimination rest on the Equal Protection Clause of the United States Constitution (or its equivalent at state levels). The relevant language, that "any person" shall not be denied the "equal protection of laws," may seem clear. But it arguably provides no clear guidance on how to ensure or achieve that equality. That lack of clarity allows for embracing different notions of equality and different ways to protect it. Despite the possibility of different approaches, current jurisprudence reveals the ascension of an anticlassification impulse. This impulse understands the Constitution as prohibiting governmental entities from intentionally discriminating against particular categories of individuals, even if the discrimination may remedy the lingering effects of past discrimination. The law requires formal equality as the default rule, permitting classification-specific approaches to equal protection problems in very narrow sets of circumstances. The anticlassification impulse largely has won the battle.

The ascension of the anticlassification principle explains various features of our equal protection tradition, and it provides a sense of where we are heading. Foremost among the current features is a commitment to protect individuals from all forms of racial classification, including "benign" or "reverse" discrimination. This commitment to protecting individuals rather than groups also explains why constitutional law does not treat facially neutral practices as presumptively discriminatory when they have a disparate impact on groups historically excluded from appropriate legal recognition. Debates may continue around what our constitutional understanding of equality ought to be, but equal protection law over the past half-century has expressed anticlassification, rather than antisubordination, commitments.

The consequences of the current resolution in approaching equality are very real. The antisubordination impulse had asked the legal system to recognize an expansive view of the nature and scope of harms to those disadvantaged and to embrace a broader view of potential remedies. The legal system has adopted an entirely different approach. It embraces an anticlassification impulse that seeks to limit both the instances in which differential treatment will be needed to achieve equality and the breadth of interventions that would further such an approach. The Court has adopted a minimalist, least-intrusive approach to addressing inequality.

There is no doubt that what people experience as discrimination continues, as do the prejudices supporting them. The Court's equality jurisprudence, based on the Equal Protection Clause, removes itself from having to address the vast majority of these matters. Importantly, the disparities in treatment and outcomes continue despite the social experiment that sought to ensure equality either through treating individuals the same way or through treating some differently because they were not equally situated in the first instance. These developments lead to the conclusion that equality jurisprudence must take a fresh look at what it can do to address the everyday realities of discrimination.

2

# The Nature, Developmental Roots, and Alleviation of Discrimination

Discrimination is necessarily a social event. It happens in social interactions, and it involves social contexts that influence the way differential treatment based on an individual's group status arises, manifests itself, and changes. As a result, socializing institutions become the important drivers for efforts to address the development of prejudice and responses to discrimination. Properly addressing discrimination, then, requires a close look at how social contexts can spur, sustain, and end discrimination. It requires exploring the characteristics of social forces that increase the likelihood of fostering dispositions, relationships, and institutions marked by tolerance, inclusion, and a sense of equity. Understanding the role of social contexts provides the foundation for thinking through how legal systems can address invidious discrimination by reshaping socializing institutions.

## The Nature of Prejudice and Discrimination

Before developmental research related to discrimination can be assessed, basic definitions must be established. Regrettably, research examining the differential treatment of individuals based on their group status often uses different terms to address similar matters and may even use the same terms to address different situations. It is therefore necessary to begin by describing general phenomena relating to discrimination, regardless of the terms specific research studies use to address them. For a variety of reasons, considering the nature of differential treatment for legally relevant analyses requires a focus on two aspects of discrimination: both the beliefs and the actions that support whether individuals will engage in differential treatment based on group status. The terms "prejudice" and "discrimination" most closely encapsulate the complexities relating to beliefs and actions needed for differential treatment, and thus are the most useful for our purposes.

This book approaches prejudice as a disposition consisting of three components. The first component involves a cognitive element, which constitutes basic knowledge, views, or beliefs about a target group or its members. Prejudicial beliefs tend to be viewed as faulty and inflexible generalizations directed at a group, either a group as a whole or individuals within it. The second aspect of prejudice, the affective component, involves feelings associated with the group. The most typical feelings include dislike, animosity, contempt, loathing, or antipathy. Lastly, the conative component involves the predisposition to behave in a particular manner toward the target group, and it can also include a likelihood to act differently toward another group when the target group becomes salient—for example, it can mean treating a privileged group better than an underprivileged one, or even ignoring individuals from a socially discriminated group. Importantly, and particularly for our purposes, prejudice involves intrapsychic phenomena. In that sense, prejudice involves a negative attitude, an antipathy based on faulty generalizations, that individuals use to conceptualize their social environment and orient themselves to objects and people within that environment. The term "prejudice," then, denotes the beliefs, feelings, and attitudes that predispose individuals to act in certain ways toward others.

At its core, prejudice involves actions marked by a lack of flexibility. Indeed, researchers sometimes present prejudices as hardwired, instinctual, or natural responses. Yet prejudices need not be rigid and they need not be actions in the common sense of the term. Prejudices are actions in the sense that they are loaded cognitive and emotional activities that occur in individuals' minds and that may be hidden from external observation. Their rigidity varies, depending on the purpose of the cognitive and emotional activities. The purpose may involve both psychological and social functions. For example, prejudice can serve to maintain or enhance an individual's self-esteem. People partly maintain their self-esteem by identifying with groups and believing that the groups to which they belong are better than other groups. When people experience a drop in self-esteem (e.g., when their self-esteem is threatened), they become more likely to express prejudices and stereotypes, as those expressions are common means of maintaining self-image: the denigration of others appears to be an automatic and reflexive response to personal failures and threats to one's self-esteem (Fein & Spencer 1997; Spencer et al. 1998). The link is particularly strong for individuals who have high self-esteem that is deliberately reasoned and controlled, known as "explicit self-esteem," as opposed to "implicit self-esteem," which is marked by highly efficient self-evaluation that may exist largely outside of awareness and does not lead individuals to engage in narcissistic and defensive behaviors (Jordan, Spencer, & Zanna 2005). Prejudices also can serve to preserve the integrity and hierarchical status relationships between groups (see Bobo 1999; Bobo & Tuan 2006). For example, people who adopt a social dominance orientation—individuals who view their social world hierarchically and want their own group to dominate and be superior to other groups—are more likely to hold prejudices toward low-status groups (see Perry & Sibley 2011). The more these self- and group-enhancing functions rely on group differentiation, the more the actions reflecting the prejudiced beliefs and emotions become robust and rigid.

Discrimination takes prejudicial actions one step further. Discrimination involves interpersonal actions—notably, treating individuals differently according to their group status. Like "prejudice," "discrimination" retains a pejorative meaning, as it refers to inappropriate and potentially unfair treatment based on group membership. It tends to be understood as negative behavior toward a member of a group that directly harms or disadvantages the member due to his or her association with the group in question. But it can be more than that in at least two important respects. First, discrimination need not involve overtly negative treatment; it can involve in-group favoritism that emerges from positive emotions such as admiration, sympathy, and trust rather than negative feelings and overtly negative responses to out-groups (see Brewer 1999). The tendency is well known as "in-group bias" and has been identified in societies around the world (see Aberson, Healy, & Romero 2000). Second, discrimination can occur toward a specific member of a group or the group as a whole. Discrimination, then, moves away from prejudice—thoughts, feelings, and possible actions—to actual actions with social consequences. The distinction between prejudice and discrimination appropriately highlights the critical point that individuals need not act on prejudices in their interactions with others and that discrimination retains its social significance.

## Latent or Blatant Prejudice and Discrimination

Prejudice and discrimination may be distinguishable concepts, but both can be either somewhat latent or blatantly obvious. Researchers focus on these two potential aspects to highlight the extent to which either prejudice or discrimination is within an individual's conscious control. The distinction gains significance given mounting evidence that many of the problematic prejudices and related discrimination involve implicit prejudice and subtle discrimination beyond an individual's awareness. This evidence is important to consider in light of persuasive psychological science revealing that inequality appears to be maintained by largely hidden actions, and that hidden, invidious actions pose inherent challenges to fostering equality.

The empirical study of prejudice has taken a series of dramatic turns. Research investigating prejudice emerged in the 1920s and sought to confirm American and European race theories of White superiority (Duckitt 1992). Reflecting concerns emerging from civil rights violations, wars, and the Holocaust, the study of prejudice focused on its pathological aspects, as researchers searched for personality syndromes associated with racism, anti-Semitism, and other forms of prejudice. That effort continued on the assumption that people consciously know that they hold and express prejudice in a manner deliberately under their control. That view changed as blatant expressions of prejudice declined—a development that, since the 1970s, has led researchers to focus on other sources and expressions of prejudice. Notably, researchers now have expanded the understanding of prejudice to include a lack of awareness and unintentional activation (Fazio et al. 1995). This form of bias occurs automatically, with little deliberate or conscious control, and also may occur despite well-intentioned efforts to think and act in nonprejudicial ways. Empirically, "prejudice" now means something entirely different from its original meaning: it has gone from identifying superior to identifying inferior statuses and now refers to consciously as well as unconsciously controlled beliefs.

Whether deliberately controlled or automatically activated, all forms of prejudice rely on the activation of stereotypes. Stereotypes simply are the images that typically come to mind when one is thinking about a particular social group. They are natural and common ways of thinking that serve as mental shortcuts that allow us to function in society. They work by implying information, typically overgeneralizations, about people beyond their immediately apparent external qualities. For example, research supports the "out-group homogeneity effect," indicating that people tend to deem out-group members to be more alike than in-group members when evaluating attitudes, values, personality traits, and other characteristics. The result of viewing out-group members as more alike than they actually are places them at risk of being seen as interchangeable or expendable, making them more likely to be stereotyped (Linville 1998). These stereotypes generate expectations about group members' anticipated behavior in new situations. Those expectations, in turn, produce a readiness to perceive behaviors or characteristics consistent with the stereotype. They even influence the targeted group: simply being a member of a stereotyped group can affect performance on stereotype-relevant tasks (i.e., tasks for which the stereotype might apply) in that, when a stereotyped group identity and the associated group stereotypes are made salient, performance tends to shift in the direction of the stereotype (Wheeler & Petty 2001). This phenomenon has been demonstrated by "stereotype threat," a concept identifying how anxiety about confirming a negative stereotype hampers performance on a variety of tasks that eventually confirm the negative stereotype (see Steele 1997). Stereotypes, as the supporting structures of prejudices, occur within individuals and may vary both in their transparency to others as well as in a person's harbored level of awareness. These prejudices are activated by the mere presence (even imagined presence) of the biased objects, a process that occurs automatically and without the perceiver noticing.

The importance of stereotypes stems from the evaluative processes that occur after their automatic activation. Much depends on the affective component of the prejudice (see Fazio et al. 1995). For example, some individuals automatically activate negativity toward a group characteristic. Some individuals may have no qualms about feeling negatively about a group or about expressing those feelings; these individuals would be viewed as truly prejudiced. Others with automatically activated negativity may be motivated to counter the effects of that negativity. The motivation to counter may derive from a sincere distaste for the automatically evoked negative reaction or from a more strategic self-presentation dictated by perceptions of the social norms that stereotypes raise in a particular situation. The negativity associated with the prejudice may lead to carefully and deliberately monitored behavior to avoid the appearance of the prejudicial response. Conversely, some individuals may not experience the automatic activation of any negative evaluation from memory on encountering a typically discriminated-against person. These individuals would be deemed the truly nonprejudiced. As seen below, given the current conceptualization of how the mind works, of how it necessarily categorizes individuals according to relevant characteristics, truly nonprejudiced individuals probably do not exist. What individuals do about their prejudices, then, depends on their awareness of them and the emotions attached to them.

Notions of overt and more subtle forms of discrimination have developed in parallel to those relating to implicit and explicit prejudice. Overt discrimination involves actions based on openly endorsed prejudicial beliefs. But just as individuals may be unaware of their prejudices, so individuals also may be unaware that they are discriminating and that their actions have negative implications. This latter form of discrimination has been viewed as subtle discrimination. Researchers, particularly those who focus on racial discrimination, have conceptualized multiple subtle forms of discrimination that come under the umbrella, for example, of "modern racism" (McConahay, Hardee, & Batts 1981), "symbolic racism" (Sears & Henry 2005), "ambivalent racism" (Katz 1981), and "aversive racism" (Gaertner & Dovidio 1986). Although these concepts focus on racism, particularly on White prejudice toward Black people, their conceptualization offers important models for understanding other forms of discrimination and the prejudices that support them. Even though each form of subtle racism has distinctive features, all consistently highlight one important point: people are most likely to express prejudice and discriminate when they can plausibly deny it (both to themselves and to others).

The focus on subtle forms of discrimination emerged out of necessity and highlights the importance of emotional attachments to prejudicial beliefs. The new focus of research emerged largely because of a pervasive reduction in open endorsements of explicitly prejudicial ideologies and of actions supporting them, particularly in relation to race and ethnicity (see Schuman et al. 1997). Individuals increasingly tend to endorse reduced prejudices, yet discrimination continues even in prohibited situations. The mismatch between professed attitudes and actions is what led to the growth of research examining subtle forms of bias, particularly in the context of race. Researchers have documented these more subtle forms of bias in ways that underscore how people may not be able to identify acts of discrimination and how those who discriminate have difficulty understanding that they are discriminating (Dovidio & Gaertner 2004). Although these conceptualizations all differ, all hypothesize the important role of emotional and subtle beliefs in that they view discrimination as resulting from a fundamental conflict between the denial of personal prejudice and underlying, unconscious negative feelings and beliefs.

Illustrative and influential conceptualizations of the various forms of discrimination emerged in the 1970s. Originally, researchers distinguished between dominative and aversive racism (see Kovel 1970). Dominative racism reflected the traditional, blatant form of discrimination: the "type who acts out bigoted beliefs—he represents the open flame of racial hatred" (54). In contrast, aversive racism reflected the emerging type of discrimination: actions that discriminate but are done by those who do not view themselves as racists. Aversive racists regard themselves as nonprejudiced and as supporting the principles of racial equality. Yet, they still may discriminate because they still possess nonconscious, conflicting negative feelings and beliefs about different races. Racism leading to discrimination, then, long has been viewed as involving both overt and subtle components.

Conceptualizations of explicit and implicit bias, such as dominative and aversive prejudices, understand prejudices as rooting from the same basic psychological processes that promote bias but as differing in the emotional responses to the bias. The fundamental difference is that the negative feelings held by aversive racists do not reflect open antipathy. Instead, the prejudices consist of more avoidant reactions of concern, discomfort, anxiety, or fear. As conceptualized, aversive racists find two things aversive: they find the target racial group aversive, and at the same time, they find aversive the suggestion that they might be prejudiced. The aversion leads to subtle discrimination—discrimination that tends to be hidden and that most readily occurs when individuals are confronted with ambiguous situations or those that permit reasons for differential treatment that do not rely on using the problematic characteristic. The major example of subtle discrimination is differential treatment that is overtly based on apparently nondiscriminating factors but that still discriminates on factors the individuals find aversive. For example, rather than treat people differently due to their race, aversive racists treat individuals differently due to a proxy characteristic, such as immigration status, socioeconomic status, or other characteristic related to race in a particular context. Individuals who find discrimination aversive still may end up discriminating; they do so by relying on rationales they find reasonable.

The focus on aversive racism (for our purposes, on aversive discrimination) should not detract from subtle forms of discrimination that result from deliberate efforts to discriminate. Notably, for example, private racism has emerged as an important phenomenon to study. This type of discrimination involves discrimination by individuals who privately endorse at least some aspects of a blatantly racist ideology (Schuman et al. 1997) yet are unwilling to admit such beliefs publicly. This type of discrimination also is subtle, and it also highlights the importance of the emotions attached to the beliefs that support the discrimination.

Although researchers originally focused on blatant forms of discrimination, the major thrust of research has turned to subtle forms, particularly aversive racism (Pearson, Dovidio, & Gaertner 2009). This research remains particularly challenging in that hidden belief systems, and the discriminatory behavior that may result from them, make the behavior tricky to detect. As a result, this area of research attracts considerable controversy. Although few dispute that unconscious motives may be at work, room exists for disputing the ways in which researchers identify prejudicial motives and link them to instances of discrimination. As a result, disputes continue over both the validity of unconscious-prejudice measures and the applicability of unconscious-prejudice research to real-world controversies (Blanton & Jaccard 2008).

Links between implicit and subtle prejudices and discrimination lend themselves to disputes, given the ease with which discrimination can be linked to overt and expressed forms of prejudice. Overt actions and beliefs can be taken at face value, but that is not the case for latent impulses for the simple reason that it is difficult to make something obvious when it is not, by its very nature, obvious. Still, a significant amount of research indicates that implicit bias, though subtle, links to discriminatory behavior inside the laboratory (Dasgupta 2004) as well as in everyday situations (Rooth 2010). A new comprehensive meta-analysis of fifty-seven racial attitude/discrimination studies finds a moderate relationship between overall attitudes and discrimination (Talaska, Fiske, & Chaiken 2008). Emotional prejudices are twice as closely related to racial discrimination as are negatively expressed stereotypes and beliefs. Moreover, emotional prejudices closely relate to both observed and self-reported discrimination, whereas stereotypes and beliefs relate only to self-reported discrimination. Support for implicit forms of prejudice also comes from investigations of whether implicit responses can be "overwritten" by newer, explicit forms of bias or incompletely replaced by individuals who genuinely strive for egalitarian beliefs. Researchers argue that new attitudes can override but not replace existing ones, thus creating dual attitudes. Whether an attitude is endorsed depends on the cognitive capacity to retrieve the explicit attitude and whether the explicit attitude will override the implicit attitude. The durability of implicit attitudes matters to the extent that, even if explicit attitudes change, implicit ones do not (see Wilson, Lindsey, & Schooler 2000). Despite important controversies relating to the power of these different forms of prejudice, researchers agree that both explicit and implicit manifestations of prejudices exist and reliably predict some behaviors. Stereotypes, overt beliefs, and emotional prejudices all closely relate to what people say they did or will do toward out-group members, but emotional prejudices are related more closely to what people actually do.

Investigations relating to prejudice and discrimination reveal important points. Prejudiced attitudes, and discrimination resulting from them, are not limited to a few pathological or misguided individuals. Prejudice emerges from normal human functioning, as the mind must use categories needed for normal prejudgment. The process cannot possibly be avoided, as orderly living depends upon it. Thus, all people are susceptible to prejudice to one extent or another. Prejudice itself, however, may not lead to discrimination, a not surprising finding given that it is well established that attitudes are not always strong predictors of behavior (Glasman & Albarracin 2006). Much depends on the extent to which individuals attach negative emotions to prejudicial thoughts, a finding consistent with a long history of research indicating that emotions are important determinants of behavior in general. In addition to being difficult to control because of its attachment to emotions, discrimination even becomes difficult to identify because what leads to discrimination may be subtle and beyond an individual's conscious control. Inequality, then, may be maintained by emotional reactions more than by cognitive beliefs, and many of those reactions reside beyond an individual's conscious control. To exacerbate matters, when differences are identified and become consistent with well-known stereotypes, the distortion in perception, and the actions associated with it, may be highly resistant to change.

## Personal and Institutional Discrimination

Just as the nature of discrimination has been studied under a variety of constructs, so have actual acts of discrimination. More specifically, personal discrimination refers to acts of discrimination committed by individuals, whereas institutional discrimination refers to discriminatory policies or practices undertaken by organizations and other institutions. "Discrimination" involves putting group members at a disadvantage or treating them unfairly as a result of their group membership.

Discrimination by individuals has been investigated under a variety of labels, including "interpersonal discrimination," "incivility," "microinequities," and "microaggressions" (see Cortina 2008; Hebl et al. 2002; Sue et al. 2007). Given that the concept of microaggressions now has been used to understand adolescents' discrimination, it can serve as illustrative. Microaggressions are defined as "brief and commonplace daily verbal, behavioral, or environmental indignities, whether intentional or unintentional, that communicate hostile, derogatory, or negative racial slights and insults toward the target person or group" (Sue et al. 2007, 273). Just as aggression itself can take multiple forms, so can microaggression. Microaggressions can involve microassaults, which are attacks meant to harm the victim that are similar to traditional forms of discrimination, like using racial epithets or displaying a swastika. They also can involve microinsults, which include behaviors that are insensitive, rude, or inconsiderate of a person's identity. These types of insults tend to be subtle in nature and may be unconscious and unintentional, but nonetheless demean the target or the target's group, such as assumptions about intelligence. Microaggressions also can involve microinvalidations, which are behaviors that minimize the thoughts, feelings, or experiences of targets, such as assuming that they are foreigners or dangerous because of their race. As a whole, these constructs are intended to identify and describe the multiple ways in which discrimination can occur among individuals.

A focus on discrimination appropriately centers on individuals' relationships with their social environments, but it is important not to ignore institutional levels of prejudice and discrimination. Beyond individual levels, prejudice and discrimination can operate in essentially two ways. First, individual prejudices and stereotypes can support institutional actions. For example, political support for laws and policies can lead to institutional discrimination, and prejudiced individuals can warp the application of laws and policies so that they end up discriminating. Second, prejudice and discrimination at institutional levels can operate independently from specific individuals. This type of discrimination does not require individuals' active support, their intention to discriminate, or even their awareness that institutional practices produce discriminatory effects. Instead, this form of discrimination simply emerges as institutions develop or reflect broader societal forces. Institutional discrimination, then, can result from specific individuals' actions or the actions of broader institutions themselves.

Just as interpersonal discrimination can be subtle, so can institutional discrimination, and it can be equally challenging to identify. Much of institutional discrimination actually can go unnoticed, given that it can derive from long-standing practices deemed normal and appropriate, and can receive support from laws deemed right and just. Because institutional discrimination need not depend on the overt or intentional efforts of individuals, it often must be inferred from disparate outcomes between groups traced back to differential practices and policies, even those that might appear to be unrelated to group membership. As a result, disparate experiences and outcomes may not even be deemed discrimination even though they relate closely to differential treatment, opportunities, and results.

Researchers have identified the effects of discrimination in a variety of institutions. For example, economic discrimination has occurred in areas such as loan policies, after differences in qualifying conditions are controlled for, and a variety of other forms of discrimination have occurred in employment, housing, and consumer markets (see Pager & Shepherd 2008). Educational institutions also are marked by discrimination, such as in policies that result in differential suspensions for disruptive behavior (Skiba et al. 2002). Pay gaps relating to gender also illustrate well how discrimination can occur among those similarly employed (see Blau 2012); and a variety of examples reveal well how policies may inappropriately keep groups from even gaining employment, such as height requirements and other physical characteristics required for jobs such as police officer or firefighter (Schulze 2012). Discrimination in the media also has been noted, such as exaggerations of the association between minority groups and violence or poverty (see Dowler 2004). Criminal and juvenile justice systems also are marked by discrimination, as is apparent in group differences in incarceration rates for similar crimes or disproportionate institutionalization of ethnic minority youth or girls for similar offenses (see, e.g., Moore & Padavic 2010; Brown & Sorenson 2013). Similarly, children of color are disproportionately involved in alternative care arranged through child welfare systems and are more likely to have longer placements in out-of-home care, less likely to receive comprehensive services, and less likely to reunify with their families than White children (Wells, Merritt, & Briggs 2009). Mental and physical health systems also have been marked by discrimination, resulting in less access to effective care or in medical providers playing down factors that lead to increased stress, such as poverty, which have short- as well as long-term effects on health (see Shavers et al. 2012; Fuller-Rowell, Evans, & Ong 2012). Just as with subtle discrimination, all of these forms of differential treatment can be subjected to reasonable explanations to support them and justify their continuation. Yet the effects are the same. Institutions treat some individuals differently because of their group status.

Challenges in identifying institutional discrimination associated with formal laws and policies pale in comparison to the challenges involved in identifying culturally embedded discrimination—discrimination in the fiber of a culture's history, standards, and normative ways of behaving. Cultural discrimination arises when one group exerts the power to define societal values deemed legitimate and worth upholding. This form of discrimination goes beyond simply privileging the culture, heritage, and values of the dominant group as it imposes its culture on other, less dominant groups. Cultural discrimination gives priority to the values of the majority group that are embedded in widely accepted cultural ideologies (Sidanius & Pratto 1999). As a consequence, everyday activities implicitly communicate group-based bias. Cultural discrimination shapes the way members of different groups interpret and react to group disparities; it fosters compliance to the status quo without explicit intentions, awareness, or active support for these group-based disparities. Cultural discrimination involves both beliefs about the superiority of a dominant group's cultural heritage over those of other groups and the expression of such beliefs in individual actions or institutional policies.

The way cultural discrimination works can be understood by reference to theories that focus on how groups gain dominance and how both individual and structural factors contribute to various forms of group-based subjugation. One of the most important theories to emerge, social dominance theory (see Sidanius et al. 2004), views the familiar forms of group-based oppression (e.g., racism, classism, sexism) as reflections of a more general tendency for humans to form and maintain group-based hierarchies. Understanding these group hierarchies requires considering the cultural, ideological, political, and structural aspects of societies as well as interactions between psychological and social-contextual processes. It is important to acknowledge individuals' key roles in social-contextual processes and to understand why they stereotype, harbor prejudice, discriminate, or view the world as just and fair. But it also is important to focus on the universal and subtle forms of discrimination and oppression at institutional levels because institutions allocate resources on much larger scales, more systematically, and more unwaveringly than individuals generally can. As a result, social dominance theory regards institutional discrimination as one of the major forces creating, maintaining, and re-creating systems of group-based hierarchy. According to social dominance theory, group discrimination tends to be systematic because social ideologies coordinate the actions of institutions and individuals. The argument is that people share knowledge and beliefs that legitimize discrimination, and that they most often behave in ways that endorse these ideologies, thereby upholding institutional practices.

Although it may be difficult to dispute that discrimination at cultural levels exists, examples are even more difficult to pinpoint. Still, two examples may be illustrative. The first involves controversies surrounding "acting white." As currently developed, the concept identifies a phenomenon explaining some minority youth's educational underachievement. The underachievement emerges from minority youth's rejection of efforts to achieve because they may be perceived as "acting white" when they do achieve. Researchers argue that the perception that academically successful Black students are "acting white" is a real phenomenon that results in negative consequences for Black students. Rather than view the phenomenon as problematic due to minority youth's actions, researchers view it as resulting from unintended consequences of desegregation efforts, which, for example, required Black youth to be educated with White children and undermined a key center of Black communities: schools and the role models and experiences that they provided minority youth (see Buck 2010).

The second example involves the immigrant paradox emerging from academic and public policies promoting rapid immigrant assimilation. The paradox suggests that first-generation immigrants have higher levels of adaptation than the second and that, over time, the adaptation of immigrants declines to that of nationals and even below. Highly acculturated youth may fare worse academically and developmentally than their less-assimilated peers even despite decreases in objective risk factors (e.g., improvements in socioeconomic status and English fluency). The immigrant paradox has been documented in studies investigating a variety of outcomes, including substance use, mental health, sexual behavior, and education (see Schwartz et al. 2010). Some ethnic-minority youth may be at risk for negative outcomes (e.g., internalizing problems, externalizing problems, academic failure, and drug and alcohol abuse) because the demands to adapt to both the mainstream and ethnic cultures require adherence to the behavioral expectations and values of both cultures (e.g., Gonzales et al. 2002; Szapocznik & Kurtines 1993). However, some authors have suggested that a strong connection to the ethnic culture may be protective and may suppress these negative effects because these youth may be less differentiated from their parents, less likely to experience family conflict, and more likely to receive strong social support from their families (e.g., Atzaba-Poria & Pike 2007; Schwartz, Montgomery, & Briones 2006; Szapocznik & Kurtines 1993). For example, researchers have found that Mexican immigrant culture represents a unique segment of Mexican culture that is selective with respect to occupational, educational, and psychological characteristics conducive to success, but that these traits tend to erode over generations because of negative acculturating experiences in the United States (Buriel 2012). Assimilation into a dominant group need not mean a similar experience and outcome for individuals who actually feel different.

These two examples relating to institutional effects reveal that even broader cultural forces may not be readily distinguishable from individual-level effects. Both necessarily interact. The "acting white" phenomenon relies on the external forces of peer pressure that influence individuals' experiences, and the immigrant paradox relies on acculturation experiences as well as broad policies relating to the relative support for ethnic groups. Because of the absence of intention and awareness involved in much of contemporary institutional and individual racism, Whites may not be sensitive to the extent of racial bias in the United States and particularly to their own expressions of bias (Dovidio et al. 2002). Even though racism relates directly to the coordinated interaction of stereotypes, prejudice, and discrimination, it involves more than individual biases. Racism reflects institutional, social, and cultural influences. The very essence of racism involves not only negative attitudes and beliefs but also the social power that translates them into disparate outcomes that disadvantage other races or offer unique advantages to one's own race at the expense of others. Thus, although the study of prejudice and discrimination focuses on the roles of individuals and interpersonal processes, racism encompasses institutional, social, and cultural processes that serve as an influential backdrop to individual-level perspectives.

## The Ubiquity and Developmental Origins of Adolescent Discrimination

A sense of differential treatment due to group status imbues most adolescents' lives. Some adolescents directly experience the effects of prejudice and discrimination, some perpetrate it, and all live in a society with institutions exhibiting differential treatment because of group status. Still, consistent with the understanding of discrimination's subtle qualities, much differential treatment can go unnoticed. Even if it is noticed, and even if it is invidious, much differential treatment may not be deemed worth addressing. Though our understandings of discrimination typically derive from adults' experiences, researchers now have sought to expand that understanding to adolescents.

## Personal Experiences of Discrimination

Research addressing discrimination during the period of adolescence has focused mainly on racial and ethnic discrimination, and most of it focuses on those who feel discriminated against. That research reveals that perceptions of racially discriminatory treatment are quite prevalent among minority youth. For example, 77% of African American adolescents reported experiencing at least one discriminatory incident in the preceding three months (Prelow et al. 2004), 87% of African American youth reported experiencing discrimination in the preceding year (Seaton et al. 2008), and 91% of preadolescent African Americans reported experiencing at least one racially discriminatory experience in their lifetime (Gibbons et al. 2004). Research now even reveals perceptions of racial discrimination in online settings, with 32% of African American adolescents reporting online racial discrimination at least once in their lifetime, and a small minority (~2%) reporting some form of online racial discrimination every day (Tynes et al. 2012). Empirical research consistently reveals that the majority of Black youth perceive themselves as being discriminated against because of their group status.

Analyses of racial discrimination also have examined perceptions of discriminatory treatment among Hispanic or Latino youth. For example, approximately half of Puerto Rican adolescents (49%) report perceiving racial/ethnic discrimination directed against them in at least one situation, and nearly as many (47%) indicate that they are worried about being discriminated against (Szalacha et al. 2003). The majority of Latino youth report experiencing some form of adult and peer discrimination, with 12% reporting incidents of discrimination once a day or more (see Huynh & Fuligni 2010). Similar to results from studies of African American adolescents, studies of Mexican-origin adolescents reveal that the majority of them also report at least one experience of racial/ethnic discrimination, with some studies reporting 64% (Edwards & Romero 2008), others 76% (Romero & Roberts 2003), and still others

94% (Flores et al. 2010). That research also typically reveals that nearly a quarter of them, 21%, report often experiencing racial/ethnic discrimination (Flores et al. 2010). Racially discriminatory experiences appear to be pervasive and ubiquitous for some groups of minority adolescents.

Studies of subtle discrimination similarly report high rates of discrimination. Those recent studies, however, report variation among ethnic groups (see Huynh 2012). For example, both Asian and Latino groups report similar levels of emphasis-on-difference microaggressions (e.g., "What are you?"). Yet, Latino adolescents report more frequent denial-of-racial-reality (e.g., told that they are overly sensitive about racial matters) and negative-treatment (e.g., ignored by clerk) microaggressions than Asian American adolescents. Although this new area of research necessarily reports tentative results, the results do support the important point that adolescents experience discrimination and are not immune to it.

In addition to being ubiquitous in the sense of commonly experienced, discrimination tends to be ubiquitous across contexts. The vast majority of ethnic-minority adolescents report perceptions of discrimination in a variety of social environments. Adolescents perceive discrimination by teachers and staff in educational settings (Crystal, Killen, & Ruck 2008; Gogtay et al. 2004; Rosenbloom & Way 2004). For example, Black, South Asian, and Asian high school students all are more likely than White students to perceive discrimination in the way teachers treat and discipline students from their racial or ethnic group (Ruck & Wortley 2002). Racial- and ethnic-minority adolescents also report being discriminated against in public settings. The groundbreaking study in this area, published in 2000, found that 75% of African American and 65% of Hispanic adolescents reported that, because of their race or ethnicity, they were hassled by a store clerk or security guard (Fisher, Wallace, & Fenton 2000). That study also found that minority adolescents report being hassled by the police (Fisher, Wallace, & Fenton 2000), a finding supported by other research indicating that minority youth report being suspected of wrongdoing because of their race or ethnicity (Simons et al. 2002). These findings comport with other studies indicating that racial discrimination and differential treatment by adults is common among ethnic-minority adolescents in a variety of settings (Greene, Way, & Pahl 2006).

Importantly, the bulk of research in this area has not distinguished among the perpetrators of racial discrimination (see Huynh & Fuligni 2010; Rosenbloom & Way 2004; Fisher, Wallace, & Fenton 2000). But adolescents undoubtedly are aware of discrimination not just because they are its target but also because they perpetrate it. Discrimination in interactions with peers appears to be a common type of differential treatment experienced by youth. For example, an important study sampling a large group of African American ten- to twelve-year-olds found that 67% of them reported that they had been insulted by a peer because they were African American (Simons et al. 2002). Some studies report similarly high percentages of peer differential treatment because of race or ethnicity, but the findings vary considerably. For example, a majority of East Asian (84%) and South Asian (73%) adolescents reported being the victims of racially derogatory name calling, compared to 36% of African American and 47% of Hispanic adolescents (Fisher, Wallace, & Fenton 2000). Name calling that uses racial and ethnic slurs also is a common form of discrimination directed toward ethnic-minority adolescents (e.g., Aboud & Joong 2008; Verkuyten & Thijs 2002).

The role of peers' discriminating actions against one another has been highlighted by research on bullying and a variety of aggressive behaviors. Racial and ethnic bullying is a common form of discrimination directed toward ethnic-minority adolescents (e.g., Aboud & Joong 2008; Verkuyten & Thijs 2002). In addition, adolescents use race and ethnicity as major sources of social exclusion and marginalization, which are relational forms of aggression deemed to be as problematic as overt aggressive behavior. This line of research nicely highlights how the concept of discrimination becomes increasingly elastic, as it includes a variety of differential treatment that reveals both its breadth and its depth.

Although research on the experience of discrimination centers on ethnicity and race, those group characteristics constitute only one source of prejudice and discrimination. For example, adolescents experience high rates of discrimination on the basis of their gender (Brown & Bigler 2005). Gender roles, traditions, customs, and rituals, prescribed by societal standards, are reflected in children's and adolescents' social environment, where they appear even more pervasive than in the adult world (Horn 2006; Tenenbaum & Leaper 2002). Stereotypes and social exclusion based on gender remain pervasive and relate to negative social outcomes (Gillen-O'Neel, Ruble, & Fuligni 2011). Unlike their view of discrimination based on race and ethnicity, adolescents tend to view gender discrimination as more legitimate and readily condone it as reflecting conventional expectations about gender roles (Killen, Sinno, & Margie 2007).

Like racial and ethnic prejudice and discrimination, those based on gender involve adolescents as both recipients and perpetrators. Sexual harassment serves as the most illustrative example. National studies on sexual harassment in schools, conducted in 1993 and 2001, reported similar results for both years: 81% of students experienced some form of sexual harassment during their school years. Fifty-nine percent of students were harassed occasionally, and 27% were targeted often (American Association of University Women 1993, 2001). In addition, 54% of students said that they sexually harassed someone during their school years. As with bullying, grade level makes a difference in the frequency of sexual harassment, but in contrast to bullying, it increases with grade level: 55% of eighth and ninth graders and 61% of tenth and eleventh graders reported that they had been physically sexually harassed at school (Hand & Sanchez 2000).

Harassment due to sexual orientation also emerges as an important form of differential treatment based on group status. In a national survey of LGBT youth, 40% reported physical harassment because of their sexual orientation (Kosciw 2004). Sexual-minority youth also report environments that do not view them favorably. One study indicated that 91% of LGBT middle school and high school students sometimes or frequently heard homophobic epithets such as "faggot," "dyke," or "queer" (Kosciw & Diaz 2006). Although these remarks come from other students, 39.2% of students report hearing them from faculty or school staff as well (Kosciw & Diaz 2006). Homophobic bias-based harassment is especially common. Nearly 85% of sexual-minority youth experience verbal harassment, and 40% experience physical harassment at school (Kosciw et al. 2010). Heterosexual youth also report homophobic victimization (Pascoe 2007; Poteat et al. 2011). In one of the largest studies on bias-based victimization, which included over six hundred thousand students, nearly 40% of those who had experienced victimization in the preceding year considered at least some of it to be based on either sexual orientation, gender, race, ethnicity, religion, or physical or mental disability (Russell et al. 2012). These types of bias-based experiences carry heightened consequences for victimized youth compared to bullying absent these forms of perceived bias (Poteat et al. 2011; Russell et al. 2012).

Current research on the experience of discrimination, then, reveals at least three key points. First, the experience of differential treatment is pervasive, and it occurs because of group status that is supposed to be protected, such as race, ethnicity, gender, and sexual orientation. Second, other forms of differential treatment are beginning to be investigated, such as differential treatment due to weight (Puhl & Luedicke 2012; Puhl & King 2013). That emerging research, however, tends to reveal similar results. Third, some forms of differential treatment remain essentially ignored, such as experiences relating to adolescents' mental health (see Lebowitz 2013), refugee status (Montgomery & Foldspang 2008), religion (Aroian 2012), and social dispositions like shyness (see Blöte et al. 2012; Tillfors et al. 2012). And existing research relating to differential treatment based on those characteristics reveals that adolescents experience it by being both targets and perpetrators, and that they are aware of discrimination that occurs in multiple settings.

## The Developmental Origins of Discrimination

The general recognition that adolescents and children themselves are the primary sources of their socialization now guides the study of how adolescents develop and experience discrimination and prejudice. As they develop, adolescents learn to interpret complex individual-environmental interactions that reflect how they acquire social orientations and become members of society (see Turiel 2002). Ever since they were young children, adolescents have been able to make moral judgments about fairness, societal judgments about groups, and psychological judgments about personal choice (see Nucci 2001; Smetana 2006). They also have learned whether to act on those beliefs. In fact, "development" essentially refers to the growing sophistication of the ability to make judgments and to act on those judgments. As adolescents gain this psychological and social sophistication, they gain not only the capacity to make appropriate judgments but also the possibility of being held responsible for them. The study of adolescent development comports with the manner in which both adolescents and society view adolescents as increasingly capable individuals responsible for their actions.

Theories of prejudice formation and discriminatory treatment correlate directly with adolescents' ability to judge and act on those judgments. Those theoretical formulations span levels of analysis that address both individuals (such as prejudice as a function of personality type) and contexts (such as prejudice learned from parents, peers, or the environment). Although much has been written about the nature of prejudice and the behaviors resulting from it (see, e.g., Nelson 2009), fewer studies focus explicitly on its actual development. Instead, research centers on determining when prejudicial attitudes begin, on expanding theories by exploring developmental differences, and on examining how the general developmental characteristics of adolescence relate to prejudice and discrimination. Together, these studies reveal important insights necessary for understanding how to respond to discrimination.

The emergence of prejudicial attitudes serves as an important starting point for understanding its expression. Children as young as three or four years of age are able to recognize group differences, and that ability has been linked to in-group biases and the ensuing development of, for example, racial and gender stereotyping (Aboud 1988; Cameron et al. 2001; Morrongiello, Midgett, & Stanton 2000; Aboud 2005; Martin, Ruble, & Szkrybalo 2002). The ability to recognize and act on group differences at that age, however, has even earlier roots. Implicit social cognitions and social preferences, such as racial in-group preferences, are visible in early infancy (Dunham, Baron, & Banaji 2008). Some theories even propose that prejudice has roots in early human ancestors (as highlighted by evolutionary theory, see Fishbein 1996). This important line of research reveals the key points that biases exist, emerge early, and are understood in the context of groups rather than individuals.

Efforts to understand developmental differences and expand theories have sought to apply insights from child development to theories of prejudice. For example, research has fruitfully applied understanding of children's prejudicial thinking to further understanding of prejudice among adults. Notably, research has drawn from children's tendency to see the world in dichotomous categories and has applied that insight to the understanding of prejudice in other age groups. That research led to the study of numerous individual characteristics that relate to prejudiced attitudes and discrimination. Among the attitudes and dispositions linked most strongly to discrimination are the constructs of the authoritarian personality (Adorno et al. 1950), right-wing authoritarianism (Altemeyer 1981), social dominance orientation (Pratto et al. 1994), and extrinsic religiosity (Batson & Ventis 1982). Research continues as these lines of inquiry have become considerably more nuanced (see Sibley & Duckitt 2008).

Although the focus on individual dispositions and cognitive abilities continues, that line of research offers only limited insights for understanding prejudice and discrimination among adolescents. Rather than focus on adolescents, this area of research seeks to understand personality or prejudice in general. Research that includes adolescents tends simply to use them as a group to be studied rather than as a group through which to acquire understanding of the development of prejudice (see Degner & Jonas 2013). Even more importantly, however, this line of research has become overshadowed by research that focuses on social contexts rather than individual dispositions, as the understanding of how individuals in groups are treated focuses on group influences themselves. Indeed, some researchers now reject the entire personality explanation and argue that prejudice fundamentally roots in social factors like social identity (e.g., Reynolds & Turner 2006).

Rather than using understandings of child development to help explain prejudice, another important line of research has extended different theoretical models from adults to children and adolescents. For example, some of the most successful efforts include extending social learning approaches that explore the influences of peers and parents on adolescents' prejudicial attitudes (Aboud & Doyle 1996). The focus on peer groups also has led to the use of cognitive-developmental approaches that view prejudice as influenced by adolescents' abilities to think about groups in complex ways, and this line of research has extended concepts of social cognition to achieve understanding of peer groups and networks (see Levy & Dweck 1999). These approaches continue to proliferate, as efforts now have developed theories that explicitly seek to explain adolescents' prejudice and discrimination, such as social identity development theory (Nesdale et al. 2005), developmental intergroup theory (Bigler & Liben 2006), moral and social reasoning theory (Killen et al. 2002), and related societal-social-cognitive-motivational theory (SSCMT) (Barrett 2007; Barrett & Davis 2008). This broadening understanding of prejudice and differential treatment among adolescents emphasizes well the importance of developmental factors, such as peer groups, in understanding the expression of prejudice.

Just as with research focusing on individual characteristics, research extending theories to adolescents' experiences also has its strengths and limitations. The research tends not to be developmental in the sense of exploring how a phenomenon develops in individuals. Empirical findings and developmental theories explain well how prejudice and discrimination exist, but not their actual development in specific individuals. Still, this line of research makes one critical contribution: it focuses on social contexts rather than on individual characteristics and personality dispositions. At its core, research examining prejudice and discrimination highlights the futility of ignoring context and the importance of recognizing that social contexts shape the expression of prejudicial beliefs.

Researchers now recognize that biases exist, emerge early, run deep, and are understood in the context of group interactions rather than purely individual dispositions. Emphasizing developmental contexts reveals that a focus on individual differences provides only a limited view of why and how adolescents develop and maintain prejudiced values and of how those translate to discrimination. For example, by the age of six or seven, children not only are able to identify their own ethnic group but also show increased in-group positivity and out-group negativity (Aboud 1988; Nesdale 2001). Beginning around nine years of age, however, children's innate prejudiced attitudes appear to dissipate, and by the time they enter middle childhood, children begin to report lower levels of prejudiced attitudes (Black-Gutman & Hickson 1996; Doyle & Aboud 1995). That diminution does not mean an absence of prejudiced attitudes. Rather, it means that cognitive development no longer reliably predicts them, as some studies report no changes in age-related prejudiced attitudes among adolescents and young adults, and others report increased levels of prejudice with age (Black-Gutman & Hickson 1996; Hoover & Fishbein 1999). That research reveals that, beginning in early adolescence, other factors besides age and developmental abilities appear to become important predictors of the formation and expression of prejudiced attitudes (Nesdale 2008).

Explaining how adolescents express and maintain prejudiced attitudes requires a look at influences important to them. Historically, researchers assumed that children learned prejudice from adults who transmitted negative messages and explicit stereotypes. As a result, parental attitudes and practices have been among the most studied influences on the formation of adolescents' prejudicial attitudes. However, few studies have found significant direct correlations between parental attitudes and children's level of prejudice (see Aboud & Levy 1999). Parents' prejudiced attitudes do not always match their children's attitudes. For example, early studies in this area examined African American children's attitudes; they reported that their attitudes differed from those of their parents, with children often having more negative racial attitudes (Branch & Newcombe 1986; Carlson & Iovini 1985). Additionally, various studies have reported that correlations between parents' and their children's prejudiced attitudes may be small or nonexistent (Davey 1983; Aboud & Doyle 1996; Fishbein 2002).

Although few studies find a one-to-one correlation between parental levels of prejudice and children's levels, adults (and parents) clearly are significant sources of influence on children's development of group identity. Parents provide direct and indirect messages about group distinctiveness (see Bigler & Liben 2006). In addition, parents can determine exposure to other groups (e.g., out-groups) and the value of intergroup tolerance and mutual respect. Relatedly, research has shown that the role of parents in passing on stereotypes to their children may be a far from obvious process fraught with complexities: a recent study found that, although children's racial attitudes were not related to their parents' explicit racial attitudes, they did seem to be impacted by the mothers' (but not the fathers') implicit beliefs (Castelli, Zogmaister, & Tomelleri 2009). Meta-analyses attempting to decipher influences as children age reveal some correlations between parents and their older children, but they note that such correlations may derive from contexts and that studies have not examined differences between parental and peer influences (Degner & Jonas 2013). Importantly, another meta-analysis confirmed that prejudice changes systematically with age during childhood, but that no developmental trend is found in adolescence, indicating the stronger influence of the social context on prejudice with increasing age (Raabe & Beelman 2011).

The wide recognition that peer groups influence attitudes has not resulted in numerous studies examining how peer groups influence prejudice (for exceptions see Aboud 1989; Poteat 2007). The studies that have examined peer influence on prejudice have focused mostly on racial attitudes (Aboud 1989; Aboud & Doyle 1996; Schofield 1982). For example, Aboud and Doyle (1996) used an experimental manipulation to show that discussing racial issues with peers can lower prejudice. In their study, eight- to eleven-year-old children first completed a measure of racial prejudice. High-prejudiced children were then paired with low-prejudiced children to discuss their ratings on the measures. Students who originally reported high racial prejudice reported lower levels of prejudice after this discussion. Poteat (2007) extended previous work on peer contextual effects to homophobic attitudes and behaviors. His research revealed significant similarity in homophobic attitudes within friendship groups at the initial time point. Additionally, evidence of peer group socialization was found, as adolescents' attitudes resembled those of their peers eight months later even after controlling for their original attitudes (Poteat 2007). Another study indicated that aggressive peer groups influenced the use of more homophobic epithets (Poteat, Espelage, & Green 2007). In addition, research also shows that even well-adjusted children have the potential to perpetuate negative peer treatment, sometimes explicitly but often implicitly. Notably, children in high-status groups are at risk for perpetuating negative treatment of others based on status and societal expectations. As an example, ethnic-majority children often perpetuate negative societal expectations about ethnic-minority children, contributing to the cycle of prejudice (Killen & Rutland 2011). As another illustration, boys who hold negative expectations about girls based solely on group membership (gender) can contribute to gender discrimination as well (Arthur et al. 2008). The few studies that exist, then, underscore that peer socialization underlies the development and proliferation of prejudiced attitudes.

One of the main places from which children and adults learn stereotypes is the mass media. Content analyses have found advertisements, television programs, movies, and other media saturated with racial and gender stereotypes (Entman & Rojecki 2000; Furnham & Paltzer 2010; Plous & Neptune 1997). The media perpetuates these stereotypes over time, in spite of decreases in real-world stereotyped behaviors (Davis

2003), and even creates markets based on stereotypes (Kahlenberg & Hein 2010). These stereotyped portrayals have important effects. Studies have long shown that even exposure to brief advertisements profoundly influences the way people perceive and relate to one another, as advertisements have an effect on social perceptions and behaviors (see Rudman & Borgida 1995). And as is well known, the media perpetuates stereotypical images of youth that become part of public consciousness, as revealed by portrayals of minority youth as problematic and subject to criminal behavior (Gilliam & Bales 2001). The media continues to be seen as a powerful tool that influences attitudes and behaviors (for a review, see Levesque 2008).

Although research examining the development of prejudice reveals important points, mainstream social expectations expressed by parents, peers, and the wider society contribute to the development of adolescents' prejudices and prejudicial experiences and, in many cases, reflect normative expectations about what it means to be socialized, adjusted, and acculturated (Fisher, Jackson, & Villarruel 1998; McLoyd 2006; Sellers 2003). As noted earlier, discrimination, prejudice, and bias often stem from normative expectations in societies, expressed in messages that are disseminated as an outcome of social categorization, social identity, and group processes (Dovidio & Gaertner 2004; Sellers & Shelton 2003). Being raised in a prejudiced environment does not necessarily translate into developing prejudiced attitudes, and the converse is also true: being raised in a tolerant environment does not necessarily lead to tolerant attitudes. Equally importantly, prejudice and discrimination may be normative expressions of relationships played out in a variety of contexts. These findings reflect the reality that adolescents are socialized by, and also influence, numerous agents in their environments, ranging from parents, peers, and media to other socializing institutions like schools that bring youth together and shape their interactions.

## Alleviating Adolescent Prejudice and Discrimination

To alleviate discrimination and prejudice it is crucial to understand how adolescents experience and make discriminatory and prejudiced judgments. Adolescents interpret a wide array of often-conflicting messages from their environment as they make judgments about them.

They make those judgments through social evaluative processes based on their social experiences; and the way they express those judgments relies primarily on the contexts that shape them. The way judgments are formed, shaped, and expressed suggests that efforts to alleviate prejudice and discrimination will reach their greatest effectiveness if they address adolescents' social experiences, consider adolescents' interpretations and evaluations of these experiences, and provide contexts that enable adolescents to make decisions that reflect fairness and justice. Efforts also, of course, will fail to achieve intended results if they do not address adolescents' social experiences and shape their environments to enable intended outcomes. The way these considerations work together is exemplified by the most studied and popular approaches to reducing prejudice and discrimination, namely, those intended to develop multicultural learning environments, foster empathy and perspective, and increase intergroup contact. These three related approaches are but a few of many others, but they have become appropriate exemplars of the promise and limitations of efforts to address prejudice and discrimination. They also happen to point toward similar themes with regard to methods for effectively alleviating prejudice and discrimination.

## Multicultural Learning Environments

Given that prejudice involves learning about others and how to respond to them, efforts have reasonably sought to address the development and expression of prejudice through formal and informal learning experiences focused on understanding difference. Multicultural approaches serve as the key example, as these have a long history. These approaches suggest that prejudice and discrimination develop partly because of a lack of knowledge of and appreciation for diverse groups. As a result, multicultural approaches champion the notions that individuals will respect groups when they learn more about them, and that a better understanding of diversity reduces negative attitudes and inappropriate treatment. By recognizing that cultural understanding and awareness of discrimination contributes to promoting tolerance and reducing prejudice, these efforts address the complex problem of both celebrating diversity by respecting cultural identities and, at the same time, recognizing that the majority group often views such identities in negative terms (see Verkuyten 2008). At their core, multicultural efforts would validate the cultures of marginalized racial and ethnic groups by challenging the notion that everyone shares a common culture and countering beliefs of cultural superiority (e.g., Banks 2004).

The continued growth and popularity of multicultural efforts to address prejudice have led to variation in their specific aims and methods. Perhaps the most popular way to foster multicultural learning environments has been through formal curricula, such as "multiethnic readers" with stories that feature characters from a diverse range of racial groups or narratives depicting children from minority racial groups in counterstereotypical ways. Multicultural efforts also can involve out-of-classroom experiences, such as art projects in observance of cultural holidays, trips to museums with a cultural focus, and direct learning about cultures through cultural immersion. In addition to including different methods, multiculturalism can include different goals. Some focus on drawing attention to cultural differences between different racial and ethnic groups to help participants understand the lives, experiences, and perspectives of diverse others (Ryan, Casas, & Thompson 2010; Wolsko et al. 2000; Wolsko, Park, & Judd 2006). Other approaches focus on appreciating and valuing different groups' positive contributions to a diverse society in order to improve intergroup attitudes (e.g., Ryan et al. 2007; Ryan, Casas, & Thompson 2010; Wolsko et al. 2000; Wolsko, Park, & Judd 2006). Still others focus on maintaining groups' own cultures or relationships to dominant cultures, such as through opposing assimilation (see Berry & Kalin 1995). Despite the diversity in aims and methods, all generally seek to highlight the histories, cultures, and contributions of particular racial and ethnic groups.

Variation in the nature of multicultural efforts unsurprisingly contributes to variation in their overall effectiveness. Although even the most popular methods have not been subjected to rigorous evaluations (see Zirkel 2008), efforts to determine effectiveness that do exist reveal mixed findings. For example, early reviews of multicultural education programs in classrooms found the modification of attitudes difficult to achieve (Williams & Moreland 1976), and others found intervention effects either nonsignificant or inconsistent across populations (Bigler 1999). Some found that effectiveness depends on who is asked. An important study found that multicultural interventions with fourth-grade children led to significant improvements in social interaction according to teachers' ratings but not according to children's own self-ratings (Salzman & D'Andrea 2001). The most popular approach, the use of readers, tends to be the least effective (see Pfeifer, Spears Brown, & Juvonen 2007). Although these types of findings appear disappointing, they actually are to be expected, given the variation in goals and methods, as well as given that reviews of multiple programs may disagree on what makes for successful outcomes.

Despite the failure to find consistent effectiveness, research still reveals important points that help shed light on how to alleviate prejudice and the discrimination that can come from it. Notably, some evaluations of multicultural education reveal conditions under which it can gain effectiveness. Multicultural efforts can help create a school climate that promotes positive attention to cultural diversity, deals with negative interactions between children from different groups, and promotes tolerance of others from diverse cultures (see Verkuyten 2008). For example, explicitly teaching six- to eleven-year-old European American children about historical racial discrimination can improve their racial attitudes (Pfeifer et al. 2007). European American children who have learned about historical racism have been shown to hold more positive and less negative attitudes toward African Americans as well as to increase the degree to which they value racial fairness (Hughes, Bigler, & Levy 2007). Formal aspects of multicultural education (e.g., teaching children about cultural traditions held by different ethnic groups) also have been shown to limit negative attitudes by improving children's knowledge and understanding (Verkuyten 2008). Without doubt, multicultural efforts can increase awareness and understanding of different groups.

The above types of findings appear to have a greater impact on attitudes as well as actions when the school context also takes diversity into account. Actual practices in the classroom (e.g., teachers who provide examples of ethnic exclusion and discuss the need for fairness toward all cultures) help establish positive, inclusive group norms within classrooms and discourage social exclusion (Verkuyten 2008). Children experience less exclusion if they believe that they could tell teachers about unfair behavior toward them and that teachers would take appropriate action (Verkuyten & Thijs 2001). Multicultural readers also may be more effective in changing attitudes in contexts in which children have little or no other opportunity to meet and form friendships with actual members of other groups (Cameron, Rutland, & Brown 2007). And diversity in schools and classrooms creates the local multicultural contexts that can help limit ethnic exclusion and negative ethnic intergroup attitudes. These findings support the argument that effective multicultural efforts emerge most when total school environments reflect diversity and help all individuals experience equality (see Banks 1995).

With older children, particularly college students, multicultural approaches include direct discussions of prejudice and discrimination (Bigler 1999). Among the most notable efforts, the Teaching Tolerance project (Aboud & Levy 1999; Bigler 1999; Derman-Sparks & Phillips 1997; Sleeter & Grant 1987) encourages students to discuss racism and teaches ways to recognize and confront racism and discrimination. These efforts have revealed some positive effects, but it remains to be seen whether the effects extend beyond those discussions. Still, the focus on recognizing difference and confronting discrimination probably is more effective than simply focusing on and celebrating difference. The effectiveness of such efforts again reveals a key reason for so much variation in the effectiveness of multicultural programs: they are diverse.

The diversity of multicultural intervention can help identify the program elements that contribute to such positive outcomes as attitude change, awareness of societal inequality, and tolerance, but the reasons for their effectiveness remain debatable. Some programs' successes may be attributable to contact among groups. For example, a meta-analysis of multicultural education programs (Stephan, Renfro, & Stephan 2004), one that defined "multicultural" very broadly, found significant positive effects of multicultural education on immediate as well as delayed intergroup attitudes and behavioral change. But the study identified only one significant component of the programs as contributing to these positive effects: having contact with the target group. Findings like these suggest that the positive effect of multicultural education programs might simply derive from the positive effect of intergroup contact components (e.g., see Brown & Hewstone 2005; Pettigrew & Tropp 2006), a finding supported by research indicating that greater knowledge of other groups is not a strong mediator of the positive effects of intergroup contact (Pettigrew & Tropp 2008). Thus, intergroup contact may account for the positive effects of multicultural programs, but not the reverse.

Importantly, however, the more common forms of multicultural programs, such as those that are integrated into the curriculum, often are not evaluated (see Zirkel 2008). Other successful efforts and methods may exist, but they have yet to be identified and subjected to rigorous empirical scrutiny.

The pervasive lack of evaluations of multicultural programs should not lead to the conclusion that they receive no support, as arguably the strongest factor supporting multiculturalism is the negative effect of color-blind approaches. Color-blind approaches view prejudice as derived from an emphasis on superficial and irrelevant group categories (e.g., race). That view suggests that prejudice can be decreased by deemphasizing group memberships. Ignoring or avoiding discussion of group categories actually may be effective, but only in the short term; preexisting prejudice seems likely to rebound in the longer term (e.g., see Correll, Park, & Smith 2008). As with other studies in this area, however, the results can be complex and may not indicate failure. Notably, color-blind approaches that do explore similarities among groups have received some empirical support because focusing on a common in-group identity ("we") transcends intergroup distinctions ("us" vs. "them") (Gaertner & Dovidio 2000). Still, these efforts have been deemed problematic in the longer term as individuals from nondominant groups are well aware of their disadvantage (see McKown 2004). Another approach focuses on individuals' uniqueness rather than that of their group, which has multiple positive effects, such as participants' viewing individuals as not conforming to stereotypes. But a focus on individuality is likely to lead to viewing stereotype-disconfirming group members as exceptions or subcategories, leaving group stereotypes intact (for a review, see Hewstone 1996). A long line of research supports the conclusion that even when people encounter a stereotyped group member who violates the group stereotype, they often continue to maintain the stereotype by splitting it into subtypes (Judd, Park, & Wolsko 2001; Richards & Hewstone 2001). Color-blind approaches may hold promise, at both the theoretical and the empirical levels, for facilitating positive intergroup interactions, but they also have important weaknesses that suggest a need to recognize that differences exist.

Despite signs of effectiveness and indications that a lack of consideration of multicultural features of groups leads to negative outcomes, available research relating to multicultural interventions still reveals important limitations. First, the successful programs have been conducted with young children (Cameron et al. 2006; Cameron & Rutland 2006; Cameron, Rutland, & Brown 2007), and indeed most programs tend to focus on children. Some focus on adolescents, including late adolescents, but those programs are remarkable for their rarity. Second, successful programs may change attitudes in the short term but not necessarily in the long term (Turner & Brown 2008). Importantly, however, long-term studies are rare; programs that do present pre- and postintervention evaluations typically report results that occur right after the intervention, and many of these interventions are short-term laboratory experiments. Third, multicultural interventions actually can be detrimental to the development of intergroup attitudes. Highlighting certain stereotypical activities (e.g., songs or cultural practices) and emphasizing the distinctness of racial and ethnic groups can increase the likelihood that adolescents will place individuals in rigid categories and increase racial and ethnic stereotyping and prejudice (see Bigler 1999; Bigler, Brown, & Markell 2001). Multicultural programs that highlight the positive contributions of various groups have led to greater racial bias among racially and ethnically diverse middle and high school students (Wittig & Molina 2000), and the fostering of stereotypes also has been documented in college students (e.g., see Wolsko et al. 2000). Fourth, multicultural programs generally are intended to manage diversity and improve intergroup relationships. Although these are inherently worthy goals, these approaches become limited to the extent that they emphasize the establishment of intergroup harmony rather than recognize the need to address intergroup inequalities (see Dixon et al. 2010; Dovidio, Gaertner, & Saguy 2009). Fostering positive feelings toward stigmatized groups may inadvertently obscure the need for social change, and the more relationships among groups continue to improve, the more majority groups view discrimination as vanquished despite evidence to the contrary (Todd, Galinsky, & Bodenhausen 2012). Although research does reveal that multicultural programs lead to improved attitudes, then, multiple reasons exist for caution as existing studies also reveal important limitations. Approaches to intergroup relationships may promote more positive intergroup sentiments, but they do not necessarily lead to greater recognition of ongoing discrimination, nor do they address discrimination itself.

## Fostering Empathy and Supporting Alternative Perspectives

Improving knowledge about a group need not result in treating its members or the group any better. Perspective taking and empathy have emerged as likely candidates for reducing prejudices and discrimination. Although often presented as different types of interventions, alternative perspective taking and empathy are closely related and highlight similar principles. Given that these approaches have received the most interest and empirical analyses, focusing on both highlights well the importance and nature of efforts intended to address attitudes that necessarily figure centrally in efforts to alleviate prejudice and discrimination.

Several reasons support the potential role of empathy and taking others' perspectives in mediating between intergroup attitudes and intergroup behavior. As we have seen, emotions substantially motivate intergroup behavior. Stereotypes and attributions guide individuals' feelings, but emotional reactions provide the motor for behavior and direct it. In addition, intergroup attitudes actually are only a moderate predictor of discrimination that occurs among groups and their members (see Dovidio et al. 1996). Even interventions demonstrated to improve intergroup attitudes (such as intergroup contact; see below) often fail to translate into support for policies that would promote equality among groups (Dixon, Durrheim, & Tredoux 2005). Lastly, empathy involves deepened connections with others. Empathizing with a member of a group, seeing the world through that member's perspective, may produce a "self-other merging" in which the member becomes included more fully as part of one's self-representation (Cialdini et al. 1997). Developing more closely related representations of group members and one's self-representation leads to generalizing positive orientations to the group and increases the possibility of treating them more positively.

The reasonable belief that prejudice essentially results from a lack of empathy, from simply not appreciating and understanding others' situations, contributed to the development of role-playing and perspective-taking approaches to reducing prejudice and conflict relating to it. These approaches typically involve participants' adopting the role or perspective of a member of a stigmatized group. Essentially, individuals imagine themselves in the situation of a member of the discriminated group. Doing so allows individuals to adopt the perspective of a member of the other group and experience how it feels to be a member of that group and be discriminated against. The argument is that imagining themselves in other positions or imagining others in different positions leads individuals to empathize with members of the discriminated-against out-group. In the end, these interventions would have individuals see themselves as being similar to members of the other group. This will lead them to empathize by feeling as others feel or feeling for them, which will then reduce prejudice because individuals will want to alleviate the pain and hurt of discrimination as if it were their own (see Aboud & Levy 1999).

Illustrative of the empathy-inducing approach is the most well-known perspective-taking, prejudice-reduction intervention involving the "Blue Eyes/Brown Eyes" experiment (Aboud & Levy 1999). That intervention involves giving discriminatory versus preferential treatment to blue-eyed and brown-eyed exercise participants, respectively, a procedure purportedly designed to sensitize participants to the emotional and behavioral consequences of discrimination. Evaluations report, for example, that nine-year-olds who received the intervention, compared to those who did not, expressed greater willingness to engage in an activity with the out-group (Weiner & Wright 1973), and studies with adolescents also reveal that they expressed a greater willingness to engage in cross-race activities (Breckheimer & Nelson 1976). When applied to adolescents, however, the results often are mixed, as highlighted by the most recent study involving college students (Stewart et al. 2003). For White students, participating in the exercise associates with significantly more positive attitudes toward Asian American and Latino/Latina individuals, but it associates with only marginally more positive attitudes toward African American individuals. Students also report anger with themselves when noticing themselves engaging in prejudiced thoughts or actions. That negative affect theoretically could prove to be either helpful or detrimental in promoting long-term reduction of stereotyping and prejudice. As the authors of the study highlight, some researchers view the aversive experience as key to motivating more positive intergroup attitudes, while others would argue that these aggressive inclinations might even be directed toward the very groups for whom reduction of prejudice and discriminatory treatment was the goal. Together, findings like these support the persisting observation that interventions can have varying outcomes depending on the composition of the involved groups and that the interventions can result in both positive and negative effects.

Other approaches involving older adolescents (those in college) have revealed more positive effects. Notably, intergroup dialogue groups, in which racially and ethnically diverse students share information about their groups and develop greater awareness of the richness of other groups as well as of societal inequality, can be quite successful at improving intergroup attitudes (e.g., Dovidio et al. 2004; Lopez 2004; Nagda, Kim, & Truelove 2004; Nagda & Zuñiga 2003). These groups provide opportunities for personalized contact with members from different groups and sharing of personal experiences that foster awareness of out-group needs and encourage perspective taking. Evaluations of the leading program in this area, involving students at the University of Michigan, revealed positive effects three years after the course; and students reported more positive interactions with other groups (see Gurin et al. 1999). Participants apparently benefited from expressing deeply felt emotions and opinions regarding central issues of contention between groups and hearing these concerns expressed openly and honestly. The researchers argued that the process leads people to value the opinions and welfare of people who differ from them. Despite these positive findings, the study itself remains limited given that it may not generalize well to other contexts. The study was limited because it made use of small groups, the students were well educated (and had high intellectual skills and were motivated, given that they selected the classes), and the classes took place in environments concerned about diversity. Yet the findings, particularly their long-term effects, reveal that interventions can have positive effects.

The effects of the intergroup dialogue, even if in a narrow set of circumstances, find parallels in other interventions seeking to induce empathy. Studies seeking to induce empathy simply by role playing suggest that this type of reversal in perspective can reduce prejudice, stereotyping, and discrimination (Batson 2009; Galinsky & Moskowitz 2000; Stephan & Finlay 1999). Indeed, empathy training programs appear to reduce prejudice regardless of the age, sex, and race of participants (Aboud & Levy 1999). These programs have the practical advantage of being relatively easy to apply in a wide range of situations. Empathy can be increased merely by asking participants to consider how they would feel in a situation, how they are feeling when thinking about how they would feel, and why they are behaving that way. Role-playing exercises also have been used to practice responding effectively to prejudiced comments (Plous 2000; Lawson, McDonough, & Bodle 2010), which also can help alleviate prejudice and discrimination.

Although empathy training programs can attain success, it is not always clear why they do. The reductions in prejudice may result from people's awareness of inconsistencies in their values, attitudes, and behaviors. Early seminal research has shown, for example, that when students spent roughly half an hour considering how their values, attitudes, and behaviors were inconsistent with the ideal of social equality, they showed significantly greater support for civil rights more than a year later (Rokeach 1971). Research indicating that fundamental value changes can be effected through the relatively simple tactic of identifying logical inconsistencies in an individual's belief system are consistent with cognitive dissonance theory, which postulates that holding psychologically incompatible thoughts creates a sense of internal discomfort (dissonance) that people then try to avoid or reduce whenever possible (Festinger 1957). Studies have shown dissonance-related techniques to reduce antigay, anti-Asian, and anti-Black prejudice (Son Hing, Li, & Zanna 2002; Leippe & Eisenstadt 1994; Monteith 1993). Again, however, reducing prejudice need not lead to a reduction in prejudiced behavior. Awareness in and of itself, as already shown, may not suffice to motivate behavioral changes.

The apparent success of the perspective-taking programs reveals that more is at work than mere information exchanges; empathy remains the likely key contributing factor that can emerge from interactions with individuals from different groups. Support for this claim comes from multiple sources. The leading meta-analysis of more than five hundred studies established that empathy was an essential factor that mediated the effects of contact among members of different groups and reductions in prejudice; simply enhancing knowledge of the group did not suffice (Pettigrew & Tropp 2008). That finding gains support from yet another meta-analysis that examined the effects of cross-group friendships on intergroup attitudes, which found that time spent and self-disclosure with out-group friends yielded significantly greater associations with attitudes than other aspects of friendships, suggesting that attitudes are most likely to improve when cross-group friendships involve behavioral engagement, particularly disclosure, which would be the root of empathic responses emerging from intimacy, trust, and other hallmarks of equal friendships (Davies et al. 2011). These findings comport with the well-supported hypotheses that stereotypes can be reduced successfully and social perceptions made more accurate when people are motivated to achieve these results (Fiske 2000; Sinclair & Kunda 1999), and that empathy can serve as that motivation. Taking the perspective of out-group members and "looking at the world through their eyes" can significantly reduce in-group bias and stereotype accessibility (Galinsky & Moskowitz 2000). Perspective taking can short-circuit processes that enable the perpetuation of stereotypes (Todd, Galinsky, & Bodenhausen 2012), and adopting the perspective of a particular out-group member can engender more positive evaluations of that person's group (see Todd et al. 2011). Even implicit stereotypes can be modified (Blair 2002). In addition, empathy actually is necessary for successful perspective taking. If an individual places a negative value on another's welfare—that is, if an individual has antipathy toward another person—then imagining the other's response to suffering and discrimination more likely produces pleasure than empathic concern and positive change (Batson et al. 2007). Still, experimental research reveals that empathy only partially mediates the relationship between perspective taking and stereotypic intergroup attitudes; situational attributions are a stronger and more reliable mediator (Vescio, Sechrist, & Paolucci 2003). Stereotypes may be widespread and persistent, then, but they also are amenable to change when people seek to reduce them; and change probably moves toward positive feelings when motivated by empathy. Empathy-inducing interventions, including perspective taking, suggest promise.

## Intergroup Experiences

A popular intervention to reduce prejudice involves simply bringing together individuals from different social groups that have a history of prejudice and discrimination. The approach stems from the enduring proposition that interaction between members of different social groups can foster positive attitudes and reduce hostility and prejudice. This form of intervention retains considerable intuitive appeal, which may help account for its being one of a relatively few social scientific theories to engage policy makers and practitioners. Yet, despite its successes, it too is marked by important limitations—limitations that nevertheless point to promising directions for addressing discrimination.

Intergroup-contact interventions have been among the most studied and promising. Hundreds of studies, now the subject of important meta-analyses and reviews, have examined the effectiveness of these efforts. Across a variety of contexts, situations, and even ages of participants, the studies overwhelmingly report positive results (see Dovidio, Glick, & Rudman 2005; Pettigrew & Tropp 2006; Wagner et al. 2008; Tropp & Prenovost 2008). For example, an early review of 203 studies involving 90,000 participants from 25 countries revealed that 94% of studies supported the central tenet of the contact hypothesis, which is that prejudice diminishes as intergroup contact increases (Pettigrew & Tropp 2000). Another, even more robust review, a meta-analysis of over 500 studies that collectively involved 250,000 participants, found that greater levels of contact among different groups typically associate with lower levels of intergroup prejudice, a consistent and significant finding from samples of children, adolescents, and adults (Pettigrew & Tropp 2006). Findings like these leave little doubt that intergroup contact can influence people's attitudes about groups.

Reviews of studies, conducted mainly in educational contexts, examining the influence of contact on ethnic or racial intergroup attitudes also conclude that contact is especially likely to result in positive outcomes when it occurs in contexts characterized by several well-identified optimal conditions for reducing prejudice (Tropp & Prenovost 2008). Those conditions, identified decades ago by Allport (1954), include equal status between groups (i.e., groups are equally valued and respected), support of institutional authorities like schools (i.e., authority figures support and promote positive contact between different group members), common goals (i.e., individual group members share the same goals when they meet), and cooperation rather than competition between groups (i.e., group members work together to achieve their common goals). The benefits of structured contact among diverse groups certainly appear to be well established. In fact, research now supports Allport's proposition that prejudice declines when individuals from different ethnic and racial groups, even when not part of interventions, work together on common goals, share equal status in situations, work cooperatively, and are sanctioned by authorities, the law, or custom.

Encouraging cross-group relationships may be one of the most effective methods by which to reduce prejudice in children and adults. Cooperative learning interventions that mix together individuals from different groups are illustrative. These techniques have been reported to increase the self-esteem, morale, and empathy of students across racial and ethnic divisions; they also have been found to improve the academic performance of minority students without compromising the performance of majority students (Aronson & Bridgeman 1979). The "jigsaw classroom" technique, for example, originally was developed to reduce racial prejudice and now has been used to address other forms of prejudice. The technique assigns students into small, racially diverse work groups. Teachers give each student a vital piece of information about the assigned topic, which makes each group member indispensable. Decades of research suggest that the technique effectively promotes positive interracial contact (Aronson & Patnoe 1997). These types of interventions appear to work because they involve the conditions deemed optimal: cooperation and common goals resulting in inclusion, increased self-worth, and empathic concern. These conditions receive considerable support from social psychological studies that reduce group conflict by crafting situations that lead to cooperative and interdependent interactions in pursuit of common goals, situations that shift people's thinking from "us and them" to "we" (Desforges et al. 1991; Dovidio & Gaertner 1999). Structured cooperative learning allows individuals to recategorize others.

Although interventions reveal that intergroup contact can be quite effective even without any of the optimal conditions (Pettigrew & Tropp 2006), research not focused on contact interventions reveals that intergroup contact without the optimal conditions can be problematic. Intergroup contact can have both alleviating as well as exacerbating effects. With students of all ages, ethnically diverse schools or classrooms can promote more positive interethnic attitudes than more ethnically homogenous schools or classrooms (Feddes, Noack, & Rutland 2009; McGlothlin & Killen 2010; Rutland et al. 2005). Yet intergroup contact may exacerbate feelings of frustration and prejudice between groups, especially when the groups are of unequal status and in competition. Real-life experiences support the claim. A review of studies conducted during and after school desegregation in the United States found that 46% reported an increase in prejudice among White students, 17% reported a decline in prejudice, and the remainder reported no change (Stephan 1986). In addition, research relating to the negative effects of contact finds parallels in research indicating that the same imbalance may contribute to violence. Self-reported victimization has been reported as higher in contexts with less ethnic diversity, suggesting that youth tend to be targeted more frequently for victimization in contexts of obvious imbalance in the racial/ethnic composition of classrooms or schools (Graham 2006). The imbalance of victimization appears to have a greater impact on minority youth. Minority students attending racially segregated schools are exposed to more social disorder and violence than either Whites or minorities who attend integrated schools (Massey 2006); some studies report that Black youths attending racially integrated schools are exposed to higher levels of school violence than peers attending segregated ones (Eitle & McNulty Eitle 2003). But not all research points in the same direction. Some studies have found that attending racially inclusive schools reduces the risk of involvement in the criminal justice system. Blacks attending schools with higher proportions of Whites have a reduced likelihood of ending up in prison, but there is no effect on White incarceration rates (LaFree & Arum 2006). Intergroup contact may lead to positive effects, but the likelihood of positive outcomes does appear related to the presence of enabling conditions.

Although research generally does support the finding that cross-group relationships contribute to reductions in prejudice, cross-group relationships remain difficult to obtain and maintain. Notably, intergroup segregation challenges the positive outcomes that can emerge from intergroup contact. Segregation makes the potential that contact will change perceptions unlikely due to limited encounters among group members. Even when opportunities for cross-racial/ethnic relationships exist, they frequently do not come to fruition. For example, children's friendships do not always reflect the mix of racial groups in the classroom. Instead, children often select friends on the basis of social group membership, such as ethnicity or race (Aboud 2003). Cross-ethnic friendships are not only relatively rare but also less stable than same-ethnic friendships (Kao & Joyner 2004; Schneider, Dixon, & Udvari 2007). Cross-race friendships also decrease with age. From the age of six years, children and adolescents show a preference for same-race as opposed to cross-race friendships; preference for cross-race friendship typically begins to show a rapid decline from around age ten to age twelve (e.g., Aboud 2003). These "naturally" occurring segregation patterns render direct contact between different ethnic groups uncommon even when they formally are together. These findings support the claim that obtaining and sustaining positive attitude change requires structural intervention.

The limited interactions that members of different groups can have, and the potential for unintended segregation, has led to the development of other forms of intervention that take a different approach to intergroup "contact." Notably, studies have focused on "extended contact" rather than only face-to-face interactions. These studies reveal that merely being aware of cross-ethnic friendships between members of one's own group and another group can reduce prejudice (Wright et al. 1997; Paolini et al. 2004; Paolini, Hewstone, & Cairns 2007). These interventions have been shown to reduce prejudice and promote positive attitudes to other groups in both adolescents and young children, at least in terms of what participants report regarding their views of friendships between in-group and out-group members after having read stories portraying such relationships (see Cameron & Rutland 2008; Cameron et al. 2011). These studies lead researchers to conclude that extended contact can change norms and expectations about friendship from those based on a notion that friendships are composed of same-group relationships to conceptions that friendship also can consist of cross-group relationships. These interventions help change perceptions of who is in the in-group and help individuals to view the out-group as connected to a close member of the in-group, thus bringing the out-group closer to the self and reducing prejudice.

Interventions framed by extended-contact hypotheses have taken the notion of contact quite a bit further. For example, media interventions have built on parasocial hypotheses suggesting that contact with a media character can result in learning about the out-group, developing affective ties with an out-group member, and inducing positive attributions.

This has led to efforts to expose individuals to different groups, which has resulted in some positive effects (see Schiappa, Gregg, & Hewes 2005; Ortiz & Harwood 2007; Cameron & Rutland 2006). But the strongest support for parasocial hypotheses already exists in the form of the power of negative stereotypes. Research has long shown that negative and limited portrayals of minority groups in the media result in negative attitude changes (Mastro 2009). These studies support the proposition that negative parasocial contact leads to the reinforcement of negative stereotypes and attitudes about out-groups and results in negative attitude change. The converse still may not be true, but it at least leaves open the possibility that positive portrayals contribute to positive changes.

Notions similar to those relating to the effectiveness of imaginary media characters have led to interventions that focus even more on imaginary relationships. Notably, some interventions have individuals imagine a positive contact with an out-group member. This exercise yields more positive attitudes toward the out-group than either a neutral control condition or a condition in which people imagine an out-group member, but without imagining contact (Turner, Crisp, & Lambert 2007; Crisp & Turner 2009). Some studies mix imagined and extended contact, and have shown that imagining a close friend having out-group friends reduces fear of rejection by the out-group (Shelton & Richeson 2005), an important finding given that anxiety and fear about groups link to prejudice and discrimination against them. Although these efforts have been part of laboratory experiments, they do reveal the importance of contact, and how contact can cover a wide range of quite structurally distinct situations.

## Conclusion: The Significance of Sites of Inculcation

Adolescents abstract, interpret, transform, and evaluate social events in their world, activities that involve complex social cognitive processes. Interventions gain effectiveness in reducing prejudice and discrimination when they address the types of social experiences contributing to those processes. Notably, such interventions must address the relationships that adolescents have with peers and adults, incorporate their interpretations and evaluations of these experiences, and provide strategies for enabling them to make decisions that reflect fairness and justice rather than invidious prejudice and discrimination. In doing so, they must address the multiple sites through which adolescents both learn basic values about how to treat others and experience the effects of appropriate treatment. These efforts reach effectiveness only to the extent that they recognize and respond to the social embeddedness of behaviors and attitudes that support them. Responding to those social conditions makes it possible to address the fundamental conclusions that emerge from research relating to prejudice and discrimination: no individual is immune from harboring prejudice, reducing prejudice requires deliberate effort and awareness, and with sufficient motivation, institutions and the individuals in them can reduce prejudice and its expression.

The above conclusions reveal that systematic policy efforts to shape the development of attitudes and values supportive of equality are unlikely to move forward without the guidance of well-established research. Robust research reveals several key points that could help shape social contexts to alleviate the development of prejudice and its expression. Numerous implications arise from research that confirms the importance of addressing the multiple social contexts in which adolescents interact and are socialized. For example, although schools have been the primary site of interest, families, media, communities, and other social contexts such as justice systems also can play important roles as they reinforce attitudes and provide opportunities to exercise them. Research also suggests the need to frame policies so that they encourage contact among different groups, provide them with opportunities to form positive relationships, and structure social situations to reduce competitiveness among different groups. Policies can also play a key role through guiding those in authority so that they, in turn, can send clear signals and discourage inappropriate differential treatment. Policies can also play a role in addressing when individuals from different groups may *not* come into contact, as they can foster social environments that reduce the expression of prejudice when they do interact or otherwise must consider each other's interests. In such cases, reductions in invidious treatment probably occurs when adolescents develop a sense of empathic concern and have experiences taking others' perspectives, and policies can support opportunities for youth to gain these experiences. Policies also can influence broader macrosystem factors (e.g., media), which may prove helpful, as they may not directly affect behaviors but inevitably do trickle down through multiple systems as they help structure social environments that shape thoughts and permit their expression. In short, there is no dearth of compelling ideas that policies can enlist to foster socializing environments committed to equality and its ideals.

Empirical findings and the theories supporting them may appear increasingly compelling, but whether they can effect change depends on how seriously they are taken. Whether they are the types of findings that legal and policy systems actually can embrace remains to be determined. For example, as we saw earlier, some long-established and well-supported propositions, such as those relating to increasing contact, can no longer rely on a receptive legal system committed to enhancing diversity in groups through affirmative action. The legal system's drift from some of the ideals previously embraced during the civil rights era necessitates a close look at what the legal system now can support. It requires an examination of what the law permits, what the research deems it important to foster, and how to take concrete steps toward the law's ideals of equality. What is crucial, then, is a different look at how the legal system can ensure equality beyond the embrace of neutral treatment that has been equality jurisprudence's focus.

# 3

## Addressing Necessary Shifts in Equality Jurisprudence

Empirical evidence reveals paths forward. Notably, efforts to decrease discrimination will gain increased effectiveness if they foster structural changes supportive of equality and if they inculcate values and personal dispositions that embrace the importance of equal treatment as well as equal outcomes. These conclusions mean that equality jurisprudence must turn in different directions while remaining true to its time-tested ideals and current legal realities. Future legal efforts to address invidious disparities in opportunities and treatment must therefore focus on understanding how to further equal treatment without resorting to classification- or group-based distinctions. In practice, this means recognizing that not all groups are situated similarly. It also means addressing the negative effects of a subjugated group status, such as reduced self-esteem, achievement, and civic engagement as well as increased intolerance, group conflict, and group isolation. Addressing these negative effects must involve supporting systems that foster the inculcation of equality. Whether the legal system can support a government in that manner remains to be determined; this question is the focus of this chapter as well as the next.

Examinations of the potential for the government to support key socializing institutions in inculcating values and dispositions that foster equality require two foundational analyses. The first analysis, the topic of this chapter, involves understanding the extent to which the legal system can support practices, beliefs, and systems that increase tolerance, alleviate subjugation, and permit rigorous respect for diversity without resorting to group classifications to achieve those ends. This possibility leads us to the second analysis, the topic of the next chapter. That analysis involves more precisely articulating how the legal system addresses the legal regulation of key institutions that may inculcate values of respect, tolerance, and even inclusiveness as the foundation of responsible citizenship. In essence, it addresses how to inculcate the very ideals of equality jurisprudence.

## Government-Supported Inculcation of Equality

The possibility of having government-imposed inculcation certainly faces important challenges given the United States' firm commitment to freedom from governmental interference as expressed by such highly respected fundamental liberties as freedom of expression, privacy, and belief. But even the most profoundly respected rights can give way to compelling government interests and, equally importantly, they also may give way to neutral government policies. Analyses relating to these matters necessarily focus on the government's power, particularly its potential to coerce and impose orthodoxy rather than ensure individual freedom by limiting governmental intrusions in people's beliefs and ways of living.

Governmental powers, and the laws supporting them, are inherently coercive, but vary in the degree of coerciveness. The legal system's power runs the continuum from imposing sanctions to urging compliance. Indeed, the government retains the power to control, guide, explain, persuade, force, deplore, congratulate, admonish, implore, teach, censor, inspire, defend, support, inform, educate, and much more. The wide range of potential governmental actions certainly buttresses arguments that the government always uses some form of coercion. This appears especially so given that the government retains the power to coerce, defines the parameters of acceptable behavior, and simply distributes coercion in different ways when it chooses to leave certain matters to private actors to decide whether to act coercively. The government retains the power to regulate, as well as to determine whether to regulate, and all that that entails.

Analytically, the broad range of potentially coercive governmental power manifests itself along a continuum from "hard" to "soft" law. Hard law rests on the ability to coerce, support, or endorse; it demarks and enforces prohibitions. Soft law seeks to attract, as it suggests approved courses of action. Although soft law may appear meaningless due to its unenforceability, it remains an important part of the law's power. Thoughtful commentators suggest that soft law may even produce the same behavioral effects, and the mindset to produce them, as those of an otherwise equivalent hard law (see Gersen & Posner 2008). Their point highlights how a focus on government-created potentials for sanctions (through the imposition of liability or punishment) obscures the manner in which the law influences behavior expressively by what it says in addition to what it does. And the legal system, and its representatives, can say much more than it actually does. To get its work done, then, the government benefits from a wide variety of "coercive" options at its disposal to inform people what they can and cannot do and to shape their thinking and behaviors.

Laws relating to equality provide no exception to the legal system's varying use of its coercive powers. As expected, laws addressing equality exist between the two potential extremes of coercion, as they can take either hard or soft approaches. At one extreme, hard law takes the form of explicitly banning government-imposed segregation or differential treatment of individuals based on race, gender, or other protected class status. The Court finds this type of differentiation as generally violating the Equal Protection Clause except in those rare instances in which the government's action survives the rigorous demands of heightened scrutiny needed when the government infringes on a highly protected right. At the other extreme, soft law takes the form of government speech that communicates the government's views, such as a resolution condemning or supporting particular actions or even public officials' recommendations when acting on behalf of the government. That extreme also can take the form of more subtle expressions in that all governmental actions necessarily have meaning. The Court finds these types of articulations permissible, as we will see below, on the grounds that the First Amendment grants the government wide latitude to further its policy objectives. As the government seeks to shape behavior to define and equalize justice, fairness, and liberty, the government necessarily gets into the business of using hard and soft approaches. It does so as its laws fall along a continuum of efforts, from those that essentially engage in indoctrination to those that passively support inculcation.

Regardless of the hard or soft approach taken, the legal system seeks to send messages of its authority and expectations. Indeed, equality jurisprudence is rooted in the law's expression, in the law's vision of equality, and in the government's role in it. For example, although *Brown v. Board of Education* (1954) arguably contained multiple visions of equality, the Supreme Court recently rested on the language focusing on the inappropriateness of using the law to segregate solely on the basis of race, on the grounds that doing so sends a divisive message that harms youth's sense of self. This interpretation emerged in *Parents Involved in Community Schools v. Seattle School District No. 1* (2007), which rejected the voluntary efforts of public school districts to prevent the negative effects of *de facto* segregation by using race as a factor in assigning students to their schools. In so ruling, the plurality opinion enlisted *Brown* to condemn such programs as "demeaning" (727) to the individuals subject to them, because they "promoted," "reinforced," and "endorsed" race consciousness (746), which inevitably causes hostility, contributes to stereotypes of racial inferiority, and reinforces the misguided notion that individuals should be "judged by ancestry instead of by [their] own merit and essential qualities" (746).

The Court's concern for messages was made even more explicit by a concurring opinion by Justice Kennedy, who argued that indisputably race-conscious but facially race-neutral plans could pass constitutional muster. The argument was that governmental classifications based on racial typologies can cause divisiveness, but "race-conscious measures that do not rely on differential treatment based on [express] individual classifications present these problems to a lesser degree" (*Brown*, 1954, 797). The justice went so far as to list a variety of ways that school districts could pursue the goal of bringing together students of diverse backgrounds and races, such as strategically placing schools at particular sites, drawing attendance zones on the basis of neighborhood demographics, targeting the recruitment of faculty and students, and using statistical procedures to track education. He suggested that such mechanisms can be race-conscious but are probably permissible if they "do not lead to different treatment based on a classification that tells each student he or she is to be defined by race" (789). Whether the Court actually would let stand an approach motivated by race-consciousness but not manifesting differential racial treatment remains to be seen. And such an approach actually may not even be possible. Still, the Court makes clear that harm comes from the law's expressed messages. Without the message of differential treatment, the government does not inflict harm deemed impermissible or irremediable. In adopting this approach, the Court removes the legal system from considering race-conscious policies. In doing so, it broadly leaves matters of racial disparities to the private sector or to governmental policies that can address disparities without expressing racial preferences.

*Parents Involved* will not be the Court's last statement on the law's expression relating to differential treatment, but at this juncture, it serves to highlight three key points. First, both the plurality and concurring opinions in *Parents Involved* pronounce race-conscious public school assignments objectionable on the grounds that they express and reinforce the impermissible perception that race matters. When dealing with equality, the Court fundamentally concerns itself with the law's messages. The Court could not be more clear. The legal system should avoid differential treatment based on race because doing so sends harmful signals. Second, the case highlights the interplay between hard and soft law. The case stands for hard law's finding it impermissible that the law would express group-based distinctions on the grounds that such law contributes to intolerable divisiveness. Yet the Court also invites ways around the hard law by noting mechanisms that would avoid strict scrutiny to achieve race-conscious ends. It offers a guide that would permit the government to engage in race-conscious approaches to address apparent disparities in securing the benefits of public education. Lastly, by taking a hard law stance on equal protection and offering a soft law invitation to remedy existing ills of racial disparity, the Court evinces a strong anticlassification position but notes possible directions that could result in taking antisubordination approaches to dealing with inequality. Despite apparently clear articulations endorsing anticlassification approaches as sending the correct messages, then, the Court openly wonders whether mechanisms exist for the government to maintain the strong stance on remaining neutral toward protected group classifications while still addressing concerns about subjugation.

The ability of federal, state, and local governments to circumvent the Court's mandate that they endorse neutral messages may raise important concerns, as examined below. But the Court's anticlassification doctrine, centered on governmental neutrality in the messages it sends, does not find full expression in other doctrinal areas. Over the past two decades, the Supreme Court essentially has minted new doctrine that avoids the anticlassification mandate and even close judicial scrutiny altogether. Notably, under First Amendment law, government entities need not remain neutral, both in the messages that they express and the policies that they wish to support. The government remains perfectly free to seek the inculcation of values it finds important, to further the societal interests it deems worthy. The parameters of this broad power continue to be determined, as examined below, but the power remains indisputable and remarkably broad.

Given societal interest in fostering equality, it appears clear that the government may seek to support, through its inculcation powers, dispositions congruent with concern for respect, tolerance, and even inclusiveness as the foundation of responsible citizenship—in essence, the very ideals of equality jurisprudence. Whether it wishes to do so is a different matter. Determining whether it should do so requires, for now, two analyses: one analysis that identifies the breadth of inculcation law's parameters, and another analysis that turns to whether the legal system even can permit different sites of inculcation to harness what empirical evidence suggests will reduce the development of prejudicial attitudes and, eventually, harmful actions toward individuals because of their group status. Both analyses are important to understanding the reasonableness of embracing approaches intended to inculcate values consistent with equality's ideals. This chapter provides the former analysis, while the next one details the latter. Together, these analyses reveal the legal system's flexibility, which can be enlisted to address the limitations of current visions of equality jurisprudence.

## The Broad Parameters of Inculcation Law

The legal system always has engaged in inculcating values, but this engagement appears to have gained new momentum. As explored more fully later, the legal system actually has a long history of using its power to shape behavior and inculcate values. Indeed, that history is synonymous with the history of youth's rights. That history reveals the push and pull to determine who has the right and responsibility to instill values in the next generation: families, communities, governments, or youth themselves. The major development in this area of law, and one that usefully frames the understanding of the government's role in inculcating values, involves the extent to which the government can use its enormous resources to promote the policies that it deems worth supporting through engaging in what is becoming known as "government speech."

The extent to which governments are able to promote their own policies gains significance in that the ability determines the extent to which they affirmatively can shape environments conducive to instilling one set of values over another.

As currently interpreted, constitutional jurisprudence in this area supports the government's power to influence ideas by using its resources to promote its policies or to advance particular ideas. This is a remarkable development given the popular view, for example, that the First Amendment requires the government to take neutral positions toward speech and to guard zealously the free flow of ideas. That popular view may retain its currency, but it offers only one view of the First Amendment. The need for the government to remain neutral in matters of deep societal concern is countered by the reality that the government's effective functioning sometimes requires it to express or promote its own viewpoints through its policies and programs. In fact, government entities need to express viewpoints and take positions, and they routinely express certain messages rather than others, which makes untenable a requirement of absolute neutrality regarding the government's own speech. Recognizing this inevitability, the Court has held that the First Amendment permits selectivity and, even more importantly, that government speech avoids rigorous judicial scrutiny altogether. The profound and necessary link between what a government expresses and the values it supports makes critical the need to understand its broad excision from judicial scrutiny and the potential effects of that exclusion.

## Government Speech Doctrine

Governing typically involves attempting to influence behavior and thought, not only by coercively penalizing certain behaviors or expressions but also by expressing viewpoints designed to affect the social milieu or to persuade people to think and act in a preferred manner. In such instances, governments become one of a host of speakers competing in the marketplace of ideas. With perhaps one exception that proves the rule (the establishment of religion, as discussed below), free speech protections have not demanded that the government abstain from such a role, nor have they required governments to endorse all viewpoints equally when sending messages. For example, most citizens probably would agree, and the courts would find consistent with the First Amendment, that the government need not send the message "Say yes to risky sex" when sending the alternative message "Say no to risky sex." The government can take a position, and can take only one position at the expense of another. That, in a nutshell, constitutes the basis of the government speech doctrine.

The government speech doctrine has deep roots, but it only gained independent prominence and full acceptance within the past two decades. Notably, in *Rust v. Sullivan* (1991), the Court examined the validity of prohibiting the use of Title X funds for abortion-related activities. In this instance, Congress funded clinics to facilitate family planning, but precluded participants from discussing abortion or making referrals to abortion providers, even upon specific requests from patients. As a result, the program curtailed the kinds of advice given by doctors receiving certain federal funding. Someone requesting information about abortion simply would be told that "the project does not consider abortion an appropriate method of family planning and therefore does not counsel or refer for abortion," although an exception might be made in the case of a true emergency (180). The Court ruled that the First Amendment did not forbid the government from choosing to fund certain programs to the exclusion of others in order to advance its own message. The Court reasoned that the regulations did not punish, proscribe, or privilege private speech based on the viewpoint expressed by the speech. Rather, the regulations constituted a constitutionally permissible instance of the government using public funds to promote its own antiabortion message. The government remains generally free to champion its preferred ideas and values.

*Rust* seemed like an anomaly to the rule that the government must refrain from interfering with the highly prized marketplace of ideas. But *Rust* was followed by a series of cases confirming and clarifying the rule's reach in a variety of instances of government speech. In addition to sanctioning the imposition of normally prohibited viewpoint restrictions on private speakers who accept government funds (*Rust v. Sullivan*, 1991), the Court permitted restrictions on government employees speaking on matters of public concern (such as condoning the denial of a promotion to a prosecutor on the grounds that he had challenged the basis of a search warrant approved by a superior; *Garcetti v. Ceballos*, 2006) and supported compelling private parties to fund government speech with which they disagreed (such as rejecting a claim from cattle producers who objected to governmental assessments to promote the marketing and consumption of beef and beef products; *Johanns v. Livestock Marketing Association*, 2005). This long line of cases culminated in a dispute that presented a clash between government speech and religious freedom in the context of selective exclusion of a speaker's religious message from traditional public fora. In that case, *Pleasant Grove City v. Summum* (2009), a religious order called the Summum sought to erect a monument in a public park that already contained other privately donated monuments. The monument was to the Seven Aphorisms, which according to Summum doctrine were inscribed on the original tablets given to Moses at Mount Sinai. Pleasant Grove City refused to accept the monument for permanent installation in its public park, which already contained an equally sized but clearly Christian monument of the Ten Commandments. The city rejected the proposed monument after finding it inconsistent with the city's purported message of celebrating local history and community. In supporting the city's refusal, the Court broadly stated that "[a] government entity has the right to speak for itself. It is entitled to say what it wishes, and to select the views that it wants to express" (467–68). Without doubt, government speech broadly deflects First Amendment scrutiny.

Government speech avoids rigorous judicial scrutiny mainly on the rationale that the speech remains limited by a mechanism often ignored in speech doctrine or even equality jurisprudence: democratic accountability. Courts apply strict judicial review when the government engages in content or viewpoint discrimination regarding private speech because such suppression or favoritism reflects a defect in the democratic process. When the government privileges or punishes private speech, it generally does so because it dislikes, disagrees with, or finds dangerous the disfavored speaker or the message. Given that the speakers of such messages presumably cannot protect themselves effectively through the political process, strict judicial scrutiny attaches to the government's efforts to suppress. In a real sense, the Court presumes the speaker or the speech to be the kind of "discrete and insular minority" that makes heightened scrutiny appropriate (see *United States v. Carolene Products Co.*, 1938, 153 n.4; *Board of Regents of University of Wisconsin System v.*

*Southworth*, 2000, 235). By contrast, when the government speaks, for example, to promote its own policies or to advance a particular idea, the electorate and the political process hold the government accountable for its advocacy. The government speech doctrine finds no need for a judicial check on the government's own speech because the Court rests on the assumption that normal political processes both generate and correct the government's speech. The government speech doctrine teaches us that the government generally may send the messages it chooses, need not make those messages viewpoint neutral, and need not support other messages.

## Manipulating the Marketplace of Ideas and Values

The *Rust*-inspired government speech doctrine has gained wide acceptance, even though it clearly involves manipulating the marketplace of ideas and the values those ideas support. The Court views the manipulation as tolerable and even as an example of democracy at work. Yet such faith in normal political processes probably does not always sufficiently consider efforts to protect the interests of minorities, particularly of socially subjugated groups. In addition, leaving the government to its own devices to support its speech runs the risk of drowning out or distorting private discourses, which are likely to include the voices and values of minority groups. These real possibilities raise the need to consider the breadth of the ability to manipulate ideas and values, and the potential sources of corrective measures.

The dangers of manipulation come from several sources. First, the distortion of the marketplace of ideas and values rests on the government's essentially limitless resources and powerful platforms for communication. Such powerful manipulations and distortions could lead, in some domains, to domination in the marketplace of ideas and the potential skewing of information to perpetuate control, making it difficult or impossible for citizens to change the government's messages. Second, groups may capture government speech, which might mean that the message sent to the public could be colored or controlled by particular groups not necessarily acting in the public's interest. These groups may drown out other viewpoints, resulting in the democracy-distorting effect of creating a false majority by enlisting government communications to ensure support for government policies. Third, the government may mislead the public to believe, for example, that the government's favored views are more widely and favorably held than they actually are, or that they are held by authoritative and esteemed sources when in fact they are not, and thereby may contribute to a false consent. Doing so endangers the basic premise that a democratic government rests on the consent of the governed. Democratic consent rests not on government-engineered consent but rather on citizens' ability to evaluate the government's performance and ultimately determine whether to give or withhold consent. Fourth, the immense power to manipulate endangers democracy's fundamental tenet—belief in the need to protect the minority from the tyranny of the majority. The founders probably did not intend for the elected majority to circumvent so easily the protections that the republic affords. Despite these possibilities, the Court places its faith in the government's ability to police itself—in its ability to correct the marketplace of ideas and values by creating, championing, and controlling its own marketplace.

The doctrine's dangers, coupled with its remarkable breadth, may appear like a recipe for disaster, but a close look at the doctrine as well as other areas of jurisprudence reveals important limitations and boundaries. A broad look at how the legal system inculcates values and protects messages reveals important limitations on the government's cornering of the marketplace, the types of beliefs the government can endorse, and the coercive power at the government's disposal. These limits are important to consider because they reveal the boundaries to the government's freedom to flex its power to inculcate its preferred beliefs and the values that go with them.

## SUPPORTING GOVERNMENT SPEECH

The government may manipulate the market of ideas, but it may not create a monopoly that compels adherence to its expressions. Individuals retain a right to protection from being compelled to speak, including the right not to appear to be believing the government's supported speech. The Court announced the rule barring coercion of private speech most famously in *West Virginia State Board of Education v. Barnette* (1943). In that case, the Court held that the government could not force students to recite the Pledge of Allegiance because to do so violated students' rights under the First and Fourteenth Amendments. It was in that case that the Court offered one of its most frequently cited statements: "[I]f there is any fixed star in our constitutional constellation, it is that no official, high or petty, can prescribe what shall be orthodox in politics, nationalism, religion, or other matters of opinion or force citizens to confess by word or act their faith therein" (642). Under this view, the Court finds compelled speech impermissible because the government forces a person to support or convey a message, in contrast to government speech, which protects the government's right to express its own views on an issue. Thus, the key to the doctrine of government speech is that the speech must be government speech, its own speech.

The government has to do more than not coerce private speech; it cannot manipulate it—private speech receives full First Amendment protection. The significance of this rule emerged in *Legal Services Corporation v. Velazquez* (2001). *Velazquez* involved the federal government's restrictions on the Legal Services Corporation (LSC), a private, nonprofit corporation established and supported by Congress. The restrictions prohibited LSC attorneys from representing clients attempting to amend (or challenge) existing welfare law. Velazquez, through her LSC-funded attorneys, sought to challenge existing welfare provisions, as doing so presented her the only avenue for financial relief. The Court ruled that the specific restriction violated the First Amendment's free speech guarantees. Because LSC facilitated the "private" speech of its grantees, the restrictions simply did not regulate government speech. Further, because the restrictions blocked attempts to change only a specific area of law, the Court held that they could not be considered viewpoint neutral. The First Amendment prohibits the government from making viewpoint-based restrictions on private speech—the government cannot manipulate private speech by supporting favored views. Importantly, the Court concluded that a government program of furnishing legal aid to the indigent vitally differed from the program in *Rust* in that attorneys who represent clients in welfare disputes advocate against the government, which created an assumption that counsel would be free of governmental control. The Court concluded that the restriction on advocacy in such welfare disputes would distort the usual functioning of the legal profession; the limitations also would distort the function of the federal and state courts before which the attorneys appeared. The system needed to operate on the assumption that it was free of any conditions that their benefactors might attach to the use of donated funds or other assistance. By so ruling, the Court was able to retain the general rule relating to government speech, which finds the funded manipulation schemes permissible so long as they do not reach those who do not hold the subsidized position.

## ESTABLISHING RELIGIOUS BELIEFS AND VALUES

The government's relationship to religious beliefs and values reveals a challenging part of constitutional law that relates closely to the government speech doctrine. As with the government speech doctrine, the government may not coerce individuals to accept (or to act as though they accept) what could be construed as the government's favored religious beliefs and values. But unlike with government speech doctrine, the Constitution explicitly bars the government from endorsing any religious beliefs over others. This rule emerges from a relatively ignored area of jurisprudence that relates closely to the power of the government to support speech: the context of the Establishment Clause. The Establishment Clause provides that "Congress shall make no law respecting an establishment of religion." The breadth of that part of the First Amendment's language gives the judiciary the difficult task of developing rules and principles to realize the goals of the constitutional guarantee. This jurisprudence asserts the basic premise of the Establishment Clause. It prohibits sponsorship, financial support, and active involvement of the sovereign in religious activity. As the Court has wrestled with the constitutional implications of government endorsement of religious beliefs and their expression, this area of law actually has developed to permit the government to support religious beliefs and values that coincide with the policies it deems worth supporting. In this regard, the government speech doctrine finds reflections in Establishment Clause doctrine in that both adopt the position that the government does not violate the Constitution unless and until it coerces private behavior, nor does the government violate the Constitution if it happens to support other messages when it supports its own.

*Lee v. Weisman* (1992) reveals the extent to which the Court limits the power of the government to coerce individuals into expressing thoughts and behaviors. The case stands for the government's general lack of power to coerce individuals to agree, including coercing them to appear to agree, with specific ideas and values. In that case, the Court overturned what it deemed a government's religious message at a graduation ceremony at the request of a school principal, Robert E. Lee, who had invited a Jewish rabbi to deliver a nonsectarian prayer. The Court ruled against the school partly on the grounds that the message fostered subtle and indirect coercion (students must stand respectfully and silently) and, by doing so, forced students to act in ways that establish a state religion. In that case, the majority defined impermissible "coercion" relatively broadly to include government-sponsored religious speech that influences onlookers' behavior through peer pressure and other social dynamics, as it found to be the case with a prayer at a public high school graduation that students feel pressure to attend and not to leave. Also in that case, the dissent took a much narrower approach to coercion and found impermissible "coercion" to include only the threat or imposition of government punishment. The Court accepted the reality that enormous variance exists between the persecutions of old and the many subtle ways in which government action can distort religious choice and coerce, leaving a wide continuum between coercion and reduced choice. *Weisman* makes clear the Court's willingness to take an expansive view of coercion in the Establishment Clause context and its steadfast commitment to protect private beliefs.

The Court may take a broad view of coercion and prohibit the government from forcing religious beliefs on individuals, but the Court's jurisprudence in this area still gives the government the freedom to support the religious values it wishes. As we will see in the next chapter, the Court has developed many important mechanisms for doing so. For now, it suffices to show how the government can support religious groups in order to inculcate the values that the government deems fitting. This rule emerged in *Bowen v. Kendrick* (1988), which addressed the constitutionality of the Adolescent Family Life Act of 1981. The act sought to provide counseling and other related services to adolescents to help them cope with the complex and controversial issues surrounding teenage pregnancy. To do so, the act provided financial support to private and public organizations so long as they did not perform abortions or provide abortion counseling, nor could the organizations advocate, promote, or encourage abortion. As a result of this focus, many of the grant recipients were religious institutions. The inclusion of religious institutions, which the statute specifically permitted, led to the constitutional challenge. The Court rejected the argument that religious institutions must be excluded from groups of eligible grantees. The Court reasoned that the government's direct financial support did not unavoidably result in an impermissible inculcation of religious beliefs. The Court so ruled because the act was facially neutral, the act did not require grantees to be religiously affiliated, and the possibility of aid flowing to some pervasively sectarian institutions (and thereby advancing the religious mission of that institution) did not preclude all grants to religiously affiliated institutions. The Court contended that simply because Congress intended to deliver a message to adolescents through the act—a message that may coincide with some religious doctrines—the statute did not necessarily have a primary effect of advancing religion.

The Establishment Clause's limit on what would be viewed as government speech rests on the fundamental distinction between impermissible government support for religious activities per se and permissible government support intended to accomplish secular, social welfare–oriented goals. Importantly, however, the *Bowen* case actually left unclear whether the religious providers in question may use religious approaches to accomplish government-supported secular goals—and if so, to what extent they may do so. Unlike religious exemptions and accommodations, the government-speech approach might lead to greater permissibility for religious approaches to solving social problems. For example, the government might conclude that "meaning-oriented" or "spiritual" approaches to problems like addiction are more effective than any other approach. This is not really that far-fetched given that Alcoholics Anonymous–type recovery programs, which currently are the most popular type of therapeutic approaches to alcohol abuse, remain centered on participants' relationship to higher beings (see Levesque 2002). Public funding, then, would go to this general category of programs, which, in theory, could be religious or nonreligious. Though most of the money undoubtedly would go to religious organizations and most of the spiritual instruction would end up being traditionally religious, the program might be upheld because, under the current approach, the Court approves of government expression that includes both religious and nonreligious language. Importantly, *Bowen* was decided before *Rust*, the key government speech case. How a court would interpret more en-tanglement between religious and secular messages remains to be seen, but we now know that the Court finds itself highly supportive of the government's messages, including messages in its social services.

### DEALING WITH HARMFUL MESSAGES

Another potential limit on the government's ability to choose the ideas and values it wishes to support relates to those that might be harmful. Although the Court permits some regulation of harmful speech, it rou-tinely rejects efforts to stifle intentionally harmful private speech. Two cases are again illustrative. In the first case, *R.A.V. v. City of St. Paul* (1992), a juvenile allegedly fashioned a cross out of broken chair legs and then burned it inside the fenced yard of an African American family who lived in his neighborhood. The city charged the juvenile with vio-lating its Bias-Motivated Crime Ordinance. On appeal to the Supreme Court, the Court held that the ordinance unconstitutionally censored expression protected by the First Amendment, and that the government could not regulate private actors' bias-motivated or hateful speech. The second case, *Snyder v. Phelps* (2011), involved patently hateful pro-tests at military funerals. In that case, Fred Phelps and his followers, members of the Westboro Church, protested homosexuals, the United States for tolerating homosexuals, the American military for defending the United States, and anyone or any religion that did not completely share his dogma. The Court ruled that the First Amendment protects a private party's "hurtful" speech. Although Westboro's messages "may fall short of refined social or political commentary," the Court admit-ted, "the issues they highlight—the political and moral conduct of the United States and its citizens, the fate of our nation, homosexuality in the military, and scandals involving the Catholic clergy—are matters of public import" (1217). Private parties' hateful speech generally remains protected from government regulation.

The Court's approach to hateful speech exemplifies the extent to which the Court rejects the notion that the government should interfere in private exchanges of ideas. Rather than evaluate the content or sub-stance of the expressed views, the Court primarily relies on formalistic time, place, and manner considerations to guide its judgment in such cases. Although the Court takes a morally neutral approach toward issues involving the freedom of expression, it still has carved out noteworthy exceptions to this general rule; but as we will see in the next chapter, these important exceptions do not come close to swallowing the rule. When governments intervene in contexts relating to youth, they do so to support the inculcation of appropriate values and the direction of youth's appropriate development. But some contexts simply do not offer much room for intervention.

The government may protect private parties' rights to express harmful speech, but whether the government must refrain from expressing such speech itself is an entirely different question. The danger exists that governments can communicate hostility or animus toward a group within an otherwise protected class status. Indeed, this danger mirrors the Court's reason for being neutral when dealing with race-based classifications, and why the Court increasingly frowns on affirmative action efforts that may result in "reverse discrimination" and feelings of animosity toward majority-status groups. The danger arises from the ease with which the government's engagement in harmful speech can drown out other viewpoints, raise the risk of facilitating private parties' discriminatory behavior, and deter their targets from certain important opportunities or activities. Under the Court's current doctrine, whether such speech violates the Equal Protection Clause remains unclear. Without doubt, the Court has embraced, in its most recent relevant case, the unsurprising view that government speech may not contravene other constitutional protections (*Pleasant Grove City v. Summum*, 2009). *Brown* and *Parents Involved* support the claim that the government may not engage in differential treatment that sends messages harmful to protected group classifications. But the issue remains whether the government can endorse one view over another. As *Summum* makes clear, the First Amendment permits selectivity provided that the government does not suppress competing private speech or violate another constitutional provision in effectuating its own speech.

Importantly, no doubt exists that the government can choose to support expressions that it deems good, including expressions of diverse beliefs and those not deemed offensive. The Court announced this general rule in *National Endowment for the Arts v. Finley* (1998). In that case, a group of artists challenged standards used to award competitive artistic grants. The government had imposed an obligation on the National

Endowment for the Arts chairperson to ensure that judgments of merit and excellence "take into consideration general standards of decency and respect for the diverse beliefs and values of the American public" (569). The artists had argued that the language amounted to an unconstitutional viewpoint-discriminatory regulation and that the "decency and respect" language was too vague to be constitutional. The Court disposed of the first challenge on three grounds. First, the Court viewed the amendment as discretionary, and thus not as a regulation of speech. Second, it viewed the decency and respect criteria not as viewpoint discriminatory but rather as appropriate viewpoint-neutral criteria of merit. Finally, it reasoned that, even if the criteria were based on viewpoint, the government's action in deciding on grants was that of "patron" and not sovereign, which permitted viewpoint-based judgments. The Court disposed of the second challenge also on the grounds that the government acted as a patron, which rendered the consequences of imprecision less severe and therefore constitutionally permissible. In *Finley*, then, the Court reasoned that the government was a participant in the market, not its regulator. As a participant, the government could express its own preference and take a position against competing viewpoints. In the end, the Court's analysis placed *Finley* among the long line of cases supporting the government's very business of favoring and disfavoring points of view on innumerable subjects.

The government can do more than favor or disfavor; it can use its resources to censor information it disfavors, even information the First Amendment otherwise protects. The leading case in this area, *United States v. American Library Association* (2003), directly addressed this issue. The case emerged from the government's concern about private citizens using computers at public libraries to surf the Internet for pornography. To address that concern, Congress had enacted the Children's Internet Protection Act (CIPA), which required that any library receiving federal money to help connect to the Internet install filtering software that protects against access by all persons to "visual depictions" that constitute "obscen[ity]" or "child pornography," and that protects against access by minors to "visual depictions" that are "harmful to minors" (201). The American Library Association, a group of public libraries, library associations, library patrons, and website publishers challenged the law. They claimed that the act improperly required them to restrict the First

Amendment rights of library patrons, particularly since the programs had a tendency to "overblock" access to information. The Court addressed whether the government could use its spending power to require libraries to censor information the government did not like. The Court found that libraries necessarily consider content in making collection decisions and enjoy broad discretion in making them. The Court did not view libraries as forums for publishers to express themselves but rather as places "to facilitate research, learning, and recreational pursuits by furnishing materials of requisite and appropriate quality" (206). Because the purpose of the library was not to facilitate "speech" but to facilitate research, learning, and recreational pursuits, the government could control the content made available by libraries that accepted government dollars.

The result of *American Library Association* diverged from prior cases that had rejected congressional attempts to censor the Internet and other media in the name of child protection. In *Reno v. American Civil Liberties Union* (1997), for example, the Court rejected a congressional effort to shield children from pornography on the Internet through the anti-indecency provisions of the Communications Decency Act of 1996. The act sought to protect minors from explicit material on the Internet by criminalizing the knowing transmission of "obscene or indecent" messages to any recipient under eighteen, and knowingly sending to a person under eighteen anything "that, in context, depicts or describes, in terms patently offensive as measured by contemporary community standards, sexual or excretory activities or organs" (*Reno*, 877–78). The Court unanimously found the act unconstitutional primarily on the grounds that the restriction relied on imprecise filtering tools and was worded too broadly, and thus would capture too much constitutionally protected speech. In *United States v. Playboy Entertainment Group, Inc.* (2000), the Court rejected another congressional effort to protect children. This time, the medium was cable television, and the statute in question addressed signal bleed from pornographic cable stations. The language at issue stemmed from Section 505 of the Telecommunications Act of 1996, which required cable television operators to scramble or block completely channels "primarily dedicated to sexually-oriented programming" from 6:00 a.m. to 10:00 p.m. The Court ruled against the limitation on the grounds that the government had failed to demonstrate that the statute was the least restrictive means to reach the articulated compelling interest and, thus, imposed an excessive burden on adults' free speech rights. The divergence between these two important media cases and *American Library Association* highlights the critical difference between highly protected private speech and speech supported by the government. The Court places very few limits, if any, on adults' access to First Amendment speech, even if efforts to censor aim to protect children. When the government supports speech, on the other hand, the government gains wide latitude to attach conditions to further its policy objectives.

Cases in this area make one point abundantly clear: the government has the power to support one message favoring one set of values over another, and can select speech by others as part of its own expressive freedom. These are merely examples of the wide variety of situations in which the government can invoke the government speech doctrine to shield its actions from judicial scrutiny. To bring its actions within the government speech doctrine, the government needs to exercise control only over what is said and what is not said. Other contexts tar this type of control as "censorship," but here that control marks the speech in question as belonging to the government. Many of the cases examined in the next chapter support the possibility that the government could reject divisive, prejudicial, and intolerant messages, but inclusivity and tolerance do not always result in positive and beneficial messages to some groups (e.g., those seeking pornography and seeking to create art generally deemed indecent or offensive, two activities that generally garner First Amendment protection). Diversity in beliefs and values that contribute to perceptions of harm spur the major dilemma faced by the doctrine of government speech that permits the government to support one set of values over another. In fact, that very diversity served as the foundational rationale for erecting a wall between private and governmental support of expressions and values, a wall that continues to crumble as the nature of government changes and as we recognize that governments necessarily support some values and expressions over others.

## Conclusion: The Multiplicative Effects of Inculcation Powers

Legal doctrine relating to the government's inculcation powers reveals important developments. Through a variety of mechanisms, the government can seek to inculcate values and manipulate the marketplace of values. Although the government cannot totally ban private expressions of specific viewpoints, government speech doctrine allows what previously had been thought to be impermissible: the burdening, if not silencing, of private viewpoints because the government disagrees with them. The power appears to be quite robust, as it avoids searching scrutiny by the courts and rests on the will of the democratic process. This development finds reflection in doctrinal developments relating to the major institutions whose very existence centers on meaning making and value inculcation—religions. The government may support religious practices, beliefs, and institutions that express messages the government wishes to support. Although the Court anchors its interpretations of these developments deep in precedent, these important doctrinal developments reveal a shift in what previously was thought to be forbidden.

Developments permitting active governmental support for some values and ideas over others can foster multiplicative effects in and of themselves, but they do so even more when they infiltrate traditional domains of inculcation. Although the Court (and commentators) have recently centered on doctrine relating to government speech and religion when considering the potentially coercive power of a government seeking to inculcate values, the government actually heavily influences other domains that necessarily shape values. Included among the most obvious sites of inculcation are families, schools, health systems, and, especially, justice systems. These systems offer their own long-established principles relating to the government's potential role in the inculcation of values. These domains already are starting to be influenced by doctrinal developments relating to government speech and religion. Putting together recent doctrinal developments and long-standing doctrine allows for the conclusion that our legal system grants the government a wealth of opportunities to shape messages, values, and the social environments in which those will thrive. How such opportunities could be used effectively to address the inculcation of values supportive of equality's ideals remains to be determined, but current doctrine opens windows to possibilities heretofore unimaginable.

4

# Supporting Equality Jurisprudence's Sites of Inculcation

The legal system may be founded on the principle of limited intrusion in our lives, but the government still serves as the dominant socializing force. The government regulates all individuals and institutions. It sets the boundaries for what can and cannot be done, both by individuals and by social institutions. Thus, despite such articulated freedoms as freedom of expression, privacy, and belief, the legal system can support practices that can increase tolerance, alleviate subjugation, and permit rigorous respect for diversity without resorting to group classifications to achieve those ends.

The reach of the government cannot be underestimated. Given that traditional and especially current equality jurisprudence anchored in equal protection mandates forbids the use of classifications to ensure equality, the anticlassification approach reigns. Yet the government may support more antisubordination impulses in two ways. First, even the most highly respected rights can give way to compelling governmental interests, and equally importantly, they also may give way to neutral government policies. Second, even if highly respected rights may not be infringed, the government generally remains free to counter and shape the influence of their expression. This possibility leads to the rationale for this chapter: the need to think through how to further the variety of interests associated with the inculcation of dispositions congruent with concern for respect, tolerance, and even inclusiveness as the foundation of responsible citizenship—in essence, the very ideals of equality jurisprudence.

Addressing how the legal system maneuvers the legal regulation of key institutions that inculcate the ideals of equality jurisprudence requires examining the parameters of those institutions' rights and responsibilities, particularly as they relate to the government and the minors they would inculcate. The analysis necessarily first centers on families and schools, as the legal system historically focused on those contexts, and their associated rights and responsibilities exemplify the government's potential role in fostering the inculcation of values that urge equality of treatment. Having established the general rules relating to those contexts, the chapter then turns to institutions outside of families and schools. That analysis focuses on socializing institutions at the heart of civil society's inculcation efforts, such as religious institutions, child welfare systems, community organizations, justice systems, and the media, as well as medical and mental health care systems. Together, these analyses provide a snapshot of the rules supporting the foundation of rights and responsibilities that necessarily play key roles in inculcating values consistent with the ideals of equality jurisprudence.

The analysis of the government's potential role in inculcating values also reveals the striking resurgence of the tensions between the anticlassification and antisubordination impulses. The different sites of inculcation developed in ways that range from urging the legal system either to remove itself from inculcation efforts (by staying neutral) or to assert itself and address subjugations (by affirmatively inculcating tolerance, respect, and other dispositions associated with ideals of equality in a democratic society). Unlike equal protection jurisprudence based on the Equal Protection Clause, however, this line of jurisprudence provides governments with considerably more freedom and even permits them to act affirmatively to address subjugations. Given that analyses of equality jurisprudence have yet to consider these alternative ways to achieve its ideals, the analyses that follow consider the legal background for understanding the promise of specific inculcation sites.

## Inculcation Rights and Responsibilities in Families and Schools

Efforts to inculcate values in youth eventually involve youth, but they historically have ignored directly addressing youth's rights and responsibilities. Traditionally, the legal system framed rights and responsibilities relating to the inculcation of youth's values as potential conflicts between parents and the government. Not surprisingly, given that schools— like families—exist to inculcate values and dispositions into the next generation, legal conflicts between parents and the government arose in the context of schooling. As a result, understanding the rights and responsibilities of either of these institutions requires understanding those of the other. This understanding is of great significance given that it inevitably relates to the power of the government to inculcate values, as well as the relative freedom that the government might have in doing so. The relative freedom, in turn, reveals the nature of the compelling interests the government must further if it wishes to shape the inculcation of youth's values in a manner that would guide them toward particular dispositions. Accordingly, the tug among parents, schools, and governmental powers gives a sense of the nature of adolescents' rights. Equally importantly for our purposes, however, the two contexts reveal the two very different approaches that the legal system can take to preserve respect for diversity, tolerance, and the ideals of equality jurisprudence.

*Families*

Without doubt, the family has long been recognized as the institution that serves as the foundation for adolescents' development, and that development includes controlling youth, even to the extent of controlling their rights. The Supreme Court has noted, for example, that society leaves to families the task of inculcating and passing down many of its most cherished values, moral and cultural. The Supreme Court first articulated the inculcation rights and responsibilities of parents in a pair of cases, decided in the 1920s, that addressed the government's ability to interfere in parents' power to direct their children's upbringing. Although the cases did not seem to address that issue directly, the Court interpreted the legal issues raised as involving the rights of parents. In doing so, the Court went even further and provided the rationales for supporting parental rights, rationales that remain key to understanding the government's ability to infringe on the rights of parents. As a result, the cases would serve as the foundation for determining the boundaries of parental rights and responsibilities relating to inculcation. They also would provide the groundwork for the way the legal system envisions families' roles in fostering equality's ideals.

The two cases that initiated articulations of parental rights involved state education laws, and the fundamental rationales for supporting the rights of parents related to assumptions about the socialization of children in a democratic society. The first of these cases, *Meyer v. Nebraska* (1923), considered a challenge to a state law that forbade the teaching of any modern language other than English to primary school children. Although a teacher had challenged the statute, the Court used the case to note that its jurisprudence historically had reflected Western civilization's concepts of the family as a unit with broad parental authority over minor children and that parents retained the right to choose their children's education and guide their upbringing. After identifying the right within the realm of liberty, the Court found that the state could not bar students from learning all foreign languages in schools when parents were not against the education unless the legislature could identify a harm that would come from such learning. While acknowledging that "the State may do much, go very far, indeed, in order to improve the quality of its citizens, physically, mentally and morally," the Court nevertheless held that the statute unconstitutionally intruded, "in time of peace and domestic tranquility," into the parents' right to control their children's education under the Fourteenth Amendment (401–2). That type of language, and the Court's findings, set the tone around the principle that legislatures and courts should not interfere unreasonably with parental decisions regarding the direction of their children's educations, very broadly defined to include the children's general upbringing and the inculcation of their values.

The Court most notably would repeat its *Meyer* reasoning in *Pierce v. Society of Sisters* (1925), a case in which the Court rejected laws requiring children to attend public schools. *Pierce* involved the constitutionality of an Oregon statute that required children to attend public school through the eighth grade. The Court took the opportunity to state more firmly the notion that parents have the responsibility to guide children in their own households and that such responsibilities were basic in the structure of our society. It even went so far as to find that "[t]he fundamental theory of liberty upon which all governments in this Union repose excludes any general power of the State to standardize its children by forcing them to accept instruction from public teachers only" (535). The Court continued by noting that "[t]he child is not the mere creature of the State; those who nurture him and direct his destiny have the right, coupled with the high duty, to recognize and prepare him for additional obligations" (535). The Court ruled that the legislature could not unreasonably interfere with the liberty of parents and guardians to direct the upbringing and education of children under their control. That standard for interference meant that the liberty of parents can only be "abridged by legislation which has . . . [a] reasonable relation to some purpose within the competency of the state" (535). *Pierce* thus stands for restrictions placed on the state that protect the liberty of parents from arbitrary intrusions, and serves as the rationale for giving parents the right to direct their children's upbringing. It also stands for confirming the view that parents' duties and rights parallel one another.

Although *Pierce* rejected state intrusions in parents' rights to inculcate their children, it left the door open. The standard does not reject potential intrusion; it merely requires that (1) the intrusion be reasonable and (2) the state have the ability to perform what it deems the parents to be unwilling or unable to perform. Clearly, the state can provide much, and education would seem to be the hallmark of what states can provide. Yet the Court chose not to give educational authority to the state. What *Pierce* tells us is that the legal system takes a broad view of education and associates it with the more general upbringing of children. As a result, it is too important to leave to states alone. *Pierce* rejects the notion of the state's general competency to raise children on its own; and even if the state had the ability to do so, *Pierce* reminds us that it still remains an inappropriate medium because our society rejects the standardization of children. This rejection led the Court to create a protected zone of family privacy supported by the parental rights doctrine, which permits a state to infringe on these rights only for a compelling reason and only insofar as that infringement is necessary to protect the state's interest. Without doubt, the Court granted parents significant rights matched with the responsibility to raise children.

Importantly, *Pierce* left open what the Court actually meant by "additional obligations" attached to the responsibilities of parents that support the need to give parents rights in the form of protected family privacy; and it would take the Court nearly half a century to offer an interpretation. When the Court did address the issue, it chose a case that permitted it to confirm the broad rights of parents to inculcate their children with their values and even essentially determine their future development. That case, *Wisconsin v. Yoder* (1972), involved the right of Amish parents to withdraw their children from public school after the eighth grade. As it ruled for the parents and affirmed their parental rights to raise their children as they see fit, the Court elaborated that "the duty to prepare the child for 'additional obligations' . . . must be read to include the inculcation of moral standards, religious beliefs, and elements of good citizenship" (233). In a democratic republic, according to the Court, parents (rather than the state) assume the proper role to "prepare" children for citizenship. In evaluating the state's interest in compulsory education beyond the eighth grade, the Court concluded that there was "strong evidence that [the Amish children] are capable of fulfilling the social and political responsibilities of citizenship" (225). In so ruling, the Court recognized the important role that parental rights play in shielding young children from state indoctrination and fostering the development of democratic citizens free from state control.

*Wisconsin v. Yoder* still stands as the Supreme Court's most important statement on the socialization of youth. The socialization of youth in a democratic society rests on providing parents with the freedom to raise their children as they see fit—free from state indoctrination. Equally importantly, the socialization also necessarily involves education that prepares youth for assuming such roles, as the Court clearly recognized that the Amish children received a basic education conducive to their being competent and responsible members of society. Despite the heightened protection (and responsibilities) granted to parents, then, their rights are not absolute, as the state retains the obligation to ensure that parents raise their children in a manner that prepares them for effective citizenship. Still, parents retain a fundamental role.

Parents' responsibilities to raise their children as they see fit but in a manner that prepares them for citizenship meant that one of the key rationales for intruding in parents' rights would directly address parents' relative ability properly to execute those responsibilities, particularly the inculcation of democratic values. The case that directly addressed that issue, *Prince v. Massachusetts* (1944), involved the right of Jehovah's Witness parents to raise their children in accordance with their religious beliefs. In that case, a legal guardian was convicted of violating the Massachusetts child labor laws after she allowed her nine-year-old niece to distribute religious publications on the street at night in her company. The Court upheld the conviction as it invoked the constitutional rights of parents: "It is cardinal with us that the custody, care and nurture of the child reside first in the parents, whose primary function and free-dom include preparation for obligations the state can neither supply nor hinder" (166). Yet, despite that heightened protection, the Court ruled that "these sacred private interests, basic in a democracy," were outweighed by "the interest of youth itself, and of the whole community, that children be both safeguarded from abuses and given opportuni-ties for growth into free and independent well-developed men and citi-zens" (65). The Court asserted that a "democratic society rests, for its continuance, upon the healthy, well-rounded growth of young people into full maturity as citizens, with all that implies." The importance of well-developed citizens has led the Court to conclude, in yet another often-quoted passage, that "[p]arents may be free to become martyrs themselves. But it does not follow that they are free, in identical cir-cumstances, to make martyrs of their children before they have reached the age of full and legal discretion when they can make that choice for themselves" (170). In affirming the limits of parental rights, the *Prince* Court identified limits to parental authority aimed at reducing the power of parents to foster values inconsistent with children's growth into independent democratic citizens. In contrast to the earlier decisions in *Meyer* and *Pierce*, the Court in *Prince* sustained a role for the com-munity in inculcating democratic values over the objection of parents and guardians. Yet, the Court set quite a high standard in permitting the community—through the government—to intervene in families: parents would need to make their children martyrs. Exactly what that would entail remains disputed, but the state clearly resists intruding on the rights of parents unless cause exists to believe that their children would be (or are being) harmed. These proclamations essentially distill down to the point that the legal system allows parents to structure their relationships with their children as they choose. Although mandatory schooling laws, child labor restrictions, and the outside boundaries of abuse and neglect do limit the broad parameters of parental rights, for the most part, the government steers clear of interfering with the paren-tal relationship. Although there may be limitations, the Court supports the view that parents are presumed to act in their children's best interest (see, generally and as discussed below, *Parham v. J. R.*, 1979). The Court also champions the view that the most effective way to ensure positive youth development, the integrity of family life, and the foundations of democracy is to support parents' far-reaching right to raise their children as they deem fitting.

The doctrine serving as the foundation of parental rights provides an important perspective on how the legal system views families as performing essential socializing functions necessary to the life of the polity. The responsibilities of parenting involve the cultivation of diverse private preferences, moral values, and religious beliefs, rather than the inculcation of uniform civic values and skills. The legal system protects democratic ideals of equality and tolerance for diversity through the constitutional commitment to freedom from state interference in families. The notion of family privacy, as developed by the Court, directly rejects the claim that families have an obligation to instill particular attitudes or ways of thinking in their children; it rejects the notion that families play an essential unifying role in the political socialization of children. Instead, families protect diversity and shelter family members from governmentally imposed ideas and values. Thus, the legal system does not make direct connections between families and any given set of moral values of good citizenship. Instead, it provides families with broad parameters as they take on the responsibility to ensure development that would foster effective engagement in a diverse society. In a real sense, the state seeks to remain neutral to family life on the theory that doing so respects diversity and fosters the inculcation of values needed for effective citizenship.

## Schools

Parents may retain the broad right to direct their children's upbringing and vigorously inculcate their own values, but once their children start moving outside of families, parents' rights and responsibilities begin to diminish. When that happens, the state undertakes the obligation to inculcate their children. The reduction in parental rights most readily occurs when parents send their children to public schools. Indeed, the general rule that emerges from leading cases in this area asserts that schools essentially act as parents, which means that they have considerable discretion in the inculcation of values. And as with families, that discretion finds limits especially in extreme cases (e.g., schools may not be abusive), but even those extreme cases are known for the incredible extent to which school officials have discretion to develop the minds and personalities of youth. Sending children to school means entrusting the schools with the broad freedom to inculcate the values that the schools deem fitting.

Schools' inculcation of values may range between two extremes: either they can seek to free children from formal inculcation so as to enable them to develop quite independently of one set of approved values (at least to the extent that adults do), or they can seek to restrict children's freedoms in an effort to inculcate particular sets of values and essentially indoctrinate them. Unlike the broad freedom of parents to move toward either of those two extremes, public schools' authority to inculcate becomes narrowed for the simple reason that minors have more rights against the state than they do against their parents. As a result, students retain constitutionally protected rights (such as free speech), and those rights would be exercised in the context of a state-controlled system (involving state action, which automatically initiates the need to protect constitutional rights, unlike private situations like families). Although minors have rights, it need not follow that those rights be respected highly. Indeed, a long line of cases constituting established Supreme Court precedent, including the most recent cases on this matter, indicates that students have reduced rights to the extent that school officials retain the general right to make curricular and administrative decisions. These types of decisions essentially are those that parents would make in families, and they are decisions that ultimately bear considerable weight, given that much of schooling falls under them. As a result, schools have considerable power to inculcate values and provide a context particularly ripe for interventions conducive to inculcation. Indeed, that power is so strong that it almost reaches within the boundaries of indoctrination.

Schools may remain an area ripe for inculcation, but the earliest Supreme Court cases essentially had recognized the opposite, as they dealt with students' protection from governmental intrusion in their rights to engage in speech and to be protected from government-compelled speech. In *West Virginia State Board of Education v. Barnette* (1943), for example, the Court used unusually powerful language to find "that no official, high or petty, can prescribe what shall be orthodox in politics, nationalism, religion, or other matters of opinion or force citizens to confess by word or act their faith therein" (642). The Court found a school's requirement that all students salute the U.S. flag an unconstitutional exercise of governmental authority.

Another leading case also was thought to be a bellwether of future cases that would give students more rights to resist the inculcation of values, and the Court delineated even more strongly its commitment to students' individual rights against the state. In *Tinker v. Des Moines Independent Community School District* (1969), which involved a school's prohibition against students' wearing black armbands to protest the Vietnam War, the Court struck down the ban, finding that students may not be confined to the expression of "officially approved" sentiments (511). According to this approach, schools should encourage students to participate in the learning process, rather than impose values. *Tinker* harkened back to the notion that democracy demanded respect for "hazardous" freedoms and that students had a right to those freedoms. Even granting students such freedoms, however, did not mean removing school officials' power to guide and direct students' ability to participate effectively in democracy. In a series of cases considering who should retain the broad power to choose the values worth inculcating and controlling the system that instills them, the Court placed the power squarely on the schools—on local school officials and teachers.

In curricular matters, for example, the Supreme Court has announced that school boards essentially retain complete discretion in deciding the values they wish to transmit. The leading case in which the Court asserted this blanket claim, *Board of Education, Island Trees v. Pico* (1982), actually was one in which the Court had ruled against school officials. In that case, a school board had removed a slew of books from its library and had justified the removal on the basis that the books were "anti-American, anti-Christian, anti-Semitic, and just plain filthy" (857). The Court found that school boards could not remove books on the basis of partisan politics. Although clearly limiting the power of school boards, the Court did so in a way that left the power of schools quite expansive. Most notably, schools still had discretion to remove books based on educationally relevant criteria. Indeed, the Court granted schools the broad authority to determine which books they could place in the library in the first place. The Court construed the school board's rights as "vitally important 'in the preparation of individuals for participation as citizens'

and . . . for 'inculcating fundamental values necessary to the maintenance of a democratic political system'" (864). In curricular matters, the
Court concluded that school boards "might well defend their claim of
absolute discretion" to transmit community values (869).

The cases that followed firmly shifted the control of school gover-
nance in the direction of school officials. In *Bethel School District No.
403 v. Fraser* (1986), a seventeen-year-old senior delivered a sexually
charged speech nominating a fellow student for elective office. The
Court defined students' constitutional rights in public school settings
more narrowly than those of adults in other settings. The limitation allowed school officials to curb forms of speech deemed threatening to
others, disruptive, and contrary to "shared values" (683). Importantly,
the Court reiterated its focus on community standards and the inculcative function of schools. Public education must inculcate "fundamental
values necessary to the maintenance of a democratic political system"
(681). Included in these values is tolerance of diverse and unpopular
political and religious views, which views must be balanced against
another value—that society has an interest in teaching the bounds of
"socially appropriate behavior" (681). The power of school authorities,
acting as the inculcators of proper community values, was supported
and developed further in *Hazelwood School District v. Kuhlmeier* (1988).
In *Hazelwood*, students alleged that their free speech rights had been
violated when the principal deleted two articles from a school newspaper, one that addressed issues of teen pregnancy and another that
described the impact of parental divorce on students. The *Hazelwood*
Court upheld the authority of school officials to control the content of
school-sponsored speech on the basis of "legitimate pedagogical concerns" (273). The *Hazelwood* majority emphasized the role of schools
as the primary vehicles for transmitting cultural values, including their
discretion in refusing to sponsor student speech that might be perceived
as advocating conduct otherwise inconsistent with "the shared values of
a civilized social order" (272).

It took the Court nearly two decades to revisit the state's power to
foster school environments conducive to inculcating the school's values.
When it did, the Court confirmed that students do not enjoy much free
speech in public schools—that schools are a place for the inculcation
of values determined by school officials. That case, *Morse v. Frederick*

(2007), involved school officials who permitted students to leave school grounds to watch the Olympic Torch Relay pass through their city. Once camera crews arrived from area news channels, Joseph Frederick and his friends unfurled a fourteen-foot banner that read "BONG HiTS 4 JESUS." When Frederick rebuffed the principal's request to take the banner down, he subsequently was suspended from school for ten days. The Court declined to apply *Tinker's* "substantial disruption" standard and instead held that "[t]he 'special circumstances of the school environment' and the governmental interest in stopping student drug abuse . . . allow[s] schools to restrict student expression that they reasonably regard as promoting illegal drug use" (408). Despite a vigorous dissent, the case stood as yet another example of the limits placed on the expressive rights of students. The cases further installed school authorities as the inculcators of proper community values; schools were to determine both community standards and the manner in which they wished to teach the bounds of socially appropriate behavior.

The Court also has granted local school officials immense discretion in the way they discipline students, and in so doing the Court has affirmed that it more narrowly defines students' constitutional rights in public school settings than it does those of adults in other settings. Illustrative are cases dealing with the extent to which students can be punished and with the way they can be treated to determine whether they can be punished or given opportunities to reform themselves. In terms of the punishments that students can be required to endure, the Supreme Court directly addressed the matter in determining the constitutionality of schools' use of corporal punishment in *Ingraham v. Wright* (1977). In *Ingraham*, two assistant principals and a principal had disciplined students with brass knuckles and a large wooden paddle, with the imposed punishments being quite brutal. The Supreme Court rejected the claim that the paddling was "cruel and unusual punishment" and that students should have a right to be heard before suffering physical punishment. Rather than being found in the basic principles of the Constitution, the protections were to be found at the local level—in the openness of the school, the professionalism of those who impose punishment, and the civil and criminal remedies available to those who get too severely beaten. As a result of *Ingraham*, states can and many of them do impose corporal punishment in their schools to instill discipline when students fail to abide by the values that schools seek to inculcate—a remarkable position given that even imprisoned criminals cannot be subjected to corporal punishment (Levesque 2006).

In terms of identifying students in need of punishment or treatment for wrongdoing, illustrative are cases dealing with infringements on students' privacy, which the Constitution protects by prohibiting unreasonable search and seizure. Generally, the Court has provided a school exemption to much of what the Constitution would require in other contexts. An example involves policies that permit schools to infringe on students' privacy to determine whether they are using drugs. The leading Supreme Court case leaves school officials considerable discretion. That case, *Vernonia School District 47J v. Acton* (1995), involved a challenge by a seventh grader who was ineligible to play football because he and his parents refused to submit him to mandatory random drug testing. The Court refused to require testing based on individualized suspicion that the student was engaging in prohibited behavior, a type of suspicion typically required to protect individuals from arbitrary intrusions. The Court found individualized suspicion unnecessary on the grounds that school officials exercised their duties, even as state actors, in a manner that was "custodial and tutelary, permitting a degree of supervision and control that could not be exercised over free adults" (655). The Court even took the decision beyond its immediate context to conclude that "when the government acts as guardian and tutor the relevant question is whether the search is one that a reasonable guardian and tutor might undertake" (655).

The Court would rule similarly in the next case that challenged suspicionless drug-testing policies, *Board of Education of Independent School District No. 92 of Pottawatomie County v. Earls* (2002). The Court did so even when the school had established neither the proven need for the testing nor the promise to bring any benefit to students or the school. The rights of students to be protected from schools' intrusions into their privacy would remain reduced, with the notable and extreme exception of strip searches, which the Supreme Court has deemed to be categorically different from other searches but still permits (see *Safford Unified School District No. 1 v. Redding*, 2009). The Court grants school officials broad authority to control the development of youth, including their school environment and, eventually, what adolescents can keep private and express within that environment.

The Supreme Court has long held that, just because they are children, youth do not shed their rights at the schoolhouse gate. Yet the development of jurisprudence in this area evinces a turn toward granting school officials broad control over the nature of the schooling they offer as well as the values they seek to inculcate. Parents certainly need not send their children to particular schools, and a growth in schools being publicly supported through vouchers permits the option. But those options remain rather constricted, and schools' mandates necessarily include inculcation and socialization into values that communities support and that the legal system will allow. The Court clearly has ceded the authority to regulate curricula and the school environment to the schools. Accordingly, school officials have emerged as having rights and responsibilities akin to those of parents, including the duty to inculcate values they deem central to their views of effective citizenship.

## Inculcation Rights and Responsibilities beyond Families and Schools

The law's views of socialization, as well as legal commentators' analyses, generally tend to ignore the reality that neither home nor school serves as the exclusive site of inculcation. Yet socialization and the inculcation that goes with it occur in many other contexts. Those contexts range widely in terms of the direct influence that they may have on youth, their potential ability to use coercive means to inculcate values and dispositions deemed appropriate, and their relative freedom to determine the nature of the values they wish to inculcate. As expected, the legal system adopts different approaches to these contexts, which is understandable given the institutions' relative rights and responsibilities. Also as expected, the legal system's responses to those rights and responsibilities again range along the continuum from mandated state neutrality to more directed state intrusion intended to foster specific forms of tolerance, diversity, and inclusion associated with antisubordination's ideals.

In considerations of who legally retains rights and responsibilities in contexts outside of schools and families, three alternatives generally arise. The first alternative involves simply extending parental rights. As we have seen, legal doctrine generally protects parents' prerogatives to rear their children free from state intrusion and, in particular, protects parents' right to exclude whomever they wish from the family home. Thus, notions of family privacy could attach to inculcation performed outside of the home by institutions that function as parental surrogates in that they take on parental duties in caring for and inculcating children. The second alternative would reflect an extension of schools' rights and responsibilities, given that the school context is one in which the state's interests in inculcation may trump the private inculcation decisions of families. By extension, the context would envelop the state's interest in educating children and preparing them for their duties of citizenship.

Rather than confining parental prerogatives to the privacy of the home or expanding the inculcating prerogatives of schools, the third approach simply would view youth as retaining rights and responsibilities of socialization coextensive with those of adults. From this perspective, parents still would have a right, at home, to impart to their children whatever values they choose; and schools still could continue to inculcate the values they choose. But once adolescents are outside of those contexts, the legal system would deem them capable of socializing themselves or able to engage, just as an adult would, the state's typical efforts to inculcate values consistent with citizenship in civil society.

This third approach would not leave adolescents with unfettered freedom. In situations where youth are deemed to be similarly situated to adults, they could be treated similarly; and if they are different, then special accommodations could be made (with those accommodations generally being additional protections, such as prohibiting their access to harmful materials). A twist to this third alternative, however, is that the rights of other adults (those not related to particular adolescents) could serve as a rationale for resisting efforts to control the inculcation of adolescents. The alternative leaves the state with more limited abilities to socialize and guide, but the state still enjoys considerable power to use the same tools it has (through, e.g., enforcing criminal laws and supporting certain social services and freedoms). Thus, just as the state's interest in educating future citizens and in enforcing the bounds of proper behavior tempers both notions of family privacy and schools' freedom to inculcate values, so would the third alternative for the simple reason that youth live in civil society and necessarily must abide by its laws. The place of adolescents in law and society, then, certainly provides the state with several alternatives to instilling the values it deems fitting.

The above three theoretical alternatives gain significance for at least two important reasons. First, the state adopts all three approaches and sometimes all of them at once, depending on context and the state's interests. Doing so has its strengths, but it also has important limitations for those seeking the development of a clear-cut, fair, and easily applied jurisprudence. Second, the alternatives point to possible avenues for addressing potential interventions. Indeed, and as noted earlier, a rather robust wall appears between families' and states' efforts to inculcate children into specific values; the legal system assumes that parents act on their child's best interests and that family privacy assures the best protection from problematic governmental indoctrination. The educational system has taken an entirely different route, with a heavy focus on inculcating values as part of its mandate to educate and produce responsible citizens. The third context leaves much room for inculcating youth, as youth spend an increasing amount of time outside of both families and schools, and as the rights and responsibilities of individuals and institutions defining those contexts generally remain in flux. That flux provides the state with the opportunity to guide the nature of values deemed important to inculcate. These possibilities lead us to focus on the major sites that serve as sources for inculcating values, again through impulses that either remove the state from involvement or actively insert it.

## Juvenile and Criminal Justice Systems

Although hardly ever framed as such, both juvenile and criminal justice systems exist to inculcate values. Whereas the rights of youth within schools have developed in a manner that provides school officials with considerable discretion, the juvenile justice system explicitly has taken a different turn. Indeed, the leading Supreme Court cases in this area evince a move away from providing juvenile justice personnel discretion that had served as the very foundation of the system. A close look at those cases, however, uncovers a system still fraught with discretion, with the major exception to the rules relating to how and whether juveniles enter the system. A look at how the criminal justice system treats youth demonstrates a similar trend, with increasing concern about the protections that youth have before they would enter the system, but also, unlike in the juvenile justice system, clear cases that involve limitations on the types of punishments youth can receive, limitations imposed largely in the hope that they can be inculcated properly and develop into responsible citizens. In a real sense, this area of law reveals immense discretion in that it serves as the system with the most power to inculcate values and direct youth's upbringing.

Initially, the recognition of youth's rights centered on society's interest in inculcating them and youth's special amenability to that inculcation. That recognition is what led to the creation of a juvenile justice system that would treat youth differently from adults. The creation of juvenile courts and systems focusing on youth's needs was the product of the nineteenth-century "child-saving movement." That movement, in part, sought to rehabilitate youth in the name of benefiting both them and society. The shift made full use of the concept of *parens patriae*, which permitted the state to provide supervision and control over delinquent youth. Charged as essentially acting as parents (since parents whose children were delinquent were viewed as having failed, hence permitting the state to intervene at least temporarily), the system explicitly sought to ensure the child's best interests as it focused on protection and treatment of the child rather than on punishment. The focus on treatment and protection that would permit the inculcation of values necessary for juveniles' return to society provided the rationale for the immense discretion exercised by juvenile justice system personnel. Their duties were deemed to be most appropriately executed if they had the requisite freedom to act as parents would, with little limitation on their ability to guide the development of youth.

Rather than challenge the states' ability to create separate systems devoted to inculcating youth and rehabilitating them, the first major Supreme Court cases addressing the jurisdiction of juvenile court systems sought to resist youth's unfair transfer out of them. In *Kent v. United States* (1966), the Supreme Court held that a juvenile court could not transfer a juvenile to an adult criminal court without following specified judicial procedures, including holding a hearing and providing effective assistance of counsel and a statement of reasons. The Court emphasized that, although the statute in question gave the juvenile court "a substantial degree of discretion," it did not confer "a license for arbitrary procedure" (553). Although important exceptions to the need for hearings eventually would emerge, this case was significant for recognizing not only that adolescents had rights but also that they had the right to be tried in juvenile courts that had original jurisdiction over them, and that they had the right to the system that embraced discretion and served to rehabilitate youth and foster their reintegration into society, probably through their families or adult surrogates.

Arguably the major case in this area, *In re Gault* (1967), also dealt with jurisdictional matters. The case recognized that strong arguments could be made to support the claim that juvenile justice systems were not as rehabilitative as hoped, and that some were even punitive. That reality challenged the very foundation of the juvenile court system in that it was the system's rehabilitative features that served as the rationale for giving minors reduced rights when involved in that court system. That the system could be problematic was made obvious by the *Gault* case itself. *Gault* involved considering the detention of a fifteen-year-old boy who was deemed a juvenile delinquent and sent to a state industrial school. His serious offense was a prank phone call, of an "adolescent nature," to a neighbor. For that misbehavior, Gault was sent to be institutionalized until age twenty-one (given that he was fifteen, that was very much longer than the penalty he would have received had he been an adult, which would have been two months maximum). The Court took the opportunity to highlight the importance of procedural protections for youth, and reversed the juvenile court's decision. The Court held that certain due process rights apply equally to both juveniles and adults, such as the right to counsel, adequate notice of the charges (comparable to the notice given in criminal or civil proceedings), the privilege against self-incrimination, and the right to confrontation and sworn testimony by witnesses available for cross-examination. The Court sought to introduce procedural regularity, fairness, and orderliness into the juvenile court system, emphasizing that "unbridled discretion [was] a poor substitute for principle and procedure" (18).

Given the panoply of rights that were recognized, it is unsurprising to find that commentators view *Gault* as having revolutionized the rights of youth by recognizing that they have basic, due process rights similar to those of adults. But *Gault* simply dealt with the group of rights that would be implicated in giving juvenile court jurisdiction over the youth in the first instance. The Court simply gave greater protections to youth who could be brought erroneously into the system; it left alone what states could do once youth were admitted properly into the system. In a real sense, the Court ignored the very reason it took the case in the first place: that juvenile court dispositions could be exceedingly punitive compared to those in adult courts and that, once in juvenile court systems, juveniles might not receive the rehabilitation that provided the rationale for the juvenile court's jurisdiction. As a result, the system retained the freedom to inculcate youth. *Gault* simply sought to ensure that the state would leave alone those who were not in need of intervention—those who already were deemed inculcated appropriately into society or under the appropriate control of those who ensured that they were being inculcated properly.

Focusing on the actual treatment of juveniles—what they receive once adjudicated delinquent or deemed as having offended—reveals that the system retains immense discretion. As with the school context, the Court protects adolescents from extreme treatments. In this regard, the Court has removed minors from being considered eligible for specific types of extreme penalties. Even if a juvenile could be deemed essentially as an adult and transferred to adult court, the juvenile may be exempt from specific punishments. The first limit is the prohibition against the death penalty, as announced in *Roper v. Simmons* (2005). *Roper* emphasized adolescents' vulnerability and comparable lack of control over their immediate surroundings, which led the Court to conclude that the differences between juvenile and adult offenders are too marked and well understood, and that the differences warranted not risking irreversible adult punishments. The second case, *Graham v. Florida* (2010), involved the imposition of life sentences without parole for nonhomicide crimes committed by juveniles. The Court found such absolute punishments unconstitutional. The Court followed rationales similar to those it had announced in *Roper*, which were that juveniles are not fully developed, that they do not have a moral sense to the same extent as adults, and that those differences required the legal system to provide them with the possibility of changing (hence, not permitting life sentences without parole for nonhomicide cases unless offenders had a chance to leave if they could show that they were rehabilitated). What the Court essentially did was recognize adolescents' ability to change and be inculcated properly into the responsibilities of citizenship. By insisting on limitations on what the state can do in extreme cases, the Court, at the same time, gives states considerable leeway by permitting a broad array of dispositions in the states' efforts to develop juvenile justice policies. Indeed, the cases involved the treatment of juveniles who had been waived to adult court, so they still leave much unsaid about the treatment that juveniles may receive in juvenile court systems. States remain free to develop programs aimed at rehabilitating youth deemed to have offended against society, and states may do so by creating special systems for youth or even using systems created for adults. Indeed, the cases illustrate the simple rule that justice systems must offer youth the chance to rehabilitate themselves, to accept the systems' inculcation.

## Health and Medical Care Systems

If examinations of the inculcation of values ignore justice systems, which exist for the sole purpose of inculcating values, they also are likely to ignore others that may do so more indirectly. This clearly is the case with health and medical care systems, as those operate within value systems and also serve to inculcate values. The systems may do so either overtly or in a largely hidden manner, depending on the nature of the services youth may require. And those services can range as widely as they can involve a wide range of values. Notably, access to medical systems can influence such values as those that guide intimate relationships, through access to treatment relating to sexual activity (such as diseases and pregnancies). They can relate to relationships that individuals have with family members, peers, and strangers through access to therapeutic services (such as treatment for fostering better relationships or integration into society). They can relate to a person's individual development, again through access to therapeutic services (such as medical treatment for a variety of personality disorders, affective disorders, or risk-taking behaviors). In all of these potential arenas, the systems can act in noncoercive ways as well as quite coercively, such as through the use of mind-altering drugs or institutionalization. Without doubt, health and medical systems can play important roles in shaping people's views of themselves and others as well as their general dispositions, all of which serve as the foundation of inculcation efforts.

The legal system typically views adolescents as incapable of making medical and health care decisions on their own volition. The reason for this is that parents are deemed as having the right to control their children's medical decision making on the assumption, for example, that they will act in their child's best interests and that adolescents do not have the maturity (ability) to make important, life-changing decisions. On grounds quite similar to those supporting juveniles' exclusion from extreme forms of punishment when they are in adult systems of punishment (that they are not necessarily mature, are subject to peer influence, or are incapable of making important decisions), the legal system acts paternalistically to protect adolescents from potential harm. The protection from even potential harm includes overriding the rights of parents to determine their children's medical treatment, in such circumstances as when the child's life would be threatened and the child is deemed unable to protect itself against its parents or the parents are unable to act in their child's best interests. The systems, however, can do much more than that. The systems can serve to reinforce parental values or they can give youth power to follow their own values and make their own decisions when they might differ from those of their parents. Two leading Supreme Court cases that have addressed the rights of minors in mental health and medical care systems provide illustrations of the limits of parents' control.

As we have seen above, in approaching the rights of adolescents within families, the Court generally has not sought to disentangle the parents' interests from those of their children. Even cases in which there could be direct conflict between parents and their children, such as when parents are seeking to institutionalize their children for therapeutic treatment, the Court has sided with the parents. That was the general rule announced in *Parham v. J. R.* (1979), which involved the institutionalization of minors for mental health care. Theoretically, everyone has the right to not be institutionalized involuntarily, and a person can be committed involuntarily only if states follow strict due process protections. In *Parham*, however, the Court noted that the child's "interest is inextricably linked with the parents' interest in and obligation for the welfare and the health of the child" (600). The Court acknowledged that "some parents may at times act against the interest of their children . . . but [that] is hardly a reason to discard wholesale those pages of human experience that teach that parents generally do act in the child's best interests" (602–3). Given the parents' presumed attachment to the child, the Court approved of significantly reduced protections from commitment to institutions. As the *Parham* case made clear, parents have a very broad right to shape their children's development, including their emotional development and general mental health.

Among the most difficult and challenging cases that have pitted parental rights directly against those of their children have been cases addressing minors' rights to abortions and other very invasive medical procedures. The leading case in this area, *Bellotti v. Baird* (1979), laid the foundation for this line of cases as well as others that would attempt to balance the rights of parents against those of their children in situations involving potential conflicts between their constitutional rights. At bottom, the legal paradigm set forth in *Bellotti* serves as the foundation for determining who controls the values that will guide decisions that not only can have a profound impact on important life decisions but also can involve deep moral conflicts between parents and their children.

*Bellotti* involved the Court's review of a Massachusetts statute requiring parental consent for abortions for unmarried minor women, with a provision allowing the minor to petition a judge if one or both of her parents refused consent. Allowing that the constitutional rights of children are not coextensive with those of adults, and recognizing a constitutional parental right against undue, adverse interference by the state in parents' authority to direct the rearing of their children, the Court reasoned that the rights of parents needed to weigh heavily in these situations. The Court reviewed key parental rights cases in this area because it recognized the duty of parents to prepare their children for "additional obligations '. . . including the inculcation of moral standards, religious beliefs, and elements of good citizenship'" (637–38). It further reasoned that "[l]egal restrictions on minors, especially those supportive of the parental role, may be important to the child's chances for the full growth and maturity that make eventual participation in a free society meaningful and rewarding" (639–40). Nonetheless, the Court concluded,

> The unique nature and consequences of the abortion decision make it inappropriate "to give a third party an absolute, and possibly arbitrary, veto over the decision of the physician and his patient to terminate the

patient's pregnancy, regardless of the reason for withholding consent." ...
We therefore conclude that if the State decides to require a pregnant minor to obtain one or both parents' consent to an abortion, it also must
provide an alternative procedure whereby authorization for the abortion
can be obtained. (642–43)

The Court, then, required a state to provide an alternative route for
minors to petition a court if they wanted to have their rights recognized. That petitioning included minors' ability to demonstrate that they
were mature enough (i.e., sufficiently adult-like) to make what would
amount to an adult decision. Importantly, the Court also found the
Massachusetts judicial bypass procedure unconstitutional, since judges
still may refuse to authorize the abortion when they conclude that an
abortion would not serve the best interests of the minor, even after finding that a woman is mature and well-informed enough to make, and has
made, a reasonable decision. The Court required judges, upon finding
the adolescent mature enough to make the decision, to leave the decision in the minor's hands. In a real sense, the Court recognized that
some adolescents can be mature enough to make adult decisions (i.e., to
make decisions without needing their parents' consent as well as without
the parents' moral guidance)—that adolescents can be adult-like enough
to follow their own values. As a result, the case became known for the
Court's sanctioning the use of the "mature minor rule," which provides
an exception to the common law rule requiring parental consent for the
medical treatment of a minor.

*Bellotti* may be viewed as championing a general and enlightened
view of the capacities of minors, but a close look shows otherwise. The
result of the *Bellotti* rule, and those following it (see Levesque 2000a), is
that minors who can be deemed mature can exercise rights without their
parents' consent or even their notification of the medical procedures
that minors are about to undergo. This rule may seem to be quite broad
and to permit adolescents considerable control over their own rights and
the ability to make decisions that follows their own values. However, the
rule only applies in situations in which adolescents can claim that they
have a constitutional right that inherently conflicts with the rights of
their parents. Indeed, *Bellotti* is known for clearly articulating why minors pervasively do not have rights against their parents and, equally im-

portantly, why their rights are not coterminous with those of adults. In reaching that conclusion, the Court identified three important reasons for not equating children's constitutional rights with those of adults: "the peculiar vulnerability of children; their inability to make critical decisions in an informed, mature manner; and the importance of the parental role in child rearing" (603). Although clearly limiting, the rule also had the benefit of highlighting what minors would need to demonstrate to retain the legal power to control their own rights and follow their own values in making important decisions: that the right at stake was a fundamentally important (constitutional) one; that exercising that right would not place them in a peculiarly vulnerable situation; that they are able to make critical decisions in an informed, mature manner; and that the recognition of their rights would not necessarily interfere with their parents' roles in raising them (e.g., they could be deemed to no longer need their parents' support, or getting their parents' support would be problematic for the child). *Bellotti* makes clear, then, that the Supreme Court retains a high regard for the rights of parents in directing their family unit, but the Court, in narrow sets of circumstances that have yet to be articulated fully, also seeks to respect the independent rights of children who can be deemed more adult than child-like.

*Bellotti* may provide a general rule that grants parents considerable rights to control their children's medical decision making, but what is quite unusual about the general rule regarding minors' access to medical care is that the rule is fraught with numerous important exceptions. Those exceptions may well swallow the general rule. For example, a common exception includes emancipation, which results in viewing minors as adults, given that their status assumes that they are able to make decisions without parental consent. Exceptions also include emergencies, in which health providers are permitted to provide treatment on the assumption that they would do what a parent would do in emergency situations and, equally importantly in law, in order to protect providers from liability. Exceptions also derive from the nature of the service that would be provided, with the most invasive and life-changing kinds typically requiring parental consent. That exception may recognize an adolescent's decision-making capacity, but it equally likely may not. Instead, for example, it simply could be granting youth rights to counter threats to public health, such as protection from diseases or burdens that come from sexual activity. For example, adolescents generally can obtain noninvasive contraception (e.g., condoms) and medical treatment for sexually transmitted diseases without parental consent. This exception rests on the rationale that it promotes access to treatment and prevents the spread of disease by eliminating the deterrent of having to inform parents of sexual activity. If the medical procedure is to be more invasive, adolescents also may be able to control their access to it by an exception known as the mature minor doctrine, which figures prominently in understanding adolescents' rights (as noted above in *Bellotti v. Baird*, 1979). Undoubtedly, the general rule prohibiting access to care leaves one to wonder why it still exists and why there is such a profound attachment to it.

The numerous exceptions are important, especially the mature minor doctrine, which permits minors to give consent to medical procedures if they can show that they are mature enough to make the decision on their own. But the exceptions remain limited. All of the exceptions, for example, tend to take into account the age and situation of minors to determine their ability to control their own rights. For example, the mature minor rule especially is used for minors who are sixteen or older, understand the medical procedures in question, have engaged in adult-like behavior, and seek a procedure that is not serious—all of which criteria reduce the need for parental involvement. Even in contexts where adolescents are deemed to have fundamental rights at stake, such as the right to access abortions, it is difficult to view their rights as fully adult-like given that they may require a court proceeding to demonstrate their maturity and ability to make important decisions on their own. Adults simply are assumed to be mature, and mature adolescents can be far from free to exercise their rights if they can do so only by being declared able by a court. Again, imagine a system where adults have to obtain a judge's permission to exercise a right (such as access to a physician); such a situation would not be deemed to be granting adults considerable freedom. Arguably even more limiting, the reality is that adolescents (like adults) may have access to care but may not actually receive care because of, for example, cost; and if they are granted access, the utility of access varies according to the nature of the needed services (e.g., confidential access to STD testing may be granted, but not necessarily confidential access to care for treating that

STD). These limitations highlight well the very practical limits that can face theoretical developments.

The above developments translate into the principle that adolescents can be treated very differently, either as adults or as children, in health care arenas. In health care contexts, adolescents typically are excluded from decision making, but they may well be able to decide on their own volition whether to make use of a service, depending on a variety of factors, including the procedure's intrusiveness and irreversibility. Despite important developments in adolescents' legal rights, then, the vast majority of adolescents are treated as children for the purposes of health and medical care. This view translates into providing adults considerable discretion in determining the foundation on which the inculcation of values can stand.

## Child Welfare Systems

As with other state-controlled large bureaucracies charged with enforcing views of appropriate behavior, child welfare systems use judicial systems, administrative agencies, and a mixture of governmental and public (often religious-based) service providers to support children in need of care (see Levesque 2008). An exceedingly complex and varied system of laws regulates these systems as they determine which children are in need of care and what type of care to provide them. Although largely governed by state laws and federal legislative mandates, constitutional parameters still guide this site of inculcation. Those parameters reveal much about the potential to inculcate values and dispositions, as they focus on the rights and responsibilities of parents and the government's obligations for children in their care.

We already have seen how the legal system grants families enormous power to inculcate values that parents deem fitting. That power has an important effect on this area of jurisprudence, as it guides governmental responses to child welfare. Much of child welfare law deals with the extent to which the state will proceed cautiously when it intervenes in families in the name of protecting children from ineffective parenting. That caution leads it to focus on preserving families, on giving careful protection to the rights of parents. Once the state removes children from their homes and parents, however, the state itself retains the broad freedom to inculcate the values it deems appropriate. The ability to use that freedom actually serves as the reason to remove children from those who care ineffectively for them. When parents fail, the state intervenes and provides children with a different socializing environment.

When undertaking the responsibility to direct a child's upbringing, the state determines the level of care it will provide and the type of social environment deemed suitable for the child. As with the juvenile justice system, jurisprudence relating to the child welfare system concerns itself mainly with the nature of the rights involved when children enter and leave the system. In this instance, however, the system concerns itself more with the rights of parents as it seeks to determine whether parents or the state should be directly responsible for children's upbringing. Despite the emphasis on parents, however, the government's interests in protecting children and the broader society from ineffective parenting clearly trump the rights of parents, as child welfare system officials essentially determine the types of values deemed permissible to inculcate in children.

## CARING FOR CHILDREN IN CUSTODY

States take on obligations when they take children under their care, but the nature of that care largely is left to the discretion of those entrusted with it. The leading Supreme Court case in this area detailed an individual's right to services in furtherance of that individual's rehabilitation when in state care: *Youngberg v. Romeo* (1982). In that case, the Supreme Court considered whether and to what extent civilly committed (as opposed to criminally committed) individuals have rights to state-provided rehabilitation and training. In this instance, a mother had become unable to provide basic physical care for her severely disabled child and had relinquished his care to the state. The Court concluded that individuals committed to state institutions have a limited positive right to receive rehabilitative training services required by minimum standards of professional judgment, in order to reduce the risk of endangering themselves or others, and to reduce or eliminate the institution's need to use bodily restraints. The Court reasoned that the failure to provide such minimal training—resulting in deterioration and the need for restraints—would amount to an additional and impermissible intrusion on an individual's liberty interests, beyond that justified by the state's interest in maintaining the individual's confinement. In rendering its ruling, the *Youngberg* Court identified the standard of care to be given to those in state custody. The government undertakes a positive obligation to provide them with basic necessities, a safe environment, and treatment designed according to minimum standards of professional judgment, all of which provisions aim to maximize their liberties. *Youngberg* recognized only minimal obligations of care, and it left that determination generally to the discretion of those charged with providing that care. Like parents, professionals caring for individuals in state custody have the responsibility to provide basic care and direct their upbringing as they see fit. Like parents, they act in children's best interests and guide their development in ways not inimical to societal interests.

The significance of formal custody cannot be underestimated. If the state intervenes to protect children, but the child's formal custody remains with a parent, parents remain in control, and equally importantly, the Constitution does not require holding the state responsible for the children. This was the result of *DeShaney v. Winnebago County Department of Social Services* (1989). That case involved a claim that the state had failed to fulfill its obligations to protect children. The Court declined to find a state duty to protect a child who was in the custody of his father, rather than in state custody, when the child had suffered permanent serious injury at the hands of his father. The Winnebago County Department of Social Services had been repeatedly informed of incidents of abuse and the risk of further abuse, and the agency had removed the young child, but then returned him to his father's care. The Court reasoned that the state's right to intervene, investigate, and monitor the situation did not implicate a duty to protect the child, who remained in his father's care. The state had not assumed the custodial right and, therefore, did not hold the accompanying duty to care for and protect the child. The right of control had been left to the father, and the child could not support a claim for denial of the state's duty based on the father's acts of private violence. The Court reasoned that the state assumes a reciprocal duty to protect and care directly for children when it restrains their freedom, such as by bringing them into state custody. The Court held that because the government has no original obligation to extend any kind of assistance to children who are abused or neglected, the Constitution cannot hold states responsible for failing to protect all children from harm caused by private actors. The majority opinion rested this area of constitutional jurisprudence on a view of the world that can neatly divide harms into two categories: those directly caused by some overt act of the state, for which the Due Process Clause provides redress, and those received in a separate, private realm, outside of the direct reach of the government and therefore beyond constitutional scrutiny. In the end, *DeShaney* would stand for the simple rule that a state owes no constitutional, affirmative duties to those not in its custody. Not having the state owe a duty to the child means that parents retain the general freedom to raise their children as they see fit, particularly when children are directly under their care.

When the legal system considers the obligations of child welfare systems, much of the focus is on the services that they provide to families. The centrality of services derives from the system's operating on a general rule and its corollary: the system presumes (1) that families can be rehabilitated with appropriate services, and (2) that those families unable to be rehabilitated should be subjected to quick dissolution and their children placed in alternate care. Given the significance of these services to assisting children and their families, much attaches to who has a right to them. Yet states, under the broad guidance of federal mandates, have discretion to determine how they will provide their services and who controls access to them. That discretion involves the nature of the services, such as therapeutic care, parenting classes, educational assistance, and other interventions that hopefully will help remedy the child's home environment and foster healthy development. Parental rights may enjoy high regard, enough to warrant assistance in some instances, but they necessarily give way to the state's discretion when parents become ineffective.

Despite the obvious importance of child welfare services to preserving highly protected parent-child relationships, state discretion in providing them means that neither parents nor children have firm rights to them. When states fail to provide appropriate services, the law limits parents' and children's ability to require the state to perform the duties that the parents or children desire; nor can families require the state to provide services that the law itself sought to provide the family. The failure to provide families with the right to have the state provide the services that the state itself determined were needed may seem illogical, but that is the rule. The legal system leaves much to the state's discretion and even permits it to fail. Although the permissiveness may seem odd, the Supreme Court condoned and embraced that approach in *Suter v. Artist M.* (1992), a case that permits states to hold parents to certain family values when, at the same time, states themselves need not provide the assistance needed to reach those standards.

*Suter v. Artist M.* (1992) involved the extent to which children poorly served in child welfare systems can gain redress in federal courts. In *Suter*, the Court specifically addressed the question of whether an individual child taken into state custody has a federal right to enforce the reasonable efforts mandate directly under the Adoption Assistance and Child Welfare Act of 1980 ("Child Welfare Act"), or through an action under 42 U.S.C. 1983 as a beneficiary of the Child Welfare Act. The facts and arguments proposed in *Suter* were straightforward and quite compelling. The Child Welfare Act is the federal statute that provides states with broad guidelines regarding how they will operate their child welfare systems, such as requiring, in some instances, reunification services. In return, the federal government provides monies to subsidize a state's child welfare system. As a condition of receiving federal funds under the Child Welfare Act, then, the state of Illinois had agreed to make, in appropriate cases, reasonable efforts to prevent the removal of children from their homes and to reunify those children with their families, should removal become necessary. Section 1983 actions provide individuals with access to federal courts to litigate claims that officials acting under state law deprived them of a recognized right. Artist M., representing a class of plaintiffs including all children who resided or would reside in the custody of Illinois' child protective services agency, argued that the state had failed to make reasonable efforts by not promptly appointing case managers to children entering the system and not reassigning children promptly to new case managers when necessary. The *Suter* Court, however, did not even reach the issue of whether the state had satisfied its agreement to make reasonable efforts. The Court instead held that individual private plaintiffs do not have a federally enforceable right to reasonable efforts on the part of the state to provide appropriate services. Rather than private enforcement by individuals, the Court believed that Congress had intended to have only the secretary of Health and Human Services enforce the reasonable-efforts provision because the Child Welfare Act granted the secretary authority to approve each state's plan, and the reasonable-efforts provision was part of that plan.

The practical impact of the *Suter* Court's rationale was to soften significantly the enforcement of the Child Welfare Act. The act had mandated the provision of services, helped set guidelines that would provide hearings to ensure the provision of services, set time frames for when services were to be provided, and permitted exceptions to the need for reunification services. These guidelines would not be effective if states were free to ignore them or to place their resources in areas that they found more important. For children and their families, their potential remedies lie at the state level—at the level that determines the nature of rights to services and has its own enforcement mechanisms to ensure that states provide reasonable care. These often strained and overburdened systems may work for children and their families, but *Suter* reveals the immense legal obstacles in the way of efforts to ensure that states enforce their own legal mandates. *Suter* joins other cases that support the immense discretion retained by states in determining how they will run their child welfare systems, and how they will care for and guide the development of children outside of families. Child welfare systems, then, do more than reveal the types of values that states wish to foster in children and guide their development; states' willingness to provide for children identified as in need of services reveals the actual value that states place on children.

## DETERMINING PARENTAL FAILURE

Parents may retain strong parental rights to raise and inculcate in their children the values that they deem appropriate, but the state has considerable freedom to intervene to rescue children whom the government deems at risk of not being raised properly. Part of that flexibility to intervene rests on the intervention's being temporary and necessary to protect vulnerable members of society. Given the temporary nature of initial interventions, the legal system permits the state to grant reduced rights to parents on the grounds that they can be made whole again in the event of error. Despite being reduced, the parents' right to raise their children still remains. In this context, this right is protected by either the right to be free from unreasonable searches and seizures or basic due process rights against state actions. Remarkably, the Supreme Court has not paid much attention to this area of law, with the notable exception of a case that actually highlights the state's flexibility when it wishes to intervene to protect children from parents who are at risk for not raising their children properly.

The only Supreme Court case squarely in this area, *Ferguson v. City of Charleston* (2001), helps to clarify how the Court approaches these issues. Ferguson addressed a public hospital's use of drug testing to deter pregnant women from harming their unborn children. The hospitals used urine screens on maternity patients who were thought to be using cocaine. Positive tests were used to "leverage" patients into formal treatment programs. Patients who refused, or who failed to live up to the treatment program's terms, were referred to law enforcement officials for possible prosecution. Potential charges included criminal charges of child neglect and unlawful delivery of a controlled substance to a child. Because the hospital's urinalysis program was not "divorced from the State's general interest in law enforcement" (79) but instead used "law enforcement to coerce the patients into substance abuse treatment" (80), the Court concluded that the program did not qualify for treatment under the special needs exception, which would have permitted the search and seizure under reasonable suspicion rather than the more exacting standard of probable cause that is needed in criminal cases. As the Court saw it, "[a]ll the available evidence" demonstrated that the hospital's "primary purpose" was "indistinguishable from the general interest in crime control" (81). Local prosecutors and police were extensively involved in the policy's day-to-day administration. Police coordinated arrests with hospital staff. Even though the hospital's motives could have been benign and did address a serious problem, the program's pervasive involvement with law enforcement rendered it unqualified for the special needs exception. As the Court reasoned, "The gravity of the threat alone cannot be dispositive of questions concerning what means law enforcement officers may employ to pursue a given purpose" (86). Despite the state's undisputedly high interest in ensuring that children will not be born addicted or raised in toxic environments, the Court required the state to protect the rights of parents in the same way that it would regarding any other serious intrusion on their rights. Notably, it did not stop the state from interfering; it simply held that the state needed to meet a high burden of proof before doing so.

*Ferguson* confirms an important rule by holding the exception to it. The case demonstrates that the Court presumes that searches motivated by law enforcement purposes should be governed by law enforcement standards, and those standards generally require some level of heightened suspicion to protect individuals from unreasonable searches. Along these same lines, child abuse investigations that further law enforcement aims should be subjected to basic law enforcement standards; at least they should not be excused outright. The law, however, currently conceptualizes child abuse investigations as civil matters, a conceptualization that supports policies that subject parents to reduced legal protections when the state seeks to intervene to investigate allegations of child maltreatment. The child welfare system does not require the typical protections when the state investigates allegations and considers the temporary removal of children from their homes. This reduced level of protection is quite different from the rights that individuals would have if the intervention involved law enforcement, the criminal justice system.

The Court may not protect parental rights as much at initial child welfare system interventions, but once the state has intervened, the rights of parents receive increased protection. This increased protection derives from the legal system's assumption of parental fitness—its assumption that parents are best situated to determine their children's upbringing. *Santosky v. Kramer* (1982) confirmed the rule and the rationales for protections given to parents. The *Santosky* case began with a determination by a New York State social agency that the Santosky parents had, for four and a half years, been both neglecting and abusing three of their children. When the state determined that the children were in danger of "irreparable harm," it ordered proceedings to determine whether to terminate legally and permanently the Santoskys' parental rights. Similarly to most states, New York divided termination hearings into two stages: one stage seeks to ensure the due process rights of parents in determinations of their fitness to raise their children, and another seeks to determine the best interests of the children. In *Santosky*, the state had met its threshold burden at the first, "fact-finding" stage. The state had shown by a preponderance of the evidence both (1) that it had provided the parents ample opportunity and assistance in rehabilitating their parental relationship with their children, but (2) that despite its doing so, the parents still had failed to improve adequately their familial situation. Thus, the Santoskys' case was headed to the second, "dispositional" stage in which the court would make a final decision about whether or not termination of their rights would, in fact, be in the children's best interests. Prior to that hearing, however, the Santosky parents challenged the constitutionality of the preponderance of the evidence standard at the fact-finding stage. While this evidentiary standard is used in most civil cases, the Santoskys argued that the critical and fundamental interests of parents required greater safeguards—especially in the context of termination. Because the taking of one's children is so traumatic and damaging to a parent, the Santoskys argued, the law must take extraordinary steps to ensure the justness of such a decision. The state countered that the legislature had already determined that there were adequate procedural measures to protect the parents' due process rights and that the standard needed to be lowered to deal more effectively with child maltreatment. Having lost in all lower courts, the Santosky parents then appealed to the U.S. Supreme Court.

The *Santosky* Court relied on the now familiar line of cases, beginning with *Meyer*, *Pierce*, and *Prince*, to demonstrate the historical recognition of parental rights.

> Freedom of personal choice in matters of family life is a fundamental liberty interest protected by the Fourteenth Amendment. The fundamental liberty interest of natural parents in the care, custody, and management of their child does not evaporate simply because they have not been model parents or have lost temporary custody of their child to the State. Even when blood relations are strained, parents retain a vital interest in preventing the irretrievable destruction of their family life. If anything, persons faced with forced dissolution of their parental rights have a more critical need for procedural protections than do those resisting state intervention into ongoing family matters. (*Santosky v. Kramer*, 1982, 753)

The Court used this framework to invalidate the use of the preponderance of the evidence standard. The Court determined that because the harm to the parental interest from termination is so "grievous," as well as "permanent," and because of the strong societal preference to err on the side of keeping families "united," the interests of the Santosky parents were deemed to be "greater" than the interests of the Santosky children (756–59). The majority thus held that the "only" way to ensure the greater status of parents—and thus to properly reflect "the value society places on individual liberty" (meaning the liberty of the Santosky parents)—was the clear and convincing evidentiary standard (756). In contrast, the "preponderance" standard was said only to afford parents an equal status with children, and therefore, it was declared to be constitutionally intolerable. Notably, the Court did not require the highest standard of proof, beyond a reasonable doubt, apparently on the grounds that such standards would be too high to meet when dealing with parent-child relationships. Still, in subsequent cases, the Court expanded parents' protections beyond the state's need to reach a high burden of proof, including the entitlement of parents to the appointment of counsel in termination proceedings (*Lassiter v. Department of Social Services*, 1981) and to a "record of sufficient completeness" to enable an appellate court to review thoroughly a termination order (*M.L.B. v. S.L.J.*, 1996, 128). These cases would stand for the strong preference to have parents raise their own children and determine the nature of their upbringing.

Child welfare systems fundamentally deal with who will be in charge of children's development. They typically focus on the basic needs of children, but that focus should not obscure that they also fundamentally deal with who will control the child's upbringing and the types of values that guide the child's development. If parents are deemed inadequate, the state intervenes and imposes its own system of values. The state's broad powers again emerge in this site of inculcation. Rooted in state and federal legislative mandates and guided by broad constitutional principles, child welfare law grants enormous power to the state once it has intervened and determined to remove children from their homes, especially when the rights of parents are terminated. Indeed, simply having these systems helps the government to ensure that parents raise their children in state-sanctioned ways. Child welfare systems, with the force of law, dictate the broad parameters that guide parents' upbringing of their children—that is, the broad societal values deemed important to instill in parents as they care for their children.

## Media Environments

Adolescents inhabit media-saturated environments that serve as contexts for youth to access information that strongly influences both their development and their interactions with others. These information-rich environments enjoy considerable freedom that stems directly from the First Amendment's command that the government shall make no law abridging the freedom of speech. At its core, that language takes the position that people should decide for themselves the ideas and beliefs deserving of expression, consideration, and adherence. Rather than supporting a government that inculcates specific views, constitutional protections in this area envision broad freedom to engage diverse ideas and ways of thinking.

Despite the broad protection granted to speech, case law has developed to offer different types of speech different degrees of protection. Most notably, the First Amendment's protections are not absolute, particularly in dealings with minors. We already have seen that the Court permits states to curtail adolescents' free speech rights in schools, and that adolescents essentially have very limited speech rights in their families. Those limitations stem from the power of both the state and parents to inculcate values they deem important, and the state permits the inculcation largely on the grounds that doing so both protects diversity and fosters responsible citizenship. When outside of those contexts, the state loses much of its power to use speech to inculcate values directly, but that power is not entirely diminished. The state still retains the power to inculcate specific values, either because of the special status of minors or because of the state's broad powers over all citizens. And of course, when not seeking to inculcate values and beliefs, the state protects the overriding value of respect for diverse speech; it embraces the well-accepted belief that the best cure for problematic speech is more speech, not less.

Just as the state must tread carefully when treating different groups of individuals differently because of their group status and must avoid targeting one group for ill treatment at the expense of another, the state generally has parallel obligations to avoid targeting the substance of a particular form of speech for regulation. Indeed, jurisprudence deems this type of targeting content-based restriction and presumptively invalid, given that such restriction seeks to prohibit a speaker's particular words, ideas, or messages. That presumption stems from the risk that the government will extract entire viewpoints from public dialogue—from the risk that such restrictions effectively impose a government-prescribed orthodoxy. Given those concerns, courts review content-based restrictions using strict scrutiny analyses, and support them only when necessary to serve a compelling state interest and as narrowly drawn to achieve that end.

*Brown v. Entertainment Merchants Association* (2011) reveals well the Supreme Court's approach. That case declared unconstitutional a California statute restricting minors' access to video games depicting violent content. The Court invalidated the statute on the grounds (1) that the restrictions failed to survive strict scrutiny given that video games qualify for First Amendment protection, (2) that research failed to establish strong links between video game playing and aggressive behavior, (3) that any demonstrated effects of video game use are both small and indistinguishable from effects produced by other media that were not the subject of similar restrictions, and (4) that the act's restrictions failed to address a substantial need of parents who wish to restrict their children's access to violent video games but cannot do so. Thus, absent an ability to show links between the restriction and a compelling interest, highly restrictive laws fail. The legal system generally seeks to stay out of the business of regulating the control of speech to inculcate specific values and beliefs.

Despite the high premium placed on protecting speech, the Supreme Court allows for categorical exclusions from First Amendment protections. These exclusions include prohibitions against obscenity (*Roth v. United States*, 1957), incitement of illegal activity (*Brandenburg v. Ohio*, 1969), and fighting words (*Chaplinsky v. New Hampshire*, 1942). The Court upholds these exclusions on the rationale that First Amendment protections do not extend to speech "utterly without redeeming social importance" (*Roth*, 1957, 484). Although speech can have no redeeming social value, it does not follow that the government can censor it; the speech must be worth stifling, and the state cannot act arbitrarily in its infringement of people's rights.

The ban on child pornography is illustrative of categorical exclusions relating directly to youth. *New York v. Ferber* (1982) upheld the constitutionality of a statute prohibiting the promotion of a sexual performance by a child under the age of sixteen, regardless of whether the material is obscene. The statute in *Ferber* was challenged by a bookstore owner who was convicted for selling, to an undercover police officer, two films depicting boys masturbating. In a unanimous decision, the Court upheld the statute on the grounds that the advertising and selling of child pornography was not entitled to First Amendment protection. The Court articulated a long list of reasons for entitling states with greater leeway in the regulation of pornographic depictions of children, not the least of which was the finding that the state had a compelling interest in safeguarding the well-being of children, the distribution of child pornography furthered the exploitation and abuse of children by creating a permanent record of the abuse, the advertising and selling of child pornography encouraged the market and created an economic motive for its production, and the social value of such material was deemed exceedingly modest, if not *de minimis*. Yet, in *Ashcroft v. Free Speech Coalition* (2002), the Court rejected provisions of a federal statute that extended the Court's lack of First Amendment protection for child pornography involving real minors to sweep up virtual child pornography, namely, sexually explicit images that appear to depict minors but were produced without the use of any real children. The rationales provided in *Ferber* simply were not persuasive enough to limit the speech in this medium given that the restrictions included categories of speech other than obscenity and child pornography, and thus were overbroad as they went well beyond the goal of prohibiting harmful conduct by restricting speech available to law-abiding adults.

In addition to the above categories that may receive no protection, the Court has reduced protections for other categories of speech. These types of speech include commercial speech and some sexually oriented speech that falls short of obscenity. Considering these types of speech as having low value, the Court reviews restrictions on them by using its most differential review—whether the prohibitions are rational. Although much could fall under the umbrella of speech deemed of low value, the Court recently announced that it no longer would add new categories of speech to the short list of those unprotected by the First Amendment. In that case, *United States v. Stevens* (2010), the Court rejected efforts to prohibit the commercial creation, sale, or possession of certain depictions of animal cruelty. The majority reasoned that protections of the First Amendment are not limited exclusively to speech that survives an "ad hoc balancing" of the costs and benefits of such speech to society, but instead, encompass all expression except speech that historically has been unprotected. The Court clearly moves toward ensuring that the state remains neutral toward speech, that it not restrict or otherwise encumber it.

In contrast to content-based restrictions, content-neutral laws do not raise the specter that the government effectively will drive certain ideas or viewpoints from the public discourse's marketplace of ideas. As a result, content-neutral restrictions allow lawmakers to limit speech on the basis of the speech's potential secondary effects. Typically, these restrictions take the form of "time, place, and manner" restrictions. Rather than concern themselves with the subject matter of speech, these restrictions exist for purposes unrelated to the speech's content. Generally, if the objectives of such statutes can be justified without reference to the restricted speech's content, then they are deemed content neutral. These content-neutral regulations are valid under the First Amendment if they advance an important governmental interest unrelated to the suppression of speech and do not substantially burden more speech than necessary to further the government's interests.

Despite free speech's broad protection, the history of the First Amendment reveals immense concern for shielding children from access to harmful speech. The leading case in this area, *Ginsberg v. New York* (1968), involved restrictions on the sale of "girlie" magazines to minors. To prohibit the sale to minors of the content that was not prohibited for adults, the New York legislature modified the prevailing obscenity test for adults by restricting only pornographic material that would be "harmful to minors." Even though the magazines were constitutionally protected speech for adults, the Supreme Court did not extend that protection for minors. Rather, the Court held that society could protect minors from the expressions deemed problematic. The Court developed what is now viewed as a variable obscenity standard by applying the same standard used for other statutes restricting unprotected speech—the rational-basis standard. Thus, as long as states act rationally, they can protect minors from materials deemed obscene as to the minors.

The *Ginsberg* Court articulated three justifications for limiting minors' access to harmful content. First, the Constitution recognizes parents' fundamental right to direct the upbringing of their children, and as a result, legislatures reasonably may enact laws to support parents' fulfillment of such responsibilities. Second, the state retains an independent interest in the well-being of its youth. Although the supervision of children's reading may best be left to their parents, the Court reasoned that the knowledge that parental control or guidance cannot always be provided and society's transcendent interest in protecting the welfare of children justify reasonable regulation of the sale of material to them. Lastly, the Court noted that the state's prohibiting access to the speech simply did not involve an invasion of minors' constitutionally protected freedoms, thus lowering the standard for review to a rational-basis standard. In doing so, the Court applied one definition of obscenity to adults and another to children, which permitted the use of different standards for review and permitted more limitations of minors' exchange of "speech."

*Ginsberg* may strike a balance between the rights of adults and the more limited rights of adolescents, but when that balance cannot be struck, states need to satisfy a high standard before it can limit expressions. As a result, *Ginsberg* also stands for the rule that the government cannot, in the name of shielding minors from objectionable content, implement a blanket ban on that content and thereby reduce the scope of speech available to adults. This pivotal principle has deep roots and finds expression in a variety of important media contexts. Indeed, it appears to become a general rule. This was the rule the Supreme Court used, in *FCC v. Pacifica Foundation* (1978), to support the FCC's power to punish over-the-air broadcasters for carrying nonobscene yet indecent content. The Court supported its power to do so on the grounds of a compelling interest in shielding minors from content deemed objectionable by a government entity and the prohibition's limitations to certain times of the day, when children would be most likely to be recipients, and left open other times for adults to receive the objectionable content. The Court emphasized, however, that its support for limitations derived from the narrow facts presented in the case.

An important slew of cases after *Pacifica Foundation* confirms that the Court generally does reject efforts to limit the protected free speech rights of adults in order to prevent youth from accessing speech. This was the case in *Bolger v. Youngs Drug Products Corp.* (1983), which found unconstitutional a federal statute prohibiting the mailing of unsolicited advertisements for contraceptives. The Court ruled the statute as impermissibly violating the First Amendment speech rights of a company engaged in the manufacturing, sale, and distribution of contraceptives. Although the Court found the corporation's flyers and mailings to fit within the scope of the Court's commercial speech jurisprudence, the Court rejected the government's asserted interests justifying the prohibition: the goals of shielding mail recipients from materials that they are likely to find offensive and of assisting parents' efforts to control the manner in which their children become informed about sensitive and important subjects such as birth control. The Court found that the parents already had to shield their children from a multitude of external stimuli that color their children's perception of sensitive subjects, but that the prohibition only achieved a marginal degree of protection, a level of protection that did not justify purging all mailboxes of unsolicited material entirely suitable for adults. In a colorful phrase that would guide other cases in this area, the Court concluded, "The level of discourse reaching a mailbox simply cannot be limited to that which would be suitable for a sandbox" (74).

The Court similarly refused to support speech limitations in the name of shielding children from access to cable, phone, and Internet content deemed objectionable for children but not for adults. In *Sable Communications of California v. FCC* (1989), the Court again rejected a federal effort to limit speech in the name of protecting minors. That case involved a total ban of dial-a-porn messages that clearly could reach minors. The Court found that the statute far exceeded what would be necessary to limit minors' access to the messages—that the legislation was not reasonably restricted to the evil with which it claimed to deal. Similarly, in *Reno v. ACLU* (1997), the Court rejected efforts to limit speech conveyed on the Internet. That case involved the provisions of the Communications Decency Act of 1996 relating to the transmission of obscene and indecent messages, as well as some patently offensive displays, to minors. The Court found the interest in protecting children to be insufficient to interfere with adult-to-adult communication. *Sable* provided an important development in the zoning of speech. The Court recognized zoning permissible in the balancing of minors' and adults' First Amendment rights when two conditions are met: the law must not unduly restrict adult access to the material, and minors must have no First Amendment right to access the banned material. The Court similarly rejected restrictions in *United States v. Playboy Entertainment Group, Inc.* (2000). That case considered the constitutionality of federal statutes requiring cable system operators either to impose scrambling and blocking measures on channels devoted primarily to sexually explicit programming or, in the absence of such technological measures, to limit the transmission of those channels to an eight-hour window from 10:00 p.m. to 6:00 a.m. The Court found the statute to present a false choice, as the only way that the cable operators could comply would be to limit the protected speech for two-thirds of the day, regardless of the presence or likely presence of children or of the wishes of the viewers. Even though the statute did not create a complete ban, the Court found that this distinction made no difference in that the objective of shielding children does not suffice to support a blanket ban if the protection can be accomplished by a less restrictive alternative. The Court rejected the argument, finding that speech that falls within the rights of adults may not be silenced completely in attempts to shield children from it.

Cases examining the regulation of speech highlight the increased protection received even by efforts that attempt to inculcate values and dispositions in youth by shielding them from unwanted information and to help parents control the nature of information accessible to their children. The Court emphasizes the various ways in which restrictive regulations would impede adults' First Amendment rights and even those of minors. In dealings with speech in media originating outside of the home and schools, the First Amendment trumps the desires of those who wish to limit children's access to information, such as through Internet activity. As much as well-intentioned lawmakers would like to limit what minors see, read, and hear—all in order to shape their development of chosen values—the legal system embraces the ideal that the state generally must remain outside of the business of indoctrination. This is not to say that the regulation of media is value free. The Constitution champions the value of limited governmental control over the creation and transmission of ideas and values. In a real sense, the government's approach to media environments epitomizes its commitment to diversity—the government protects media environments by removing itself from them, by seeking to remain neutral.

## Community Organizations

Schools and parents receive support from a variety of community organizations that exist to socialize youth. Such community organizations engage in activities that express certain values that they deem worth inculcating, and some of them exist for that express reason. Although these organizations may raise numerous important legal issues, two of them are instructive. The first major issue involves the right of individuals to form associations to express their values without governmental interference. Although the related freedoms of speech and assembly would seem to protect such associations, their focus on inculcating values may lead them to exclude members or positions that they find anathema to their very existence. The focus on exclusion may conflict with other protected rights, such as the right to be free from invidious discrimination and the state's obligation to remedy harms that would arise from it. The second issue relates to the extent to which the state may wish to support the values and messages of community organizations, at the expense of not supporting others. The fundamental concern that this second issue tends to raise is the extent to which states can support such messages without, for example, violating such important principles as the prohibitions against establishing religions and actively supporting some religious beliefs while discouraging others. Clearly, these two examples raise complex sets of issues, but they do provide two general rules: (1) the state must remain neutral to the efforts of communities to develop organizations aimed at inculcating values they deem fitting, including values that would discriminate against protected groups, and (2) the state remains generally free to support the organizations that project the values the state deems worth actively inculcating. Thus, in terms of community organizations' efforts to support the inculcation of values, the state can either remain neutral or actively support the ones that it finds favorable. Together, these rules provide organizations with immense power, and considerable opportunities, to instill their values.

### PROTECTING EXPRESSIVE ORGANIZATIONS

Expressive organizations enjoy considerable protection. Expressive association is a right embedded firmly in First Amendment jurisprudence, as it relates to both the freedom to engage in association and the freedom to advance beliefs and ideas: "Congress shall make no law abridging the freedom of speech . . . or the right of the people peaceably to assemble." Constitutionally, the right of expressive association simply extends the freedom of speech and expression from individuals to groups. Just as individuals are protected constitutionally in whatever speech or expression they might wish to convey (with a few notable exceptions), the First Amendment also protects a group of individuals who come together for the purpose of group speech or group expression, even though the word "association" appears neither in the text of the First Amendment nor anywhere else in the Constitution. Groups, then, enjoy the freedom of association so that they may more effectively exercise members' protected First Amendment rights, notably speech, assembly, petition for the redress of grievances, and exercise of religion. Importantly, expressive associations are distinct from intimate associations. First Amendment rights protect expressive associations. Intimate associations, on the other hand, are protected through the right to privacy embedded in the Due Process Clause of the Fourteenth Amendment, a right that shields human relationships resembling the intimacy of the family. Although community organizations may be like families and take on families' roles, they are viewed as expressive organizations, protected by the First Amendment rather than the right to privacy. The distinction bears stressing in light of our understanding of the role of families in inculcating values, but the state's ability to intrude still may be quite limited given the high regard given to First Amendment values. Indeed, that high regard finds reflection in the three leading cases in this area.

The first leading case found against a community organization's right to expressive association. In *Roberts v. United States Jaycees* (1984), the state of Minnesota used a state sex discrimination statute to sue a men's organization that prevented women from becoming regular members. The Court first analyzed the group's claim under the First Amendment and then asked whether the state had a compelling interest in overriding the organization's right to expressive association. The Court suggested that most expressive organizations are guaranteed a certain level of First Amendment protection.

> We have long understood as implicit in the right to engage in activities protected by the First Amendment a corresponding right to associate

with others in pursuit of a wide variety of political, social, economic, educational, religious, and cultural ends. In view of the various protected activities in which the Jaycees engages, that right is plainly implicated in this case. (622)

Given that a substantial part of the Jaycees' activities constituted protected expression on political, economic, cultural, and social affairs, the strength of the Jaycees' expressive claim was deemed quite strong. The Jaycees engaged in group activities that the First Amendment protects. Although the Jaycees had a right of expressive association, a unanimous Court held that state law overrode that right. The Court reasoned that, on balance, the Jaycees could admit women as permanent members because the state had a compelling interest in ending gender discrimination, and women's admission would have only a minimal effect on the group's expression of protected activities or dissemination of its preferred views. In the Court's view, the Jaycees' expression simply was not implicated seriously by the challenged governmental action.

The controversial case of *Hurley v. Irish-American Gay, Lesbian and Bisexual Group of Boston* (1995) provides the second instructive example. In *Hurley*, the organizers of a St. Patrick's Day parade sought to exclude a homosexual contingent (GLIB) from marching in the parade to express pride in their Irish heritage as openly gay, lesbian, and bisexual individuals. The *Hurley* Court found that the parade was a form of expression even though the parade did not contain a narrow, succinctly articulable message. The Court ruled that application of the Massachusetts public accommodations law, which would force the parade organizers to include the gay marching contingent, violated the parade organizers' First Amendment rights. Although the *Hurley* case did not present itself as an expressive association case, the parade constituted a group with a strong claim to protected expression. The challenged government action forcing inclusion of a contingent marching for Irish gay pride was found to be highly intrusive, an impermissible alteration of the parade organizers' protected expression. The parade organizers were rather lenient in admitting participants, but they still retained the right to control the content of their expression, the messages broadcast by the parade. In the end, the Court found unconstitutional the application of the state antidiscrimination law. The Court did so on the grounds that the law would force the organizers to express GLIB's message and alter their own expression for the simple reason that the dissemination of the message would be contrary to the organization's own views. In addition, in this case, the Court did not give much weight to the state's interest in ending discrimination against nonheterosexual messages. The Court made clear that it does not view the state's interest in eradicating discrimination against homosexuals as compelling. In sum, the group in *Hurley* was engaged in protected activities, as was the case in *Roberts*; unlike in *Roberts*, the government action was found to intrude too much on the messages that organizations sought to promote, and the state's interest in *Hurley* was deemed not sufficiently compelling to force the organization to change its messages.

The third case, *Boy Scouts of America v. Dale* (2000), uniquely concerned a community organization's ability to instill its system of values in young people in a context unconnected to parents or the state, at locations other than home or school. The Boy Scouts of America (BSA) sought to do so because the association seeks to instill the values of heterosexuality, as opposed to homosexuality. In *Dale*, the BSA sought to prevent James Dale, a gay man, from leading a troop of Boy Scouts in New Jersey. They wanted to exclude Dale even though New Jersey law considers the Boy Scouts a place of public accommodation, and New Jersey's public accommodations law explicitly prohibits discrimination on the basis of sexual orientation. The BSA argued that the First Amendment protected its instilling of values as well as its teaching-by-example method of expression. The U.S. Supreme Court ruled in the Boy Scouts' favor, rejecting Dale's argument that the Boys Scouts were not exempt from New Jersey's public accommodations law. The Court reached its holding on First Amendment expressive association grounds, concluding that Dale's mere presence would infringe on the Boy Scouts' First Amendment right to express its desired message regarding sexuality. Although the Supreme Court's analysis focused on the speaker of that message (the national Boy Scouts organization), the case reveals that the message would not have mattered but for its recipients: the boys of the Boy Scouts. The Court understood the BSA as an expressive association engaged in the protected First Amendment activity of inculcating values in its young members, including the message that presents homosexuality as a morally unacceptable lifestyle. If forced by New Jersey law to include Dale as an assistant scoutmaster, BSA's expression would be altered, in violation of the group's First Amendment rights, on the grounds that application of New Jersey's public accommodations law significantly would impair the Boy Scouts' ability to impart its desired values to boys.

Importantly, the *Dale* Court focused explicitly on the inculcation of values, on the internal expression that aimed to expose children to the group's unambiguous and explicit message. The BSA even went so far as to assert, and the majority accepted, that it could exclude Dale because his mere presence—not any speech or conduct—conflicted with the Boy Scouts' desired message and its teach-by-example philosophy. These are dramatic findings, as they rule that Dale's silent presence infringed on the Boy Scouts' speech. Given that a fundamental rationale for protecting expressions is that the right ones will survive in the marketplace of ideas, the focus on granting protection to internal expression, as well as to an expanded view of expression that includes one's mere presence, seems more odious than focusing on granting external speech protection by an association making similar speech. The external speech at least would be more clearly in the marketplace. To the extent that such expression can be understood as a form of raising children—of helping to instill values in young people, and in other ways preparing them to make ethical choices over their lifetimes—however, the Court affords BSA's claim of exclusion additional constitutional protection. Because BSA's expression can claim protection not merely as a form of free speech but additionally as part of parents' freedom to raise their children, it retains a stronger claim to freedom from government interference than if such expression were divorced from the childrearing context. *Dale* is thus a case about childrearing—more specifically, the socialization of boys—and who may make decisions about childrearing in one particular space between home and school.

Fraught with irony, the above ruling highlights the importance that the state places on protecting the inculcation of children. The irony is that expressive organizations that take on childrearing functions are likely to have the strongest effect on civil rights and equality; yet the Court grants them the broadest latitude in their claims of expressive association. Groups that exist to inculcate values in children are likely to be given more deference by courts in terms of the messages they wish to express. These actually also happen to be the very groups best positioned, through inculcating values in children—the most impressionable element of society—to teach the importance of equality.

Importantly, the right to associate for expressive purposes is not, however, absolute. Infringements on that right may be justified by regulations adopted to serve compelling state interests that cannot be achieved through means significantly less restrictive of associational freedoms; and they may give way to infringements arising from the state's efforts unrelated to the suppression of ideas. The most important case on point for this limit is one that relates to the extent to which private schools can discriminate on the basis of race in admissions. The Court, thus far, flatly declined to give private schools such power. The Court did so in *Runyon v. McCrary* (1976).

In *Runyon*, parents with children attending all-white private schools argued that their parental right to teach the value of segregation would be violated if the schools were forced, pursuant to federal antidiscrimination law, to admit African American students. The Court recognized that the parents, under the First and Fourteenth Amendments, had a constitutional right to impart to their children whatever values and standards they deemed desirable, including the value of segregation. The Court concluded, however, that the parents' rights would not be violated if the schools were required to admit African American students because "'there is no showing that discontinuance of [the] discriminatory admission practices would inhibit in any way the teaching in these schools of any ideas or dogma'" (176). Accordingly, the *Runyon* Court rejected the parents' First Amendment argument by drawing a distinction between speech and mere presence, finding that the mere presence of African American students would not prevent the parents or the school from teaching the desirability of segregation. Unlike in *Dale*, it could be argued that *Runyon's* holding emerges because of the heightened protections to racial classification and arguably lower protections for sexual orientation; but the state law in *Dale* had given heightened protections to sexual orientation. The organization's mission appears to distinguish *Dale*, with the Court granting increased protection to organizations devoted to the inculcation of specific values that could not be instilled if the state intervened.

With expressive associations aimed at instilling values, then, the Court adopts a position of neutrality to provide groups that inculcate values a substantial measure of sanctuary from state interference. That shelter arises for two central reasons. The Court views these group-created bonds as playing a critical role in the nation's culture and traditions as they cultivate and transmit shared ideals and beliefs in a manner that fosters diversity and buffers individuals from the power of the state. The Court views collective efforts on behalf of shared goals as especially important for preserving political and cultural diversity and for shielding dissident expression from suppression by the majority. Moreover, the constitutional shelter afforded such relationships recognizes that individuals draw much of their emotional enrichment from close ties with others. Protecting these relationships from unwarranted state interference safeguards individuals' abilities to define their identities, a protection central to any concept of liberty. *Dale* makes clear that the Court very strongly protects expressive organizations' efforts to inculcate values deemed central to the organizations' very existence.

## SUPPORTING EXPRESSIVE ORGANIZATIONS

First Amendment law is certainly complex in its consideration of the active, governmental support that expressions might receive, but two rules generally emerge. First, the amendment generally does not permit the government to restrict private expressions based on viewpoint. Thus, even though private speakers use governmental resources as conduits for their messages, such as using public land as a forum on which to speak, the government cannot deny access to public resources or support on the basis of the speakers' viewpoints. As a result, the government may be selective in the aid it grants (e.g., the resources it provides) but must use viewpoint-neutral access criteria. Second, the First Amendment generally allows the government itself to express its own particular viewpoint. The government may express viewpoints designed to affect a particular social milieu or to persuade people to think and act differently, and it even can attempt to influence behavior and thought by coercively penalizing certain behaviors or expressions. In such situations, the government simply serves as one of a host of speakers competing in the marketplace of ideas. In that role, the government can choose to support one message, including one expressive organization, over another, as the First Amendment generally does not require the government to act neutrally when it transmits its own messages. Thus, the government may be required to remain neutral in some circumstances, but it also can act affirmatively to support its own chosen messages.

The power to support expressive organizations runs deep, as illustrated by the case that confirmed the constitutional foundation for the doctrine. In *Rust v. Sullivan* (1991), the Court considered the constitutionality of Congress's limitations on the advice given by doctors who worked for federally supported programs. In *Rust*, Congress had set up clinics to facilitate family planning, but it specifically had precluded participants from discussing abortion or making referrals to abortion providers even upon specific requests by patients. For example, patients requesting information about abortion simply would be told that "the project does not consider abortion an appropriate method of family planning and therefore does not counsel or refer for abortion" (180), although an exception might be made in the case of a true emergency. The Court upheld the constitutionality of the program at issue, as it reasoned that Congress could limit funding to projects that it believed would serve the public interest: "The Government can, without violating the Constitution, selectively fund a program to encourage certain activities it believes to be in the public interest, without at the same time funding an alternative program which seeks to deal with the problem in another way" (193). The Court refused to characterize this limitation as discrimination against a point of view, reasoning instead that the government had "merely chosen to fund one activity to the exclusion of the other" (193).

For our purposes, *Rust* gains significance for two reasons. *Rust* rejected the argument that the government impermissibly had restricted the rights of those providing state-supported services, and *Rust* rejected the argument that the government impermissibly had restricted the rights of those who received the services. Regarding the former reason, the Court rejected the argument that Congress had imposed limitations on the recipients of federal funding, noting that it would be permissible for the individuals to provide abortion counseling and services as long as they did not do so while on the federal government's payroll. The Court was well aware that medical professionals seeking to provide comprehensive care would feel constrained in what they might do or say while employed in a facility receiving the restricted funds. However, the Court reasoned that such limitations did not involve an impermissible burdening of First Amendment rights since the employees' freedom of expression only was limited during the time when they actually worked for the project. The Court deemed the limitation merely as a consequence of physicians' decision to accept employment in a project, the scope of which is permissibly restricted by the funding authority. Regarding the latter reason, intrusion in what doctors can discuss with their patients seems to constitute an undue limitation on the doctor-patient relationship. The Court, however, rejected the claim that the program's regulations significantly impinged on the doctor-patient relationship in that the program had not required physicians to represent opinions they did not in fact hold. The Court's position highlights the lengths to which it will go in order to accept government-supported speech, as the sanctity of the doctor-patient relationship remains one of the most cherished, given that patients expect their doctors not only to refrain from misrepresenting their own medical views but also to present, affirmatively, all of the relevant options to ensure their self-determination. The high regard for the doctor-patient relationship, and the government's ability to intrude in it without much transparency, highlights the power of the state to support its chosen messages at the expense of others.

Understanding the effect of *Rust* over expressive community organizations requires a close look at a case decided two years before it, *Bowen v. Kendrick* (1988). By leaving funding decisions to the legislative process, the Court in *Rust* essentially followed the sensible rule that individual taxpayers do not retain a veto power over the use of their tax dollars. But other limitations probably apply. Most notably, the Constitution also provides that the government will not endorse certain groups and beliefs, such as religious institutions and their dogma, as clearly articulated in another part of the First Amendment: the prohibitions against endorsing religions or prohibiting its free exercise. Yet despite these broad proscriptions, the government actually remains free to support some of the key messages of religious groups that provide community services. *Bowen* made clear that the government may support religiously affiliated service providers in their efforts to provide services biased by their religious beliefs. Indeed, *Bowen* went even further as it endorsed the government's ability to support a narrow provision of services that includes, and actually relies on, religious providers to further governmental ends.

*Bowen v. Kendrick* (1988) involved the constitutionality of the Adolescent Family Life Act of 1981 (AFLA), which seeks to supply federal funds to both governmental and independent-sector nonprofit organizations doing research or providing services (counseling and education) for adolescents in the areas of premarital sexual relationships and teenage pregnancy. The act sought to support these programs by promoting the use of other family members, religious and charitable organizations, voluntary associations, and other groups. Rather than simply including religious organizations as possible grant recipients, however, the statute specifically calls for the active participation of religious organizations in providing the specified services and does not limit their use of granted funds to secular purposes. In addition, AFLA-sponsored programs increase the likelihood of funds being directed to religious organizations, given the stress on premarital abstinence, prohibitions against granting moneys for "family planning services," and the granting of funds to programs that "do not provide abortions or abortion counseling or referral" or encourage abortion (596–97). Because religious organizations were included among the recipients of the grants, a group of taxpayers challenged AFLA, arguing that funding to religious organizations violated the Establishment Clause. The Supreme Court upheld the statute on the grounds that the statute did not violate the clause "on its face"; the Court rejected the taxpayer group's argument and remanded for reconsideration of the "as applied" challenge for instances in which grant recipients were pervasively sectarian organizations. *Bowen* thus stands for the proposition that the government may not establish religions, but it certainly can support their messages.

The significance of *Bowen* to the state's power to support particular messages makes it important for us to closely examine the Court's reasoning in order to understand the role of the state in fostering conditions conducive to inculcating particular sets of values as well as the behaviors that go with them. The *Bowen* Court's analysis centered on the three typical concerns raised by cases involving the potential establishment of religion. First, the Court addressed whether the legislation had a secular purpose, a consideration typically highly deferential to legislatures. The Court agreed, along with both parties involved, that as a whole, religious concerns were not the sole motivation behind the act and that AFLA had a valid secular purpose to prevent teenage pregnancy and premarital sex, both of which caused economic and social injury.

Second, the Court sought to determine whether the principal or primary effect of the law impermissibly advanced religion. The Court pointed out that there was nothing "inherently religious" or "specifically religious" about the activities or social services provided by the grantees to adolescents with premarital sexuality questions and problems (613). Moreover, expressly requiring religious organizations to be considered among the available grantees, and demanding that the role of religion be taken into account by secular grantees, did not have the effect of endorsing a religious view of how to solve the problem. As to grantee eligibility, the Court interpreted AFLA as blind to religion given that Congress required that all organizations, secular and religious, be considered on an equal footing. In addition, the Court viewed the legislation as not violating the Establishment Clause despite overlap between religious beliefs and the moral values urged by AFLA. Critical to the result was the majority's refusal to hold that faith-based teenage counseling centers were necessarily pervasively sectarian. "Pervasively sectarian" refers to the religious ("sectarian") character of a program offered by a religious group. When pervasively sectarian, the religious dimensions so permeate programs that direct aid to any aspect of those programs inescapably aids religion itself. Such direct aid would violate the Establishment Clause. In this case, even though the organizations received direct aid, the programs were not pervasively sectarian. The Court reasoned that, since there was no reason to believe that any significant portion of the funds necessarily would flow to pervasively sectarian institutions, there was no risk that the funds would be used to advance the organization's religious mission.

Third, the Court considered whether the statute in question fostered an excessive administrative entanglement between religious officials and the offices of government. The Court noted that monitoring of AFLA grantees by the director of Health and Human Services was necessary only to guard against the misappropriation of federal funds. Importantly, the Court viewed the provisions of funds as permissible also on the grounds that faith-based grantees modify their programs because they are required to follow federal guidelines. Because religious grantees are not necessarily pervasively sectarian, the Court concluded that this limited oversight by the federal agency could not be deemed excessively entangling.

In deciding *Bowen*, the Court spoke in sweeping terms of allowing governmental aid on an equality-based rule. It emphasized that "religious institutions need not be quarantined from public benefits that are neutrally available to all" and that the Court had "never held that religious institutions are disabled by the First Amendment from participating in publicly sponsored social welfare programs" (609). Following this line of reasoning, the Court found that, just because some groups were denied federal funds because their programs did not support the values the government wished to inculcate, it did not follow that others should be precluded from support. *Bowen* stands for the Court's permitting support of religious doctrine aligned with the values that the state seeks to support. In producing government speech, the government may align itself with organizations that support its values and, equally importantly, refuse to support those that do not.

## Religious Groups

The power of religious groups rests on those who subscribe to them and their ability to inculcate new believers and infiltrate their beliefs into broader society. Whether groups can exert that power, however, ultimately rests on the legal system's flexibility. In that regard, individuals and religious groups retain considerable freedom given the Constitution's First Amendment mandate that "Congress shall make no law respecting an establishment of religion, or prohibiting the free exercise thereof." That language has led to two related doctrinal lines of analysis that fall under the rubric of the Free Exercise Clause, which relates to the freedom to practice religion, and the Establishment Clause, which prohibits the state from establishing religion. These separate lines of analysis still confirm the significance of religious freedom, but recent developments permit what was once thought impossible: the government may support religious beliefs and institutions. The push and pull between supporting some beliefs and practices and staying out of religious issues marks the tension between freedom from governmental interference and governmental support for inculcating values in the public interest.

Understanding recent developments requires starting with the key values that underlie religious protections, as those values have to do with the political system's approach to recognizing and protecting rights. At their core, both the Free Exercise and the Establishment Clauses reflect three commitments. First, religious protections reveal a commitment to individual free choice in the selection of values and an opposition to governmental indoctrination. The clauses support (and are supported by) a strong political statement that societies once considered radical: that people are free, that free people are free to hold diverse thoughts, and that governments must neither constrain nor direct such freedom. Given that free governments are ones that are "of and for the people," however, it is difficult to escape the influence of religion on governmental actions, and vice versa. A two-way relationship necessarily exists between "freely" selected and embraced values and governmental actions, as individuals' values inform their political choices and political life influences individuals' thoughts.

Second, the protections reflect a profound political commitment to not having the government be in the business of exclusion and of fostering strife. Thus, the clauses are intended to ensure that the state does not create outsiders—that it does not create and designate unequal groups. A government would do so, for example, when it would support one group over another, such as by imposing or denying benefits on the basis of religious beliefs. Such actions would be deemed improper in that they send messages regarding an individual's status as a full citizen, create outsiders who are not full members of their political communities, and run the risk of fomenting civic divisiveness.

Third, the clauses reflect a view that sectarian groups should not benefit from state resources in a manner that would enhance their competitive positions; the clauses are intended to free religions to gain adherents on the basis of their intrinsic merits rather than through state-subsidized incentives. This view rests on the belief that governments should avoid involvement in individuals' religious beliefs as well as in religious institutions—a belief based on the concern that governments can corrupt. The clauses' concerns with protecting all religions, and rejecting calls to determine which religious beliefs count and which do not, are deemed to be critical to avoiding the exploitation of the machinery of the state to enhance a group's position in civil society and impose one group's beliefs on others. Thus the clauses protect both the integrity of individual conscience in religious matters and the integrity of religions themselves from the potential corruption deemed inherent to state subvention. Such protections are meant to avoid both the human suffering intrinsic in coerced violations of conscience and the social conflict that inevitably arises from attempts to inflict such suffering.

The above three commitments reflect what the government fundamentally resists. It opposes involvement in indoctrination, creation of inequality, and corruption of religious beliefs. These three ideals are what remain at stake in this area of jurisprudence. But, the Court evinces surprising flexibility as it responds to the important role that religious institutions play in fostering values and living by them.

### EXERCISING RELIGIOUS BELIEF

Over a century passed before the Supreme Court would interpret the protections offered by the Constitution's Free Exercise Clause. The Court first did so in *Reynolds v. United States* (1878), which addressed the constitutionality of the prosecution of polygamy under federal law. Reynolds, a member of the Church of Jesus Christ of Latter-day Saints (LDS Church), challenged his conviction of the criminal act of bigamy under the federal Morrill Anti-Bigamy Act. Reynolds presented many claims, the most critical for our purposes being his religious duty to marry multiple times and concomitantly. The Court recognized that Congress could not pass a law that prohibits the free exercise of religion, but it did not view the prohibition of bigamy as falling under this mandate. The Court noted a distinction between religious beliefs and actions that flowed from religious beliefs. The Court grounded that distinction in the proposition that beliefs must be free from governmental intrusions, but such expansive freedom was not necessarily permissible for actions that resulted from the beliefs. Following that distinction, the Court ruled that Congress need not excuse practices emerging from religious beliefs. The Court reasoned in this way for the simple reason that doing otherwise would have made the professed religious doctrine superior to the law of the land and would, in effect, permit some citizens to be above the law. This line of reasoning resulted in *Reynolds'* standing for the Court's commitment to separating what the state and individuals could do in the practice of their religious faiths, and to recognizing that doing so awards the state power over religious practices.

The firm separation between church and state for the purposes of the Free Exercise Clause could not withstand the test of time and the development of jurisprudence in other areas. Most notably, the dramatic federal protections relating to religion were extended to the states that took on parallel obligations (see *Cantwell v. Connecticut*, 1940). And equally dramatically, the 1960s witnessed the development of civil rights, which transformed some of the Court's views of how to interpret the Constitution. The clearest example of this development was the use of the "strict scrutiny" standard to determine whether laws violated fundamental rights enumerated in the Constitution. This standard allowed for the accommodation of religious conduct. That accommodation could be had if the state could show a compelling interest in restricting particular religious conduct and could demonstrate that the limitation was the least restrictive necessary to achieve the compelling interests.

The Court's accommodating approach to constitutional challenges was used in several leading cases. *Sherbert v. Verner* (1963) provides the leading example. In that case, the Court overturned the state Employment Security Commission's decision to deny unemployment benefits to a practicing Seventh-day Adventist Church member who was forced out of work after her employer adopted a six-day work week. Working six days a week would have required her to work on Saturdays, against the dictates of her religion. In thinking through the case, the Court recognized the slippery slope between action and faith, as it found that conditioning the availability of benefits on the appellant's willingness to violate a cardinal principle of her religious faith effectively penalized the free exercise of her constitutional liberties. Equally notably, the strict scrutiny standard was applied in the landmark case of *Wisconsin v. Yoder* (1972). In that case, several Amish families appealed a decision convicting them of failing to send their children to public school through the age of fifteen. The Court ruled that a law that "unduly burdens the practice of religion" without a compelling interest, even though it might be "neutral on its face," would be unconstitutional (221). *Yoder* would be deemed a victory for the firm protection of religious rights and for the related rights of parents to raise their children as they see fit, a closely related right that the law has long recognized (see *Meyer v. Nebraska*,

1923; *Pierce v. Society of Sisters*, 1925) and that *Yoder* reaffirmed by using modern standards of constitutional interpretation.

Although the above cases seemed to cement a firm protection of religious practices, the strict scrutiny standard for evaluating challenges to constitutional rights became much narrower in 1990. That narrowing emerged in *Employment Division v. Smith* (1990), a case that sought to determine whether the state could deny unemployment benefits to a person fired for violating a state prohibition on the use of peyote, even though the use of the drug was part of a religious ritual. The Court ruled that although states have the power to accommodate otherwise illegal acts done in pursuit of religious beliefs, states are not required to do so. The general principle that emerged was that, as long it does not target a particular religious practice, a law does not violate the Free Exercise Clause. This ruling appeared to contradict *Yoder*, which had upheld the rights of parents, supported by a Free Exercise claim, to be exempt from a general law. But the Court importantly distinguished *Yoder* on the grounds that it was a hybrid rights case, presenting a constitutional right in addition to the Free Exercise right, rendering the latter worthy of greater protection.

The Court revisited this approach in *Church of Lukumi Babalu Aye v. City of Hialeah* (1993). In that case, the city of Hialeah had passed an ordinance banning ritual slaughter, a practice central to the Santería religion, while providing some exceptions such as the kosher slaughter of Judaism. Since the ordinance was not "generally applicable," the Court ruled that it was subject to the compelling interest test, which it failed to meet, and was therefore declared unconstitutional. Thus, if the ordinance (law or policy) had been general (neutral), it would have passed muster. Today, *Church of Lukumi Babalu Aye* and *Smith* confirm that the Court has settled on an important interpretation of law and that it has set clear guidelines for determining the power of the state to limit the exercise of religion.

Beyond setting a clear and useful standard, both *Smith* and *Church of Lukumi Babalu Aye* also are significant in that they held a controversial view of *Yoder*, which was that *Yoder* had evaluated the challenged policy on the strict scrutiny standard (requiring a compelling interest) because the right to religion was attached to other important rights (e.g., parental rights). The upshot of this interpretation was that the right to exercise religion, on its own, need not require the state to reach such a high standard of scrutiny from the courts. This was seen as a step back in the development of constitutional standards protecting religion. In a real sense, however, even though the Court used modern standards of constitutional interpretation, the Court essentially returned to a time when the state could not allow even firmly held religious beliefs and practices to usurp the law's power. The Court famously had held to that view in *Prince v. Massachusetts* (1944).

*Prince* involved the constitutionality of a statute used to convict a custodian for furnishing to children copies of a religious pamphlet for subsequent sale and for permitting her ward to proselytize on the streets of Boston. The custodian appealed her conviction on two grounds: as undue interference by the state with her parental right to control the activities of her children and as undue inhibition of her exercise of religion. The Court found that "against these sacred private interests, basic in a democracy, stand the interest of society to protect the welfare of children, and the State's authority to that end" (165). Equally significantly, *Prince* established that parental authority was not without limits. It signaled the beginning of the idea that a state can exercise authority over parents' control of their children's upbringing. Indeed, *Prince* retains the status of being the constitutional bedrock of modern child welfare law, as it announced that parents may become martyrs, but they are not "free . . . to make martyrs of their children" (170). *Prince* had spurred the Court's move toward the protection of societal interests as defined and asserted by the state.

Together, the cases discussed thus far in this section highlight key developments in the Court's regulation of religion. They signal the Court's move away from providing protections for religious liberty significantly stronger than the protection of belief alone, a move that had been afforded by *Reynolds*. The cases stand for the claim that the government serves as arbiter between religion and the state, and that the state can hold considerable power when it enlists its broad public health and police powers. Constitutional doctrine developed through the cases of the early 1990s held the view that the Constitution generally protected religious exercise under the First Amendment, but that this protection did not prevent the government from passing neutral laws that incidentally affect certain religious practices.

The above developments did not sit well with religious groups as they became concerned that this line of cases would be cited as precedent for further regulation of common religious practices. Congress responded by passing the Religious Freedom Restoration Act (RFRA), which sought to restore the strict scrutiny standard that would be more protective of religion, as it would require a narrowly tailored regulation serving a compelling government interest in any case that substantially burdened the free exercise of religion, regardless of the intent and general applicability of the law. By increasing the protection of religion, the RFRA sought to limit the government's power to regulate it.

The RFRA itself became victim to the Supreme Court's position. As the RFRA related to the states, the Court overturned it in *City of Boerne v. Flores* (1997). In that case, a dispute arose when the Catholic Archbishop of San Antonio, Patrick Flores, applied for a building permit to enlarge his 1923 mission-style St. Peter's Church in the historic district of Boerne, Texas. His permit was rejected on the grounds of an ordinance that governed additions and new construction in a historic district. Relying on the RFRA, Archbishop Flores argued that his congregation had outgrown the existing structure, rendering the court's ruling a substantial burden on the free exercise of religion without a compelling state interest. The Supreme Court struck down the provisions of RFRA that would have forced state and local governments to provide protections exceeding those required by the First Amendment. The Court ruled that Congress had exceeded its powers, that the Court alone retains the ability to declare which rights are protected by the Fourteenth Amendment (the amendment that the Court had used to "incorporate" the First Amendment into state law). By doing so, the Court brought an end to legislative attempts to overturn *Employment Division v. Smith*. According to the Court's ruling in *Gonzales v. UDV* (2006), the RFRA remains applicable to federal statutes, which must therefore still meet the strict scrutiny standard in Free Exercise cases. As a result of these cases, *Smith* rules: as long as a law does not target a particular religious practice, it does not violate the Free Exercise Clause. Although it does not require it, the rule does give the state considerable power to regulate religion, but that power needs to be, in a real sense, incidental. In addition, and equally notably, *Smith* revealed that the Court would not read the Free

Exercise Clause as generally requiring accommodation of religion, but it made clear that legislatures would be permitted to provide accommodation if they so desired.

ESTABLISHING RELIGIONS

History books may center on the Establishment Clause's importance for prohibiting the establishment or declaration of a national religion by Congress, but the clause's reach is much broader than that, and jurisprudence in this area essentially has ignored that narrow issue as it continues to be taken for granted. At its core, the clause is understood as focusing on prohibiting Congress (and by judicial interpretation, the states; see *Everson v. Board of Education*, 1947) from preferring one religion over another. As noted earlier, given the way religion infuses human life and social institutions, this is no easy prohibition. Although this clause has been the subject of much commentary and its interpretation remains highly nuanced (and often context specific), commentators and judicial interpretations tend to coalesce between polar points of preference to be given to religious beliefs and groups. One end point seeks to create a wall of separation between religion and the state, and thus provide no aid or support. The other end point seeks to accommodate religious beliefs and practices by permitting some support for religious groups or religiously motivated policies. Thus, the former prohibits state interference while the latter permits state entry into religious domains. As expected, adopting either of these approaches can lead to dramatically different outcomes, and both can be found in jurisprudence in this area.

*Everson v. Board of Education* (1947) served as the vehicle for the Supreme Court's modern foray into this area of jurisprudence, as it both used and challenged the metaphor of a wall of separation between church and state that had been established in *Reynolds*. *Everson* involved a New Jersey taxpayer's challenge to the use of taxes to reimburse parents of both public and private school children who took the public transportation system to school. The challenge rested on the claim that the reimbursement that went to parents of children attending religious schools violated the Establishment Clause. The Court was unanimous in its support of the need for a wall of separation between church and state, but the justices sharply differed on what that meant. The ruling opinion held that the state acted permissibly because the reimbursements were offered to all students regardless of religion and because the payments were made to parents and not any religious institution. The dissenting justices argued the opposite. They reasoned that the principles of separation required invalidating the challenged law on the grounds, for example, that parents who were getting reimbursed with state funds for sending their children to parochial schools meant that the state aid was supporting religious training and teaching, and thus violating the Constitution's Establishment Clause mandate that there be a wall of separation between church and state. Perhaps because *Everson* contained strong dissenting opinions clearly articulating opposite views that highlighted a different vision of establishment, the case would continue to frame Establishment Clause cases: it reflected not only the broad interpretation of the clause's prohibition but also the challenge of determining what that prohibition meant, with some insisting that the Constitution forbids all forms of public aid or support for religion, and others permitting incidental support (which they did not even define as support).

A flurry of cases sought to clarify the parameters of the separation between church and state. These cases are notable for their development of various standards that the Court would announce in an effort to guide lawmakers, and of the rhetoric that would support them. A key development was the construction of the rhetoric that religious organizations had beneficial and stabilizing effects, as highlighted in *Walz v. Tax Commission* (1970). In that case, the Court extended the Establishment Clause doctrine considerably as it sustained a state law providing real estate tax exemptions for churches and other religious organizations. It is difficult to play down the significance of such support, but it also is difficult to argue that the Court consistently supported religious institutions. Most notably, the line of cases from *Everson* to this point, which appeared to favor a robust protection of religions, culminated in *Lemon v. Kurtzman* (1971).

*Lemon* involved a challenge to a law that permitted reimbursement to nonpublic schools (mostly Catholic schools) for the salaries of teachers who taught secular material, and for secular textbooks and other secular instructional materials. The Court reasoned that the law violated the Establishment Clause. That result was significant, but *Lemon* became more significant for the doctrine it announced. The case provided the leading standard for analyzing Establishment Clause challenges. The Court declared that a state action was not establishment if (1) the statute (or practice) has a secular purpose, (2) its principal or primary effect neither advances nor inhibits religion, and (3) it does not foster an excessive government entanglement with religion. Although some justices (and many commentators) have criticized the approach, the Court continues to consider variations of this three-pronged test and, indeed, adds other prongs to it to address nuances in Establishment Clause challenges.

Lemon's broad impact finds reflection in establishment jurisprudence that followed it, as revealed in several cases that exemplify the breadth and depth of the factors that the Court considers in establishment challenges. Agostini v. Felton (1997) demoted the entanglement prong of the Lemon test to being merely a factor in determining the challenged statute's or practice's effect. In that case, the Court ruled that it was permissible for a state-sponsored educational initiative to allow public school teachers to instruct at religious schools, so long as the material was secular and neutral in nature and no "excessive entanglement" between government and religion was apparent. In Bowen v. Kendrick (1988), the Court rejected a challenge against using federal funds, under the federal Adolescent Family Life Act of 1981, to do research and provide services relating to adolescent sexuality. The act essentially required recipients of the funds to provide services that were more likely to mirror those of religious groups (e.g., focus on abstinence-based rather than comprehensive sexuality education), which some viewed as showing preference to religious groups. The Court, however, found that the secular concern simply mirrored those of some religious groups and that the support was merely incidental (rather than meant to direct establishment). The Court was not concerned with excessive entanglement, as it would be simple for the government to monitor where funds were spent.

In Zelman v. Simmons-Harris (2002), the Court addressed whether school vouchers, 96% of which at that point were used to support children going to religiously affiliated schools, violated the Establishment Clause. The Court expanded the Lemon test into a five-prong test to evaluate establishment: (1) the program must have a valid secular purpose, (2) aid must go to parents and not to the schools, (3) a broad class of beneficiaries must be covered, (4) the program must be neutral with respect to religion, and (5) there must be adequate nonreligious options.

Following this standard, the Court found that the aid went directly to parents and thus the benefit to religious institutions was only incidental; this was unlike in *Lemon*, in which the support went directly to the institutions themselves (and therefore was not permitted). These cases reflect much more than the expansion of factors the Court would consider in Establishment Clause jurisprudence: they reveal the Court's openness to governmental support of religion and the Court's commitment to analytical flexibility.

Use of the *Lemon* decision and other cases adding more factors did not always lead to predictable outcomes, but the Court's scrutiny of religion itself would take a decisive turn, as the Court found searching questions of religions' role increasingly problematic. Notably, the Court would use *Lemon* in *Santa Fe Independent School Dist. v. Doe* (2000), in which it ruled that a policy permitting student-led, student-initiated prayer at high school football games violated the Establishment Clause due to excessive entanglement with the school's policies and practices relating to prayers. The majority would reach this decision by finding the school district's arguments of neutrality disingenuous. The Court would make a powerful statement one year later, as it would require schools to treat religious groups neutrally. In *Good News Club v. Milford Central School* (2001), the Court held that a school could not exclude a religious club, one aimed at proselytizing to young children, from meeting in the school after school hours merely because the club is religious in nature. The Court partly ruled in this manner because the government (school) was to act in a neutral manner toward religion. The Court did so even though it famously had rejected school prayers at graduation, in *Lee v. Weisman* (1992, 592), on the rationale that "[t]here are heightened concerns with protecting freedom of conscience from subtle coercive pressure in the elementary and secondary public schools . . . [and] prayer exercises in public schools carry a particular risk of indirect coercion." The group meetings in *Good News Club*, which were held after school and supported by parents, were deemed as not coercive toward children.

Perhaps the Court's most prescient opinion came in *Mitchell v. Helms* (2000). In that case, the Court rejected a challenge to the use of federal funds to support religious schools' purchase of educational materials. The Court did more than reject the request; it focused on some of the central points of analysis, such as the pervasively sectarian nature of the recipient's religious views. The Court found such an "inquiry into the recipient's religious views . . . not only unnecessary but also offensive" (828). These general developments tend to show a movement toward developing laws and policies that permit support for religious beliefs so long as they do not favor a particular sect and are consistent with the secular government's goals. In a real sense, we have a switch away from the rhetoric of separation and toward the rhetoric of equality and neutrality.

### SHIFTS THAT MATTER

Despite the commitment to religious freedom, the state still controls religion. It can choose to ignore it, infringe on it, or support it. This flexibility exists because a secular purpose could override a parochial one. Most notably, this trumping occurs in criminal law, child welfare law, health care law, family law—essentially, all laws that regulate the way people treat one another or an institution's behavior. Indeed, a look at all major institutions regulated by the state reveals instances in which the state can override religious beliefs and customs, or can use them to reach its goals.

The constitutional protections from encroachment on religious rights concern themselves with state actions. The state need not remove itself from supporting some beliefs or religious institutions, so long, for example, as the benefits are incidental to a secular purpose. This was decisively announced in *Employment Division v. Smith* (1990, 879), which noted "that the right of free exercise does not relieve an individual of the obligation to comply with a 'valid and neutral law of general applicability on the ground that the law proscribes (or prescribes) conduct that his religion prescribes (or proscribes).'" The Court held that it would be wise for states to avoid creating religious exemptions to generally applicable laws as a matter of individual entitlement but that, if they wished to create such exemptions, they could do so without running afoul of the Establishment Clause. Although the Court endorsed legislative accommodation, the power to make such accommodations clearly remained with the state.

The constitutional protections relating to religion belong to everyone, as do the limitations. Like other areas of First Amendment law, this area of law focuses on the liberty of the autonomous individual vis-à-vis the state in the public sphere. When some individuals may not be deemed competent to exercise their own rights, such as children and individuals with mentally debilitating conditions, others deemed legally competent serve as proxies for them. What happens in the private sphere (outside of state control, such as much of what happens in families) remains broadly beyond state regulation and, as a result, can be under the control of religious beliefs and institutions. In private, absent extremes, the law protects the rights of parents to direct the religious upbringing of their children and what adults wish to believe and practice as related to their consciences and relationships, as was noted above in *Wisconsin v. Yoder*'s (1972) strong support for the cultural norm that parents have the right to form the religious beliefs of their children. A constitutional firewall shields parents from state interference in the religious upbringing of their children.

Despite the state's immense power to regulate religion, much of the doctrine in this area remains entirely unapplied to large swaths of conduct that occurs at the intersection of religion and government. Across a whole range of government actions, religiously motivated decisions can be made, and the Court will remove itself from evaluating claims through the Establishment and Free Exercise Clauses. For example, the Court pervasively avoids inquiring deeply into the actual provenance of legislative actions as long as the laws have a legitimate secular legislative purpose. This is not a trivial matter, as it relates squarely to many of the policy controversies dividing along religious lines—abortion, contraception, stem-cell research, same-sex marriage, and end-of-life care—as well as broad policy reforms relating to highly regulated institutions foundational to the state's mission in modern civil society: health, education, criminal justice, welfare, social security, and employment. Indeed, in some of these cases, the Court does not even examine the actual provenance of government legislation.

Establishment Clause jurisprudence reveals the breadth of religious influences on both formal and informal governmental actions. Abortion probably provides the most litigated, controversial, and obvious example. In *Harris v. McRae* (1980, 319), the Court rejected an Establishment Clause challenge to restrictions on abortion funding, holding that it would not assume that religion is being advanced because a law "happens to coincide or harmonize with the tenets of some or all religions." Similar results emerged in *Bowen v. Kendrick* (1988), a case that supported a narrow view of sexuality education and prevention services that paralleled the beliefs of conservative religious groups that championed abstinence-based approaches and eschewed more comprehensive responses to sexual activity. In such cases, religiously infused and inspired policy agendas can survive if they can be justified without reference to religion. Even if a law is motivated by a particular belief or religious constituency, the Court will uphold it if a plausible secular criterion can be raised and if religious authorities are not formally exercising state powers (see *Board of Education of Kiryas Joel Village School v. Grumet*, 1994, where the Court rejected an effort to draw the boundaries of a school district on the basis of an area occupied by a religious group). Aside from restricting these formal grants of authority to religious groups, however, Establishment Clause doctrine does not easily reach informal political interactions between religious groups and government officials. Religious organizations and activists can lobby for certain laws on the basis that they are required by their religions, and legislators may vote for such legislation because of their own individual religious commitments. Indeed, the Constitution does not prohibit politicians from making political alliances with specific churches or religious groups, explicitly endorsing their messages, or seeking and receiving their financial assistance. These domains of inapplicability are of significance in that they allow courts to avoid putting the state to the burden of providing secular justifications for non-religion-specific laws, not even in instances where the laws have a religious provenance or coincide with the tenets of a particular religion.

Despite the above areas of unregulated activity that occur at the intersection of religion and the state, it is important to emphasize the lesson that regulation has real effects. Most notably, we have seen how the Court can seriously limit the free exercise of religion when it contravenes criminal and other laws. Likewise, the Court will not permit civil governments to cede their powers to religious entities, fund religious institutions directly, discriminate among religions in the disbursement of funds, and directly introduce religious practices in schools. These are quite real and potentially broad limits. Yet, we also have seen the importance of an emerging trend toward neutrality and equality that permits states, in roundabout ways, to reach ends that would otherwise have been prohibited (such as permitting prayer groups aimed at proselytizing to young children to meet in public schools, *Good News Club v. Milford Central School*, 2001). Again, the significance of these new developments cannot be understated as they provide important nuances to what have been deemed broad prohibitions.

The past two decades have witnessed a dramatic reshaping of American law relating to religion. Legislative and executive actions that led to *Employment Division v. Smith* (1990), and what often is viewed as the Supreme Court's reinterpretation of the Free Exercise Clause, have resulted in increased governmental endorsement, financial subsidization, and other privileging of religion. This governmental support may not be direct, but it is governmental support nevertheless. Similarly, legislative and executive actions also led to an altering of the Establishment Clause doctrine that has contributed to a noticeable collapse of the "wall of separation" between church and state, as highlighted by *Zelman v. Simmons-Harris* (2002), and enlarged the social status and power of religious organizations that can benefit from the government's support so long as the government acts neutrally and treats the various religions (and nonreligious institutions) equally. Lastly, despite the explicit constitutional mandate that governments will not infringe on the free exercise of religion or will not establish it, the Court remains reluctant to regulate large areas of activity that occur at the intersection of religion and the state, including the actual religious provenance of government legislation. That reluctance may have arisen from the typical reasons for judicial underenforcement (political pragmatism, institutional competence, and the privileging of democratic processes), but the result remains. Together, these developments actualize the general constitutional vision that the state, as much as practicable, must maintain distance from institutions and ways of thinking that give human and societal development their fullest meaning. And together, these developments reveal a discernible move toward protecting religious freedom even as they set broad parameters that grant the state ultimate authority over the exercise of religion and state support for it. Individuals certainly enjoy important religious freedoms, but their freedoms are much more curtailed than they might expect.

## Conclusion: Committing to Inculcation

The march toward ensuring equality no longer can rest solely on equal protection mandates. Protections rooted in those mandates increasingly center on state neutrality to ensure equal treatment, whereas the best evidence we have indicates that staying neutral is not only challenging but also likely to stifle the development of dispositions and social structures that foster equality's ideals. Recognizing the limitations of emerging equality jurisprudence, it is important to examine whether, and to what extent, the legal system would tolerate the inculcation of values consistent with the ideals of equality jurisprudence: tolerance, respect for diversity, and other dispositions associated with ideals of equality in a democratic society. Rather than find a system that rejects the inculcation of such values, our analysis has identified numerous domains that are devoted to the inculcation of such values or that permit their support.

From a bird's eye view, two extremes emerge when we consider the government's potential role in the inculcation of values and dispositions supportive of equality. Some sites of inculcation sought to remove themselves from governmental interference in their inculcation efforts (by the government's staying neutral to them). Other sites assert themselves to prop up government-supported inculcation efforts for addressing subjugations (by affirmatively inculcating tolerance, respect, and other dispositions associated with ideals of equality in a democratic society). As a result, some sites of inculcation are beyond the government's reach, while others actually are situated in governmental organizations. The latter group undoubtedly remains open to governmental inculcation of its preferred values, but the former does not preclude such inculcation.

The family serves as the quintessential site restricting governmental interference. The right to raise one's children free from governmental interference is, along with free speech and religious liberty, a "fixed star" in the constitutional firmament of negative liberties that curtail governmental interference. The legal system understands this parental task as involving the cultivation of diverse private preferences, moral values, and religious beliefs, rather than the inculcation of uniform civic values and skills. The doctrine of privacy reduces the family's role to that of sheltering family members from governmentally imposed ideas about proper values. Still, the government has retained the power to set important limits to what can go on in families. Perhaps more importantly, families themselves reduce their power considerably when they open themselves to outside influences.

While constitutional law no longer extols a direct connection between parents' childrearing and the maintenance of democratic institutions and values, schools have adopted the obligation to instill the moral values of good citizenship and prepare youth for entrance into civic life. Legal mandates require states to teach civic values, such as mutual respect for others and tolerance for diversity. To execute this task, the Supreme Court has granted school officials considerable freedom to inculcate their views of the community values that they deem worth supporting.

Moving outside of schools, we find a wide range of institutions that support the inculcation of youth, some of which the government can use to engage directly in inculcating values and some of which it cannot. Among the most notable sites of values inculcation are juvenile and criminal justice systems, which actually devote themselves to the inculcation of values and often directly involve governmental action. Medical systems also influence the development of dispositions supportive of particular values and behaviors. Although medical systems are highly controlled by parents, parents' own rights can be tempered by the best interests of their children and even those of society. Community organizations and religious groups remain broadly free to inculcate the values that they cherish, but the legal system can support these organizations and groups to foster the values that the government deems worth inculcating. The child welfare system also exists to inculcate values for the simple reason that the system intervenes in family life when parents have failed or are at risk for doing do. The government retains the power to infringe on parents' inculcating roles when parents fail to abide by societal views of proper child care. Lastly, and as expected in a society concerned about freedom of speech, media industries remain highly unregulated, but in some instances, they can be required to consider society's interest in values deemed worth inculcating, and states can be free to support media industries that provide messages that comport with those the government seeks to foster. The government does not lack venues through which to foster the inculcation it deems worth developing in youth, nor does it remain powerless in influencing the nature and reach of those sites of inculcation.

Despite an apparent commitment to removing the government from the business of inculcating specific values, then, legal developments reveal multiple avenues championing considerable flexibility. Funneling that flexibility remains central to the future of equality jurisprudence. The best empirical evidence indicates that existing empirical knowledge provides important starting points for establishing the structural qualities of institutions that can help foster equality's ideals. The following chapter examines those starting points and the necessary steps toward effective implementation.

5

# Harnessing Developmental Science to Broaden Equality Jurisprudence

To effectively address inequality, we must structure systems that foster the development and expression of values that embrace equality. Rather than find that our legal system rejects the inculcation of such values as it regulates social institutions and organizations, the preceding analysis identified numerous arenas devoted to their inculcation and multiple ways that permit their support. But they are currently underemphasized. These findings mean that a broader approach to equality jurisprudence not only must address the same contexts of current legal approaches to equality but also must advocate a different view of the legal system's role. In addition to focusing on equal treatment by the government itself, a more effective equality jurisprudence seeks to structure systems and contexts that shape values. It develops sites of inculcation so that they can foster greater equality.

At least three lessons have emerged from our look at diverse sites of inculcation and their ability to inculcate values embracing equality. First, the government can support, compete against, and even supplant the values that any site of inculcation embraces and seeks to impart. This power can even reach institutions deemed nongovernmental, such as families, religious groups, and other private institutions. Second, the distinction between governmental (public) and nongovernmental (private) institutions continues to blur. The government continues to infiltrate the internal workings of contexts traditionally deemed private and previously considered outside of the government's reach. And equally importantly, contexts historically deemed public now have private dimensions to them; the government increasingly relies on private groups to support its initiatives. Third, all sites of inculcation can play roles in addressing inequality, as no doubt exists that all of them influence the development and expression of deeply held values and beliefs, such as prejudices. These lessons led to the conclusion that the legal system can be developed to inculcate much more affirmatively values such as tolerance, respect, and other dispositions associated with ideals of equality in a democratic society. This inculcation can continue and complement the current trend toward ensuring formal equality (neutrality), the type of equality that the Supreme Court currently identifies as the bedrock of current equality jurisprudence.

The goal of enlisting the government to foster ideals of equality through influencing sites of inculcation, an approach that broadens current equality jurisprudence, raises the concern that our current empirical understanding of prejudice and discrimination actually may be inadequate to guide the development of appropriate policies and initiatives. This concern may initially appear valid given evidence of broad failures to inculcate equality and continued disparities in the way the government itself continues to permit unequal access to resources and opportunities. Yet the vast and often nuanced area of research on prejudice and discrimination suggests that all institutions that serve as sites of inculcation can enhance the ability to recognize the development, expression, and recognition of prejudice and that they can be shaped to reduce prejudicial attitudes and actions. Sites may do so, for example, through fostering intergroup contact by encouraging community service and interactions, focusing on common group goals, clarifying values deemed worth upholding, shaping peer interactions through adult supervision, enhancing the training of those who work with youth, and holding people accountable. None of these methods by itself can achieve the goal of fostering equality, and none of them is absolutely necessary by itself. Together, however, these types of efforts can enhance the development of dispositions conducive to increased equality. As we have seen, most of these basic findings actually have been known for decades, and have recently been buttressed by additional important studies.

Empirical findings regarding ways to reduce prejudice and discrimination yield important policy implications. They highlight the way even the dramatic shifts in equality jurisprudence, such as a move away from desegregation efforts, need not portend an end to the government's role in shaping responses to inequality. The government remains the dominant force in determining the broad parameters of values deemed worth inculcating, particularly those to be inculcated in youth. Recognizing that force, and more deliberately shaping it, will go a long way toward addressing the emergence and expression of invidious prejudices and fostering interactions that reflect democratic ideals of equality. This book has shown that this effort is well in keeping with the development of a broad equality jurisprudence, one that goes beyond the current discourse that ignores the government's expansive role in shaping values.

Although different directions can be taken, an analysis of policy and practice relating to fostering values of equality must center on the legal system's potential role as well as on the nature of legal mandates that could help address manifestations of inequality. By pointing to existing examples, we can highlight not only what could be done but also what can be done more systematically and across contexts that influence each other. Equally importantly, exploring such examples indicates what currently is not being done, as what emerges from investigating the law's role in the inculcation of values is a lack of development that would be unacceptable in other areas of law.

Two related analyses help to sharpen our understanding of the legal system's ability to take more seriously its inevitable inculcation of values. The first concerns the need to recognize the central limits of current equality jurisprudence, all of which point toward a pervasive lack of development of laws and mandates that guide institutions in their inculcation of values fostering equality. The second details how the legal system can more effectively engage in the business of fostering equality. The breadth of the legal system and the diversity of systems it regulates require offering a broad framework guided by developmental science and useful across institutions, rather than proposing a rigid set of rules. At its core, the analyses simply seek to make obvious and transparent what the legal system necessarily does: shape the development and expression of values.

## Recognizing the Limits of Current Equality Jurisprudence

As we have seen, the significant amount of activity, both empirical and legal, addressing inequality rivals any other area of law and empirical inquiry. Yet rampant invidious inequalities remain in the way the legal system treats individuals and the way individuals treat one another. These continued disparities do not point to a lack of important progress. Equal protection mandates, grounded in the Constitution, have changed the law to advantage traditionally disadvantaged groups and can be credited for transforming multiple institutions historically marked by inequality and subjugation. Recognizing the limits of equal protection law need not translate into ignoring the contribution that that legal strategy can make toward realizing true equality. It still plays, and must continue to play, a foundational role. But rather than bar other approaches to achieving equality, the ideal of equal protection can inspire them. Equal protection law deepens our understanding of equality, its importance, and the challenges faced by efforts to ensure ideals of fairness, equal justice, and equity. No inconsistency exists between a robust commitment to equal protection law and the development of broader and more varied strategies for addressing inequality. But the differences do mean that a more effective equality jurisprudence must grapple with what equal protection law does not.

If equality jurisprudence needs to expand to address the limitations of an intense attachment to equal protection mandates, then those limitations must be firmly understood. Even a cursory look at both federal and state legislative mandates reveals an impressive amount of legislation directly addressing unequal treatment. For example, in addition to the constitutional mandates that we have examined, plaintiffs claiming discrimination can allege numerous potential statutory violations of protections that reach, in some instances, beyond government actions and even prohibit discrimination in private sectors (see, e.g., Title VII of the Civil Rights Act of 1964, 2000). Laws and policies mandating the equal protection of laws and prohibiting discrimination are ubiquitous. The mere existence of these mandates makes it surprising that so much inequality remains. Yet current legislative mandates addressing inequality tend to be marked by at least three types of limitations.

First, existing legislative mandates prohibiting discrimination generally suffer from the limitations of equal protection law. Equal protection mandates provide a limited strategy for achieving equality. That limitation stems from multiple sources. Among those sources are the requirement that direct governmental action contributed to discrimination (unequal or disparate treatment) before the legal system can embark on remedies, including preemptive remedies. And once discrimination has been indicated, remedies are difficult to obtain due to the general need to demonstrate intentional explicit discrimination. Such limitations eventually mean that equal protection mandates tend to ignore the life circumstances that led to unequal treatment and opportunities. Equal protection law has little control over the diffuse norms, expectations, and general conditions of social life that lead individuals to experience inequality. At its core, this limitation turns into a major indictment of equal protection approaches, as it has turned much of what individuals may experience or view as discrimination into something that the law does not address.

Second, the legislative mandates do not sufficiently guide actions. Existing mandates generally lack appropriate detail and comprehensiveness, which means that they rarely structure social systems' responses. This is even the case for mandates recognized as being the most comprehensive, such as the federal Juvenile Justice and Delinquency Prevention Act (2006). That act, which articulates what states must do to receive critically needed federal funds to support their juvenile justice systems, has been lauded for developing a Disproportionate Minority Contact Standard. That mandate emerged from the appropriate recognition that a focus on reducing disparities in minority confinements would be ineffective without a focus on the different contact points that minority youth have with the juvenile justice system. That focus led to this mandate, which requires states to "address juvenile delinquency prevention efforts and system improvement efforts designed to reduce, without establishing or requiring numerical standards or quotas, the disproportionate number of juvenile members of minority groups, who come into contact with the juvenile justice system" (§5633(a)(22)). Appropriately recognizing that simply asking states to "address" the issue was too vague, the office charged with implementing the act offered further guidance, which led to a series of well-funded initiatives. Regrettably, those efforts generally have not resulted in reducing disproportionate contact with the juvenile justice system, as they fail to address the factors that lead youth to the system's disparate treatment (see Jones 2012). That is, disparities will continue because the system fails to take into account broad social forces that lead individuals to the system, such as discrimination and prejudice, misperceptions of minority youth, and social structures shaping family influences (see Leiber, Bishop, & Chamlin 2010). As a result, minority youth's disproportionate representation in the system continues, even as stakeholders can firmly discount the idea that any overt discrimination exists in today's juvenile justice system.

Third, even when existing mandates are more effective, they fail to address the way individuals are influenced simultaneously by multiple laws, mandates, and systems that counter what would otherwise have been effective mandates. As a result, having one system increase its ability to ensure equality runs the risk of creating inequality in another. Schools serve as a powerful example of institutions that create reverberating effects. Schools remain deeply devoted to ensuring equality of access, and many states have statutes barring discrimination. To ensure that youth have safe, secure, and healthy learning environments, for example, states have enacted zero tolerance policies to remove disruptive youth from schools. These efforts may create more effective learning environments and ensure more equal access to education for youth not deemed disruptive, but they also inadvertently contribute to the disproportionate referral of minority youth to juvenile courts. The transfer of youth to juvenile court systems eventually results in the disproportionate confinement of minority youth and their involvement in criminal courts (Fenning & Rose 2007). Concerns about equal access to schooling, increasing safety, and increasing standards of achievement also run the risk of fostering unintended inequality within schools that, again, result in reverberating effects outside of them. They do so, for example, by playing down other aspects of educational missions, such as the need to engage and support diverse youth while they are in school. Schools that fail to do so produce high rates of truancy. Such seemingly innocuous inactivity can lead to dangerous, life-altering results, as truancy has become known as the "gateway" to juvenile delinquency and future adult criminal behavior. Delinquency prevention programs have long recognized this link, and federal studies have grouped correlates of truancy into four main areas: family factors, school factors, economic influences, and student variables (Baker, Sigmon, & Nugent 2001). Although none of these broad factors and causal categories include children's race, the negative effects of truancy disproportionately reach minority youth. In a real sense, the best way to address the disproportionate number of minority youth in juvenile and criminal justice systems requires addressing not only the biases in those systems but also those outside of them. It also requires addressing the potential negative repercussions from systems that are overtly moving toward equality but are doing so through a narrowly defined equality that contributes to other forms of inequality. This last limitation is especially relevant to the types of laws championed below, those that center on the inculcation of values, in that the mandates that currently exist pervasively fail to consider how individuals easily transfer across sites of inculcation and are influenced, in multiple and often conflicting ways, by a variety of sites.

Importantly, the limitations identified above reach further than formally developed governmental organizations and public services that affect youth. The limitations of equal protection mandates also restrict efforts to influence nongovernmental institutions that more broadly define customs and behavior patterns important to societal functioning, such as families and religious groups. These latter groups generally remain outside the reach of formal legal mandates given that equal protection law generally deems them private. The limitations are very real, but as we have seen, they offer but one vision of the government's role in addressing inequality. The government remains the final arbiter of values, as it influences social systems, social institutions, and even personal relationships by establishing the parameters within which they function and gain meaning.

A necessary first step, then, in addressing continued inequality, is to recognize the source of the limitations of current mandates prohibiting discrimination and differential treatment. With very few exceptions, the mandates are narrow, explicitly ignore broad social forces that contribute to inequality, ignore the way multiple systems regulate youth, and fail to guide and structure institutions in ways that would foster the values deemed worth inculcating in a society marked by equality. The limitations can result in missed opportunities in a wide range of institutions that serve as sites of inculcation. When systems are marked by disparities and contribute to differential treatment, or when they operate as though such disparities do not exist, they are likely to have difficulty fostering the values that contribute to equality.

## Broadening Equality Jurisprudence

No one doubts the practical and inspirational powers of equal protection mandates, but even commentators and researchers who recognize the limitations of such mandates still have not strayed far from them. Even leading legal scholars who champion equality in important book-length treatises, for example, content themselves with either documenting the failures of equal protection mandates (Colker 2013) or focusing on its impressive accomplishments without highlighting how legal reforms could address their limitations (Minow 2010). Other legal scholars focus on working through equal protection mandates, either to reduce standards of proof, liability standards, and procedural rules to make discrimination easier to prove (Robinson 2008) or to enhance voluntary enforcement mechanisms (Bartlett 2009). Although such contributions remain critical to understanding equality jurisprudence, the hesitancy to consider alternative legal means of fostering ideals of equality continues. The reluctance to move beyond equal protection mandates becomes particularly remarkable in light of emerging legal trends that limit even more the ability of equal protection strategies to address prejudices and their expression. Still, despite a pervasive lack of commitment to looking beyond narrow mandates, several suggestions emerge from the current understanding of the nature of prejudice and discrimination. Those suggestions can guide the development of a legal system that better fosters values supporting equality.

## Reinforce Broad Policies and Vague Mandates

A more comprehensive approach to equality jurisprudence would benefit from statutes and specific legally enforceable policies that create and help reinforce government policy objectives and constitutional mandates. The need for reinforcement emerges from several directions. National levels of policy making conspicuously resist developing laws that explicitly shape values, including those relating to equality. Many of the sites that have emerged to direct youth's upbringing, such as child welfare, educational, and juvenile justice systems, are notable for leaving much to the jurisdiction of states and even local agencies and individual personnel. National policies simply prohibit discrimination and pervasively leave program development to state and local officials. This approach has a very long history, as laws that are deemed "domestic" are left to states and local communities. The rationales for leaving matters to local communities vary, but many have to do with respect for the diversity of communities and individuals in them. Those commitments, however, need not come at the expense of invidious inequality recognized as unacceptable by broader community standards. Communities have an obligation to further broad mandates. Broad prohibitions against discrimination and mandates for fostering equality need reinforcement.

The need for reinforcement also emerges because, without comprehensive guidance, institutions operate without clear direction. For example, service providers who develop programs addressing inequality without statutory guidance leave themselves at the discretion of new and emergent streams of political capriciousness. The hazards emerging from lack of direction are particularly pronounced in institutions that care for youth. Currently, just as they have historically, youth-oriented systems such as educational, justice, health, and child welfare systems generally remain within the purview of local politics and are guided largely by personal relationships among parents, community members, and those who provide services. Local discretion means that the provision of services and programs will vary greatly from area to area as service providers try to cope with the wishes of multiple stakeholders. In addition to variations across areas, policies may change from year to year, depending on who takes office and the desires of different groups. Perhaps more important than variations in location and time is variation in the extent to which institutions will take no formal position on ensuring equality and shaping its development. As a result, the provision of services even could vary from one service provider to the next, which increases the risk of inappropriate differential treatment for those seeking services. Explicit mandates help ensure that institutions treat individuals equally regardless of their protected group status, something that institutions currently must do. In addition, however, the mandates can help institutions recognize that they are inculcating values and that those values must comport with broad policy objectives and legal mandates.

The entry of minority youth in criminal justice systems offers an illustrative example of the need to reinforce mandates. In most states, prosecutors make charging decisions with little guidance about whether and how to charge youth. Even when statutes and court rules express a preference for diversion or the least restrictive response to adolescent offending, these statutory provisions are often vague and rarely provide specific guidelines for charging youth in juvenile court or adult court. Even statutes that mandate transfers to adult court for some crimes leave discretion to prosecutors who determine whether the facts of a case qualify for a specific crime. Few internal standards have been published to guide prosecutorial decisions (Little 2011). The guidelines that do exist do not adequately guide prosecutors in addressing disparities in the way they treat minority youth. Guidelines focus on objective factors that, on their face, do not relate to disparities in treatment but, in practice, actually do result in differential treatment. As a result, rather than have a system that seeks to offer assistance to youth in need by offering rehabilitation and effective reintegration into society, the efforts to stem discrimination focus on ensuring that minority groups are not disproportionately overrepresented on such objective factors as the nature of the offense, the maturity of the offender, the offender's amenability to treatment, and available resources—all of which can lead to disparate treatment. Such efforts to address discrimination not only continue to fail but also fail to inculcate in youth the values needed to support the development of dispositions that would treat individuals more equally. Instead, the systems run the risk of creating the values opposite of what they intend to foster: a sense of not being treated fairly and equally, which contributes to lack of respect for others and a failure to address the roots of inequality both in individuals and in institutions that support them. Thus, failed opportunities mean more than a failure to create effective institutions and shape the values of those who control them; they also mean a failure to inculcate hoped-for values and expectations.

Reinforcing broad mandates and vague policies may be more challenging for institutions that are not devoted to specific public services or program delivery. But those systems are not out of reach. Families are illustrative. As we have seen, for example, the legal system created a "veil of family privacy" to protect families from governmental intrusions. Those laws explicitly protect parents' rights to determine the moral upbringing of their children, with all that entails (see *Wisconsin v. Yoder*, 1972). The broad right may be highly protected, but it does not prevent institutions outside of families from helping to shape children's values or helping to shape parenting. The government can enlist its powers, including its resources, to encourage families to move in particular directions, as it can fund community programs, educational institutions, media efforts, and other initiatives that can help sway families. The government particularly can embark on programs that could influence adolescents, as one of adolescents' key developmental tasks includes moving outside of familial influences. The government even may enact laws that deal directly with shaping children's values on the grounds that those laws assist parents in raising their children, as illustrated by the rationales for laws that prohibit minors' access to pornography and other products deemed hazardous to youth's health, well-being, and appropriate development (*Ginsberg v. New York*, 1968). The same rationale applies to laws that help parents shape their children's behaviors by protecting them from victimization or offending, such as curfew laws (Diviaio 2007). All of these laws not only exist to help parents but also rely on a framework that aims to support the inculcation of values. Ensuring that youth develop appropriate values and that parents are supported in guiding them serves a legitimate governmental interest. Equally importantly, those governmental interests also can be deemed compelling enough to trump the rights of parents to inculcate values in their children; they can do so when the community agrees that the values it wishes to inculcate are more important than parental freedom—as seen in child protection laws, which include protections against moral corruption (see Levesque 2008).

Efforts to shape values that reach private institutions need not be so overtly obtrusive, intrusive of parental rights, or controlling of youth. Two examples are illustrative. Media campaigns relating to the need to treat everyone equally and with respect, such as antibullying campaigns, provide a recently emerging example of leveraging technological tools to reach youth. Although these programs have not been subjected to rigorous evaluations, successful media campaigns have been used to reach youth to address a number of factors, including physical violence, that relate directly to treating individuals deemed different with respect and consideration for their rights (see Swaim & Kelly 2008). These programs can reach very wide audiences as well as targeted ones; they even can reach some that would prefer not to hear them.

The other example involves governmental support of religious institutions. Although direct support of religious groups remains impermissible under constitutional law, states and local communities can develop voucher programs that allow parents to send their children to religious schools. In turn, states can place restrictions on religious schools that take public funds, such as prohibitions against some forms of discrimination, which the private institutions could have ignored if they had not wanted to participate in the funding program (as was the case in the school voucher program eventually supported by the Supreme Court; *Zelman v. Simmons-Harris*, 2002). The state can guide parents toward inculcating values of equality by encouraging them to place their children in circumstances that embrace those values. Thus even though some sites of inculcation may be outside of immediate reach, they nevertheless can be reached—and actually already are reached by other institutions that influence them and sometimes overtly support them. Again, individuals are influenced by multiple institutions, all of which influence one another. Reinforcing how some institutions approach the inculcation of values necessarily will influence others.

### Shape Institutional Missions

A more effective legal approach to equality requires more than enacting policies that clarify and reinforce broad mandates. Values supportive of equality need to be at the core of the systems that inculcate values, and they need to be clearly stated. That clarity, in turn, involves understanding and addressing both overt and subtle values, which thereby become part of a broader system of explicitly formulated inculcation. If the institutions (and specific organizations in them) are government supported, for example, they need to embrace equality. To embrace equality properly, institutional and organizational missions need to be addressed to ensure that they will counter inequality and reshape the development of values that reject it. The content of programs, services, and the very missions of institutions can be influenced through the forthright, comprehensive articulation of the values that they will inculcate.

Educational systems illustrate the need for mandates to shape the core of institutional missions. The Supreme Court and society have long recognized that the regulation of educational institutions rests on their need to foster equality and that schools exist to prepare youth for effective participation in a diverse society (see *Pierce v. Society of Sisters*, 1925). That mandate has been formalized through a series of impressive state and federal laws intended to ensure equal protection in the form of equal access to educational services. Educational institutions (including those at state, district, and community levels) embrace that mandate, and the result has been impressive. Yet that embrace has been effected in the narrowest of ways. Despite the tendency to limit the reach of equality mandates, efforts increasingly have sought to take a broader approach to inequality and access, as they focus on opportunities and access of young people while they are in school. These approaches are not always successful, and those that fail point to the need to deeply infiltrate institutional missions.

The enactment of policies relating to youth with disabilities provides a powerful example of progress that will remain stifled unless institutions' broader commitment to equality is addressed. Equal access laws for youth with disabilities exemplify how systematic rules and regulations, along with supportive systems and resources, have fostered important progress in the equal treatment of youth with disabilities. That progress, however, remains limited, notably due to the failure to address other forms of discrimination: compared to white youth, minority youth are more likely to be labeled mentally retarded than autistic, and thus less likely to benefit from important resources; minority youth also are more likely to be suspended because of their disabilities, which disrupts educational progress and leads to other negative effects; minority youth are more likely to be relegated to separate and less resourced special education tracks; minority youth are more likely to receive less adequate services because of a lack of appropriate school funding; and minority youth are more likely to be referred to special education classes rather than mainstreamed, another practice with disproportionately negative effects on educational outcomes (see Colker 2013). The unequal effects of efforts to address inequality reveal well how reaching greater equality requires much more than a commitment to reducing one form of inequality. Broad commitments to equality must reach the heart of institutions' missions.

That the unprecedented efforts to end discrimination against youth with disabilities resulted in such differential treatment due to minority or socioeconomic status certainly gives pause to those hoping for effective responses to newly identified forms of discrimination that stifle access to educational opportunities. Illustrative is discrimination in the form of sexual harassment or bullying based, for example, on race, religion, gender, and sexual orientation. Commentators lament the lack of appropriate progress in addressing these forms of discrimination, and how they now manifest themselves in new ways, such as through cyber-bullying. These efforts do remain limited in terms of the actual existence of statutes requiring programs, what statutes protect, and how institutions are to address these forms of inequality (see Russell et al. 2010). But what is often ignored is that remediating programs remain limited by the failure to consider the forms of inequalities that they will create. It is easy to imagine, for example, that aggressive efforts against bullying will focus on overt forms, which will have a biasing effect of targeting boys, given that boys are more likely to perpetrate overt rather than more hidden bullying. Similarly, focusing on aggressive behavior tends to disadvantage minority youth. Not surprisingly, these efforts can mirror the get-tough antiviolence school initiatives that disproportionately reach minority boys. Lessons learned from the disability context, and other efforts to foster equality, lead to the conclusion that new efforts seeking equality need to be implemented with special care; otherwise they will contribute to more, not less, discrimination against those already suffering from the most discrimination.

More striking than the limitations of equal access and equal opportunity laws is the failure, despite the mandate to foster equality and effective participation in society, to develop guidelines and statutes that aim directly at the inculcation of those values. Despite the existence of programs that could help improve relationships among different ethnic groups, for example, few schools have embraced them (Killen, Rutland, & Ruck 2011). Instead, schools that have addressed ethnic diversity have done so by simply prohibiting discrimination in access to particular schools or educational programs rather than by shaping social structures and enlisting programs that could reduce discrimination. Schools also have not taken seriously the need to foster civic engagement, which has been linked to embracing equality's ideals, even though public schools exist for developing effective citizens (Kahne & Sporte 2008). Thus, despite having the technical know-how to develop and implement programs that could address a wide variety of unequal treatment and foster the development of values embracing equality, few jurisdictions have taken them seriously enough to mandate their use and implementation. When left to their own devices, institutions avoid addressing challenging issues, remain with the status quo, or address issues minimally to avoid contravening broad mandates.

Several other examples highlight the need to shape more explicitly the missions of institutions. Unlike the educational systems that have problems of inadequate access, some systems present disparities through too much access. The juvenile justice system serves as an example of institutions that cast wide nets but disproportionately ensnare minority youth. Much of the disparity in involvement in the juvenile justice system remains directly attributable to its mission. Broad and imprecise juvenile court purpose clauses have multiple and competing goals—ranging from rehabilitation to victims' rights, and from public safety to individual accountability—that allow police officers, probation staff, and judges to mask illicit motives and subconscious racial biases behind the state interest deemed politically salient at the time. For example, contemporary juvenile court purpose clauses that explicitly allow for a focus on victims' rights also implicitly allow for racial bias (Bandes 1996). In addition, the focus on protecting public safety leads to disparate treatment of minority youth. Widely held stereotypes that minority youth—African Americans in particular—are violent, aggressive, dangerous, and possess adult-like criminal intent have been shown to influence police and probation officers who endorse harsher punishment for them (Graham & Lowery 2004). Studies of probation officers reveal that their probation reports consistently portray black youth with more negative personality traits than white youth for the same or similar behavior; they also are more likely to attribute crime to character traits and personality dispositions with black rather than white youth and are more likely to view black youth as responsible for their crimes and prone to criminal behavior in the future (Bridges & Steen 1998). As a result, black youth face more severe penalties, including confinement. This finding emerged even after the severity of the youth's current and past criminal behavior was controlled for. And as expected, similar findings have been found at the point of entry into systems, as research has shown that the "youth discount" extends more to whites than to African Americans at intake proceedings (Leiber & Johnson 2008). White youth, as a group, benefit more from the leniency and rehabilitative features of juvenile justice systems, and they do so because they tend to be viewed more as the type of juveniles who could benefit from it.

The differential perceptions of groups of youth become increasingly important as the Supreme Court expresses interest in considering immaturity and malleability as key factors in youth's avoiding harsh, adult consequences (see *Miller v. Alabama*, 2012). These studies demonstrate an unwillingness among stakeholders to apply theories of immaturity and diminished culpability to youth of color, and suggest that contemporary juvenile justice policies have been implemented unevenly according to distorted perceptions of race, crime, and threat. Addressing these issues requires addressing the current missions of juvenile justice systems as well as their changing missions. Factors contributing to disparities in treatment may significantly influence public policy regarding judicial decisions in juvenile court, transfers to adult court, and the sentences that youth receive in adult systems. Trends in legal developments point not to a lessening but to an exacerbation of disparities that will come from efforts to respond to youth's particular vulnerabilities and abilities. This again points to the irony of creating more inequality by trying to ensure more equal treatment on the basis of group differences—in this instance, harsher treatment of minority youth as a result of increased consideration of the differences between youth and adult cognitive and social abilities.

Child welfare systems also reveal the failure of missions and the need to make equality central to them. All states have laws detailing the types of maltreatment that permit intrusion into families to remedy the harm or risk of harm to children (for a review, see Levesque 2008). These mandates do not explicitly discriminate according to minority or socioeconomic status. Yet the systems disproportionately serve minority and poor youth. Children from poverty and with minority backgrounds are disproportionately involved in the system, though evidence reveals that they are not necessarily more subjected to maltreatment, with the exception of neglect due to lack of resources. But their disproportionate involvement is not recognized as discrimination. Some argue that minority families actually do suffer from more maltreatment, and that the disproportionate response reflects the disproportionate rate of maltreatment (Fonts, Berger, & Slack 2012). If those claims are accurate, then the systems fail to prevent the disproportionate maltreatment and fail to provide greater support to families at risk of falling into the dysfunction that results in maltreatment (in support of this argument, see Bartholet 2009). Recognizing the need to pursue equality as a component of those systems' missions would mean thinking through the many ways in which inequality exists and taking serious steps to remedy them. That recognition necessarily would go to the core of the systems' missions and ensure equal opportunity to avoid unwarranted contact with legal systems, and equally importantly, the systems would permit the development of attitudes needed to ensure equality.

The need to shape missions appears particularly important for institutions that have an overrepresentation of minority youth. At a deep level, there is something odd about concerns that key social institutions like child welfare systems and juvenile justice systems have a disproportionate inclusion of minority youth and disproportionately serve minority families. Addressing inequality forthrightly would mean that these institutions could focus on their fundamental missions, which are to assist youth and rehabilitate them in their families and communities. If those missions were served, concern about the overinclusion of groups and about opportunities to avoid contact and access would dissipate. Equality would mean more access, not less.

The above examples reveal the potentially dramatic effect of shaping systems that embrace equality and make it central to their missions. Government-supported institutions that took equality more seriously in their missions probably eventually would be quite different and would morph into other types of systems, or other systems would take their place. Having a child welfare system that is less reactive and more preventive would lead to different types of systems, just as a juvenile justice system would transform itself if it took a similarly preventive posture. Not surprisingly, several calls have been made to focus more deliberately on assisting families and youth at risk for involvement in child welfare and juvenile justice systems. This is particularly the case since involvement in the child welfare system increases the risk of involvement in juvenile justice systems, and the child welfare system has been identified as a significant source of overrepresentation for African American youth in juvenile justice systems (Ryana et al. 2007). Yet those efforts have not become part of their missions. It is true that the systems formally have adopted a preventive approach: the child welfare system places a premium on preventing the permanent removal of children from their families, and juvenile justice systems essentially exist to prevent youth from developing into criminals. But those efforts have not been marked by a focus on ensuring equality of access to treatment and other needed resources. Part of that limitation has to do with society's weak support for socioeconomic rights, a limitation that underscores the extent to which youth-serving institutions probably will need to address different views of rights if they are to foster effectively the development of social structures marked by equality and its associated values.

The above examples again demonstrate that the shaping of institutional missions can reach multiple sites of inculcation and permit the influencing of those typically deemed outside of governmental efforts to shape the development of values. Individuals are influenced by multiple institutions, all of which influence one another. The rationales that those institutions use to influence one another rest on visions of how youth should develop and on the types of dispositions and values they need to embrace if they are to become effective members of society. Governmental institutions that influence families and other private groups can attain increased effectiveness if equality becomes part of their missions and if they recognize more fully their roles in inculcating values.

## Clarify Decision Makers' Roles

The effective inculcation of values in youth must involve clarifying the roles of those who interact with them. This clarity is significant in guiding youth more effectively and treating them more appropriately. Clarity in roles also allows for holding individuals and institutions accountable. These clarifications are most likely to materialize through legal mandates that delineate and support them. Generally, available evidence points to the need for people to feel supported and guided—not judged—by those around them in order for more fruitful outcomes to be produced. This important general rule applies to how to treat those who would interact with youth as well as how to treat youth themselves—a reminder that effectively addressing the way people treat one another requires infiltrating entire systems and influencing their values.

### CLARIFICATIONS FOR GUIDING YOUTH

Existing mandates intended to ensure equality generally do not detail the obligations of those who work with youth, and they generally fail to provide for the guidance and training of decision makers, including administrators and those directly interacting with youth. It is true that those who work with youth increasingly undergo diversity training and may understand basic rules regarding legally inappropriate discrimination. But such training and rules remain too narrow, as they rest on equal protection mandates and do not recognize fully enough the inculcation of values.

The omission is significant. Addressing inequality requires addressing controversial and challenging topics, topics that go to the heart of people's sense of self. The failure to offer appropriate guides casts a shadow over relationships and creates a tendency toward self-censorship. The manner in which discrimination works makes obvious the need for guidance and training: minority voices tend to be systematically excluded, as shown, for example, in research on heterosexism (Gorski, Davis, & Reiter 2013). Training is necessary to ensure that those who interact with youth do not make false assumptions and do realize that every adolescent is an exception to general assumptions. Indeed, prejudices rely on stereotypes that thrive on general assumptions. Addressing them requires training and clarity in terms of what one can and cannot do.

The failure to guide those who work with youth places them in awkward and compromising situations because they may not know the rights they have to address youth's situations. For example, youth dealing with difficult issues relating to inequality may seek confidential advice. The issue of what to do with confidential information, and whether it in fact can be confidential, remains murky. It remains uncertain, for example, what teachers, coaches, and those who volunteer as mentors can do when students want to discuss with them their thoughts about initiating sexual activity or about matters regarding past activities, including victimization. These are value-laden circumstances fraught with challenges. Particularly challenging are issues involving guidance with contraceptive choices and advice that relates to sexual behaviors some would consider deviant and immoral. In the absence of clear guidance from other sources, criminal law serves as the major guide for those who need to determine whether to provide youth with confidential contraceptive advice or whether to inform their parents of sexual activity below the age of consent. Child welfare law also becomes a guide, but relevant rules in this arena involve duties to report to state officials (and those laws vary considerably from one jurisdiction to the next; Levesque 2008). Note that there is not even clear Supreme Court authority with respect to the free speech rights of service providers, such as school teachers or counselors. The failure to identify the rights of service providers is significant. The complexity of this area of law itself warrants more guidance for decision makers. Yet that guidance remains minimal.

Although concerns about influencing value-laden behaviors often focus on sexual behavior and victimization, other actions raise similarly complex questions and concerns. For example, adolescents may seek or need advice regarding other types of relationships. Cross-race or cross-religious friendships may be encouraged by teachers, schools, and the broader society, for example, but those types of relationships may not be supported by some parents, particularly if the relationships move beyond friendships to intimate relationships. Similarly, those who work with youth may advise them to take risks that are not advised by others and that can have harmful consequences, such as taking a stand against bullies. The same could be said in the context of recent efforts to have youth "call out" those who unintentionally (or intentionally) use language that disparages some groups. Those who advise, shape, and foster the moral upbringing of youth can do so in myriad ways, and often inadvertently. Those who take on these roles can benefit from guidance and from knowing what they can and cannot do.

The failure to address these issues has less to do with bars against doing so than with rapid changes in the socialization of youth and the increasing influence of multiple institutions that directly shape their development, including their dispositions and values. Historically, these issues were addressed on the assumption that parents controlled the rights of their children—what their children could and could not do. That assumption is now marked by countless exceptions, as youth increasingly have been granted rights and the ability to exercise them in a variety of domains, such as in the criminal justice, health, and educational systems. In addition, rapid social changes, as evidenced by exposure to media, push the need to rethink who interacts with youth. That need becomes even more pressing as the legal system grants adolescents direct access to media that some would deem problematic, with some members of the Supreme Court even entertaining the proposition that adolescents have rights to direct access to media (*Brown v. Entertainment Merchants Association*, 2011). Thus, as adolescents gain increasing rights and as they interact more with individuals and entities beyond their parents' control, those who interact with the adolescents must be considered as they influence youth's development, including the development and expression of their values.

## CLARIFICATIONS FOR ENSURING ACCOUNTABILITY

It is clear that diverse institutions now influence the values of developing youth, that they can do so in direct as well as subtle ways, and that their ability to do so raises important considerations regarding their responsibilities. Clarifying decision makers' roles serves as an indispensable aspect of the ability to hold individuals and institutions accountable for supporting values conducive to equality. The need for clarifying decision makers' roles in this regard relates to the standards used to hold accountable both decision makers and the institutions themselves.

Addressing issues of accountability requires a close look at two standards that go to the core of the legal system's jurisprudence: reasonableness and discretion in executing one's duties and expressing one's rights. The legal system relies on individuals to be reasonable and use common sense. In fact, the reasonableness standard infiltrates much of this area of law, which means that decision makers who do not act in a preferred manner can avoid liability or other penalties. For example, the criminal justice system, prompted by the Supreme Court, has embraced the exclusionary rule to prevent police officers from acting unreasonably (Levesque 2006). That rule protects the rights of those wrongly targeted by police. As a result, police officers who act reasonably when interacting with youth from different ethnic backgrounds do not have their evidence suppressed on the grounds of discrimination. In addition, qualified immunity rules protect from civil liability those who reasonably perform their duties. In policing as well as other contexts, those responsible for youth, and who infringe on their rights, are not held accountable if they acted reasonably. The concept of qualified immunity laws not only shields from claims of civil rights violations those who act within the boundaries of their official duties but also protects from liability those who act reasonably. Infringements on youth's rights generally do not lead to liability unless the decision maker should have known that he or she was infringing on a recognized right (and therefore acted unreasonably by ignoring the law) or his or her conduct was not objectively unreasonable (as was the case in a recent Supreme Court decision finding qualified immunity for school personnel because they had not clearly violated a right when they strip-searched a thirteen-year-old girl in a fruitless hunt for ibuprofen; see *Safford Unified School District v. Redding*, 2009). Despite cases that some find egregious, the reasonableness standard may make perfect sense, and it is difficult to think of another one that would not appropriately balance the obligations and rights of decision makers and those of youth. Yet prejudice and discrimination defy people's understandings of reasonableness. Subtle discrimination relies on rational explanations. As we have seen, the nature of subtle discrimination is very much reasonable. Yet there is nothing subtle about the ultimate consequences of subtle discrimination.

In addition to discrimination emanating from reasonableness standards, the legal system introduces discrimination through broad discretion granted to those who provide services to youth or who make decisions for them. The problem with discretion lies in the risk of bias and unrecognized abuse. For example, abuses of discretion in the juvenile and criminal justice systems long have been critiqued, and literature on the disproportionate representation of minority youth in juvenile and criminal courts repeatedly has condemned the broad discretion afforded to prosecutors, judges, and probation officers as providing a safe haven for implicit or explicit racial animus (see Davis 1998). Appropriately addressing bias in the overinclusion of minority youth for punishment and control requires that decision makers be trained to understand why and how discrimination persists. Training curricula would expose decision makers to implicit-bias research and educate them on the normative similarities in adolescent development across socioeconomic and ethnic groups as well as individuals perceived as different. Lead administrators, such as chief prosecutors and directors of child welfare systems, may identify and agree to reexamine common stereotypes and presumptions that are made about different groups of youth and their families, not only by themselves but also by their system's other decision makers. Although these types of training may be assumed to exist already, especially as related to racial minority groups, they actually do not, even in the systems marked by the most blatant disparities in the way they treat

minority youth—criminal justice systems (see Henning 2013). Addressing discrimination requires supporting the professional development of
decision makers and clarifying their obligations in ways that will infiltrate the manner in which they approach others and use their discretion.
This type of training, however, would need to encompass more than the
current nature of diversity training and its dominant mode of delivery;
it would require a broad institutional response that clarifies and enforces
values of equality.

Clarifying decision makers' roles becomes important for ensuring accountability as it fosters enforceability and transparency. For example,
strategies to address disproportionate minority contact with criminal justice systems have been hampered by the lack of public accountability for
prosecutors, minimal enforcement of internal decision-making guidelines in prosecutors' offices, and Supreme Court jurisprudence shielding
prosecutors from public and judicial scrutiny (see Henning 2013). Even
more than judges, prosecutors operate in virtual secrecy with unreview-
able charging authority, especially in juvenile courts, where confidenti-
ality shields access to court records and proceedings. If prosecutors are
unwilling to develop or enforce standards on their own initiative, they
can be spurred to do so by statutory mandates. Whether voluntary or leg-
islatively mandated, standards for making charging decisions would need
to be reviewed periodically to ensure transparency and effectiveness.
Indeed, similar observations could be made about each major decision
point in the prosecutorial process, from charging through bail decisions,
plea bargain, disclosure of evidence, and trial strategies to sentencing (see
Smith & Levinson 2012). Again, it is not that these efforts are impermissible and unmanageable (see Pinard 2010); they are not barred. It is only
that they are not required and, as a result, are rare. Particularly rare, actually almost nonexistent, are legislative mandates that would guide prosecutors' charging decisions. Instead, legal systems have chosen to guide
judicial decision making involved at sentencing (Wilmot & Spohn 2004).
Ironically, the limitations placed on judges' sentencing decisions have
granted even greater power to prosecutors, who determine the charges
that relate to mandated sentencing ranges.

Understanding roles and obligations contributes to accountability,
but it most successfully leads to equality when systems move toward
proactive and preventive stances that shape norms and values. Effective

ways to combat bias facilitate tolerant instincts rather than strengthening coercive antidiscrimination laws. As we have seen, institutions increasingly are populated by individuals overtly committed to nondiscrimination and good intentions. But they operate in systems and contexts that discriminate in ways for which neither the system nor the individuals can be held accountable because of the nature of equal protection mandates and their enforcement. The danger in embarking on more coercive measures rests in the real potential to undermine the conditions necessary to motivate people to want to avoid implicit discrimination. Forceful attempts to assert equality typically feed rather than reduce implicit discrimination. Efforts to suppress stereotyping have been shown to result in a "rebound effect," which means that stereotyping returns, sometimes with greater force, when the external pressure to suppress it is relaxed or ways around it are discovered. For example, showing a sexual harassment policy to men has had the effect of activating rather than suppressing gender stereotypes (Tinkler, Li, & Mollborn 2007). In addition to fostering rebound effects, legal coercion also threatens to crowd out internal motivations and undermine a person's sense of autonomy, competence, and relatedness in ways that reduce self-regulation. As a result, legal coercion can counteract the potentially positive effects of social tuning; coercion reduces people's willingness to assimilate to a perceived social norm and to improve interactions with others who hold the norm (see Bartlett 2009). Diversity training and evaluations—practices designed to alter the attitudes and behaviors of individuals by providing education and feedback—are generally ineffective and, in some circumstances, counterproductive (Kalev, Dobbin, & Kelly 2008). More effective approaches ensure that meaningful accountability and oversight are built into the structure of the organization in such a way that both individuals' roles and those of the relevant institution are clearly delineated (see Bielby 2010; Sarine 2012). As effective approaches to addressing discrimination guide people's decision making, they reach into and shape people's values and dispositions.

*Enhance the Detection of Biases*

An effective equality jurisprudence would help move systems toward better recognition of prejudice and discrimination. The need for guidance to enhance bias detection mechanisms stems from the reality that even the current high number of checks and balances in institutions remains ineffective in countering disparate treatment and discrimination. For example, governmental institutions such as child welfare and juvenile justice systems rely on a multitude of individual participants, government entities, and private agencies, as well as a mass of informal and formal proceedings. The involvement of so many individuals and processes to support legal protections would seem to ensure a built-in system of checks and balances against all forms of discrimination. But discrimination continues. The continuation of discrimination demonstrates that addressing discrimination necessarily involves overcoming barriers to its detection.

CHALLENGES TO BIAS DETECTION

The difficulty of detecting discrimination comes from the nature of contemporary prejudices and decisions relating to them. As we have seen, abundant evidence now suggests that fewer and fewer people embrace overt forms of bigotry and that individuals are more likely than ever to condemn public expressions of prejudice. While it is true that serious social problems like terrorism, hate crimes, and other forms of fanaticism still exist, most forms of contemporary prejudice manifest themselves more subtly. The same is true of state-supported institutions that interact with youth, such as educational and justice systems, which formally have abolished discrimination but, in practice, display disparate treatment according to group status. The wide range in forms of prejudice is critical to consider in that they challenge efforts to address them.

Addressing subtle discrimination may be even more challenging than addressing blatant discrimination. The problem with subtle discrimination rests on the subtlety of the prejudices that support it. Subtle discrimination arises from normal thought processes, tends to be more ambiguous, and frequently takes place outside of one's awareness. At the system level, subtle discrimination arises from what are deemed normal, unbiased processes, but they are processes that lead to biases or that permit bias in the manner in which they allow ambiguity and discretion. As a result, discrimination typically operates too subtly to be detected easily in the course of everyday interactions, so it remains widespread.

It simply becomes part of normal, everyday life and, as a result, runs the risk of going unremarked and unrecognized as problematic.

Importantly, even if the discrimination is not subtle, people still have difficulty detecting it at individual levels. Individuals deny discrimination for a variety of reasons. Blatant discrimination remains difficult to uncover because people seek to avoid it; individuals resist feeling mistreated by others or as though they have no control over situations (Ruggiero & Taylor 1997). To complicate matters, individuals cannot serve as their own control group and test whether they would have received better treatment as a member of more privileged groups. As a result of these and other psychological mechanisms, minorities, for example, are more likely to perceive discrimination against their group than against themselves personally (see Taylor, Wright, & Porter 1994). This is not to say that individuals do not notice that they are being discriminated against or that they suffer from microaggressions because of their identification with groups. But even if they recognize the differential treatment, they may not address it because the system involved in bias detection is not one that can respond well to the vast majority of what individuals experience as biased treatment. Having a system that does not respond appropriately is a recipe for having situations go, if not unnoticed, then ignored even though they could be harmful.

The challenges of detecting discrimination also come from those who discriminate. Individual cases are easy to explain away. One of the most intractable limitations of current discrimination law, for example, is that rational explanations can be made to explain the way someone acted toward others. This result has emerged in efforts to cure systems of blatant discrimination on relatively recognizable markers, such as those based on race or gender. These efforts ask the decision makers to explain their decisions that appear biased. Although doing so may limit some blatant forms of discrimination, decision makers simply can offer nonbiased reasons for their decisions. This ineffectiveness has been found in the criminal justice system, when attorneys excuse potential jurors on the grounds that they would be biased against their case because they belong to a specific social group, such as one based on race or gender (Sommers & Norton 2007). The same has been found in prosecutors' charging decisions relating to minority youth. Prosecutors can easily provide a rational, race-neutral explanation to support each of the charging decisions they make by pointing to the dangerousness of the crime, the youth's record of prior offending, the child's lack of family support, the victim's rights, public safety, and the need to respond to community and constituent interests. Thus, regardless of whether the discrimination is intentional or not, the challenge of detection remains.

RESPONDING TO THE CHALLENGES OF DETECTION
Identifying biases that can be addressed more effectively presents daunting challenges, which can be responded to through enhancement of the legal system's detection and response systems. Legal mandates can help enhance the detection of bias. Research focusing on prejudice reveals that no one is immune from harboring prejudice, that it often takes deliberate effort and awareness to reduce prejudice, and that, with sufficient motivation, it can be done. As much as individuals are predisposed to prejudice, stereotyping, and discrimination, they also can overcome these biases if motivated to do so (Monteith, Arthur, & Flynn 2010). Motivations can be prompted by the contexts in which decisions are made, and motives can be reshaped through supportive environments—those that shape values.

Given that individual cases of discrimination are easy to explain away, targets of subtle discrimination are unlikely to possess sufficient evidence to claim remedies. For example, they are unlikely to be able to pursue a legally actionable claim of discrimination. Subtle forms of discrimination are often better detected with aggregated evidence than with single cases. Thus, an effective bias detection mechanism requires systems that monitor and aggregate data; they also require reporting. Some of these challenges have been met, in some circumstances, by using testers to detect potential biases when situations make challenging the accumulation of appropriate data. Testers take on various roles (such as renters, home buyers, job applicants, and restaurant patrons) to gather information to ensure that individuals or companies do not engage in unlawful discrimination. Still, the use of testers remains a limited mechanism because a multitude of contexts do not lend themselves to testing.

Increasing detection also can take the form of easing reporting and ensuring reasonable responses. Individuals who recognize discrimination may not report or come forward if their reports will lead to retaliation or other negative responses. Harmful responses and inadequate protections probably stifle detection and help account for continued discrimination. For example, recognizing that legal systems failed to respond appropriately to sexual violence against minors led to now-universal statutory rape laws that create strict liability offenses that facilitate holding offenders responsible. But in addition to the rationale relating to offenders' responsibility was the recognized need to help encourage victims to report and be less fearful of the repercussions that would come from the criminal justice system (Levesque 2000a). These efforts have not met universal success, as they have been seen as problematically limiting the sexual rights of some youth. But what is remarkable about these types of efforts is the extent to which creating responsive systems remains ill explored. A look at statutes relating to discrimination reveals very little attention to easing reporting and to creating standards of liability that would ease that reporting. The challenge raised by these issues again points to the need to inculcate values of equality. Systems that do not embrace equality throughout their system ensure the continuance of inequality.

Although a role remains for enhancing an individual target's sense of discrimination and appropriate response systems, a more effective approach also would address the institutions themselves. For example, policies can be set in place to increase the awareness of bias. A key example involves police interactions with minority youth. Law enforcement officials who interact directly with youth should receive training that increases their awareness of the subtle nature of contemporary racial bias. Simply raising individuals' awareness of subtle forms of racial discrimination may be effective in reducing discriminatory conduct and may be useful in limiting racial profiling and the discrimination that accompanies it. As we have seen, studies have suggested that well-intentioned actors can overcome automatic or implicit biases—that more deliberative decision making may weaken implicit biases. But the awareness is most likely to result in hoped-for outcomes when mechanisms are in place to support them.

The need for support comes from, for example, the real risk of rebound effects. As we have seen, research indicates that attempts to suppress stereotypes may actually exacerbate biases by causing people to think more about them. Yet, mechanisms can be put in place to prevent rebound effects. Researchers suggest that bias affirmation may be offset by the inclusion of motivations to control stereotyping, by the practice of stereotype control, and by the replacement of prejudicial thoughts with egalitarian ones (see Monteith, Arthur, & Flynn 2010). In the law enforcement example, the process would involve law enforcement personnel collecting and relying on information that individualizes suspects and committing to avoiding prejudice in decision making. The reduction of exacerbating effects also can be improved by an increase in exposure to positive images of people within an identified prejudiced group. This can be accomplished through the development of relationships with members of a previously stereotyped or devalued group. In the justice system context, police, prosecutors, and other law enforcement personnel interested in overcoming stereotypes may engage more closely with minority communities by attending neighborhood meetings, volunteering at neighborhood centers, or serving on collaborative task forces with community representatives to develop a better understanding of the communities they serve and alternatives to processes prone to discrimination. These types of initiatives can help remove negative biases, prevent exacerbation effects, and move institutions closer to supporting values of equality.

The focus on law enforcement as an example of the challenges to overcoming bias is deliberate. As much as individual decision makers can be assisted in overcoming bias, they nevertheless need to answer to multiple constituencies. Notably in this instance, the tools available to law enforcement must be considered in light of the system's goals, which is to prevent and respond to crime. When law enforcement personnel perform their duties, they do so by operating within the rules of the system. Those rules influence the actions of all who come into contact with the system. For example, defense attorneys seek to zealously defend their clients, and doing so may require them to do what they can to assemble a jury that is biased to their side, just as prosecutors do. Attorneys litigating cases do not want unbiased juries; they want juries to favor their sides (Levesque 2006). These forces make the detection of bias exceedingly difficult.

The above examples of challenges reveal the enormity of the task of detecting bias, but they also suggest ways in which institutions and the organizations in them can be shaped to better address inequality and foster the inculcation of values that resist inappropriate differential treatment. Clear standards are needed to stave off subtle biases that eventually have the effect of creating unequal treatment. In a variety of settings, negative implicit attitudes and stereotypes foster biased evaluations. The negative attitudes and stereotypes are more likely to influence judgments when the information at hand is ambiguous or unstructured. Similarly, bias is more likely to occur when the standards for evaluating others are ambiguous and subjective: the more subjective the procedures by which individuals are evaluated, the greater the likelihood that subtle bias may result in biased decisions. Although these biases have been identified in multiple settings, they most notably have been examined at work in the juvenile justice and criminal justice systems: ambiguous standards permitting wide discretion contribute to inappropriate differential treatment. The decisions made by those involved early in the process (e.g., probation officers, intake workers, and prosecutors) and later in the process (e.g., judges) are crucial, especially because discretion is legally much more permissible in the juvenile court than in the adult criminal justice system. In those systems, unclear standards have negative effects on minority youth, from the initial interaction with law enforcement to the ultimate disposition of their cases (see Leiber 2003). Although some aspects of law enforcement may not be as amenable as others to less ambiguous standards, other aspects are, such as formal court hearings, trials, and dispositions. Thus, just as clear standards can assist in ensuring accountability, so they can assist in bias detection.

The need to enhance mechanisms to detect bias also finds reflection in health systems. Research now well documents widespread racial/ethnic disparities in the quality of health care received, treatments offered, and health outcomes achieved. Hypothesized reasons for worse care include differential access to health care, actual health status, patient preferences, and provider bias or discrimination. Yet even after these three factors are controlled for, studies have demonstrated that racial/ethnic minorities are less likely than non-Hispanic Whites to receive equivalent care across a broad spectrum of diseases (see Kressin, Raymond, & Manze 2008). Findings like these have led to a focus on the concept of cultural competence to improve the quality and efficacy of the health care provided to families from culturally marginalized communities. Cultural competence seeks to remove unwarranted biases and has contributed to reduced disparities in treatment. Reviews of efforts to diminish bias through culturally competent service delivery emphasize the key point that bias diminishment is most likely to derive from policy directives that provide clear definitions and instructions (Gant, Parry, & Guerin 2013). Clearly articulated values help further the provision of competent services.

Efforts to increase cultural or diversity competence may well increase equal treatment, but these efforts too remain limited. Evaluations of efforts to increase cultural competence find that such programs increase practitioners' knowledge, awareness, and cultural sensitivity, but it has yet to be determined whether these reduced disparities in treatment actually translate to improved patient health outcomes (see Renzaho et al. 2013). Effects are difficult to find, apparently because of the focus on service providers and the failure to include those who would seek services but do not do so for a variety of reasons, some of which relate to discrimination. Enhancing bias detection results in thinking through where the biases lie. Biases may not only rest in those who provide services; those in need of care also have perceptions of services and needs that require addressing.

Enhancing bias detection necessarily rests, again, on the inculcation of values. Effective approaches move systems toward a more proactive, preventative stance. Although the focus above has been on those who interact with youth and shape their value systems, it is important not to ignore youth themselves. Important progress has been made, for example, in schools to address bullying and harassment. Many of those efforts, although still sporadic, focus on the identification of incidents and the creation of effective response systems. Effective efforts reach youth themselves and seek to foster environments that detect incidents and, as a result, reduce their occurrence (Merrell et al. 2008; Ttofi & Farrington 2011). These efforts work to the extent that mechanisms are in place to detect a need and respond to it. They also work to the extent that recognition contributes to changing the values of the systems in which youth operate. What is remarkable about these approaches is that, despite their successes, they remain rare and have not been used to address other forms of potential discrimination, notably those based on ethnic minority status. Again, awareness still may not be sufficient, but complementing awareness with monitoring and responsive systems can increase the effectiveness of antidiscrimination efforts.

## Ease the Implementation of Programs

An effective equality jurisprudence would address one of the most important lessons learned from efforts to counter discrimination: persistent gaps between what evidence reveals could make a difference, on the one hand, and its effective implementation, on the other. Gaps may come from a variety of sources, but they tend to relate closely to the mechanisms for reform. Those mechanisms also may come from many directions and institutions. However, since the mid-twentieth century, the principal means for instituting change and fostering programs has been litigation based on the recognition of basic rights. Litigation seeking institutional change involves modifying the framework of the procedural and substantive rules that operate in social and political institutions. For example, courts use the Fourteenth Amendment's Due Process and Equal Protection Clauses to secure and mobilize other rights, such as the right to desegregation of school districts that were segregated by law. When courts do so, they invoke these rights to affect the way institutions function. They do so by generating remedial decrees or policy directives that can include the expenditure of funds necessary to protect the rights at stake and create oversight mechanisms to ensure the continued implementation of their remedies. In doing so, the courts become the enforcers of individuals' rights and the vehicles used to ensure equality.

Although an obvious mechanism for reform, the use of court systems to address discrimination actually has served as an example of how not to embark on reform. Despite important progress in some domains, reforms relying on judicial remedies remain problematic to the extent that they unleash legal, political, and social forces that are difficult to manage. In the context of inequality, for example, notions of what constitutes the equal protection of laws continue to shift, and in some ways the courts have stifled efforts to achieve greater societal equality. The resistance comes not only from the courts but also from political responses to court decisions, as exemplified by the continued disparities in some minority groups' access to educational services and what has been called "second-generation discrimination." The resistance from multiple domains reveals how the limitations of reforms through judicial systems also often mirror those of legislative efforts to foster institutional reform. Court systems remain involved, such as in the checks and balances of legislative mandates; and the decision-making processes of legislators and administrators can be equally as ineffectual as those in judicial systems. Whether independently or together, all branches of government face important limitations when seeking to foster reform; governmental actions remain far from cure-alls. Yet limitations notwithstanding, we live in a society of laws, and the government has assumed the responsibility to create, implement, and enforce them. Laws dealing with discrimination are no different; they come with limitations, but the government holds the obligation to address inequality.

The failures and limitations of reform efforts and the focus on governmental processes, however, do more than reveal immense challenges; they also reveal factors contributing to success. Frameworks used to examine institutional change suggest important characteristics of circumstances that can lead to effective and sustainable change. Those characteristics include incentives for institutions to change (including the costs for not changing), the existence of parallel institutions to help implement changes, and the use of court or legislative orders to leverage additional resources to effectuate change or to serve as a cover for willing administrators unable to act for fear of political repercussions (see, e.g., Rosenberg 2008). All of these circumstances highlight the need to center on the implementation of programs by developing supportive statutory mandates. These mandates can focus on supporting decision makers, shaping the allocation of resources, countering reasons against reforms, and ensuring program effectiveness. Each of these components is central to easing the implementation of programs, and accordingly, each becomes a critical component of an effective equality jurisprudence.

## SUPPORTING DECISION MAKERS

Support from the legal system in the form of statutory frameworks renders decision makers' task of implementing programs less daunting. For example, state agency officials resist program review and change when they face the risk of backlash. Concern for backlash ensures that officials act conservatively in the sense that they will act to serve the most powerful and dominant groups. This tendency actually helps to explain the resistance to efforts that would reduce ingrained inequalities.

Sustainable policy reform often requires departing from the status quo, creating new models rather than merely dismantling old ones, and making short-term investments to reap long-term benefits. Economic and culturally divisive times make these efforts particularly difficult, highlighting the importance of the law's power to prevent and resolve disputes and support decision makers.

It is difficult to overestimate the need to ease the implementation of equality reforms and to support decision makers who guide systems that have an influence on youth. As noted earlier, the general rule has been that parents control the upbringing of their children, and it has been assumed that they do. Yet youth increasingly move into contexts without their parents, and parents do not control their children's rights as firmly in those situations, such as when youth interact with community members, schools, or the media, as well as when they interact with a variety of youth-serving systems like juvenile justice and child welfare systems. Quite remarkably, those who work closely with youth generally operate in systems that have not articulated the values they hope to impart nor determined who should impart them.

Of the key socializing institutions, only families give parents control over the values they hope to impart; other institutions either grant the power to the institutions themselves or have not addressed the issue directly. Notably, and as expressed in statutes, only educational institutions have determined unambiguously who controls the types of values that they wish to impart, and the general rule has been that school officials retain the power to determine the values that they inculcate in students, rather than the children or the parents who send their children to the schools (Levesque 2003). Presumably, community groups would be similar to schools, as would religious institutions. The legal system grants those groups considerable freedom to embrace and impart the values they choose, but they generally are not required to articulate those values. The control that parents retain in these contexts rests in their participation in those communities and their decisions to send their children to them. Although effective decision makers work with parents and other constituencies, their ability to shape institutions rests on the power they retain. Statutes can guide the use of that power and support decisions that move institutions toward inculcating values of equality.

The types of values that other systems, like child welfare and juvenile justice systems, could foster remains unexplored. Although parents' views could be considered, these systems take on the role of parents and do so on the assumption that parents are failing in the upbringing of their children. The lack of exploration of the types of values that these systems should impart results in the failure to address inequality effectively, as it may not even be recognized as a value of concern. As a result, these contexts do generate some disputes, such as those relating to youth's religious freedom while in foster care, race-matching in adoptions, or gay youth's rights when institutionalized (see, e.g., Estrada & Marksamer 2006), but those disputes rarely surface. The rarity of these disputes attests to the extent to which inequality in the systems themselves remains unaddressed. It also indicates the extent to which concerns about equality go unnoticed without decision makers' awareness and ability to respond effectively. And it reveals the power that these institutions have in shaping values—their power pervasively goes unchallenged.

## SHAPING THE ALLOCATION OF RESOURCES

Equality jurisprudence gains increased effectiveness when its statutes guide the allocation of resources among competing demands. Addressing inequality rests on the allocation of resources, particularly reallocating resources from one group to another. This maxim has been well recognized, and it has a firm foundation in the civil rights movement. Much of discrimination involves a lack of opportunities, many of which rest on access to resources.

Resources may be at the heart of efforts to address inequality, but what constitutes resources and their allocation can take different forms and play different roles. The allocation of resources can take the form of costs that come from failing to implement a particular policy, either the cost of missed opportunities or the cost of penalties for not adopting preferred policies. Alternatively, resource allocations can come in the form of incentives, which would be granted when decision makers move toward the successful implementation of policies. Such incentives need not be only monetary. They can include designing facilitating systems, training and credentialing personnel, and providing such basic resources as curricula and technical information to assist in implementation efforts. The way these broad types of resources are enlisted to address unequal treatment largely rests on the values used to guide their allocation.

The absence of clear mandates determining the allocation of resources, and the failure to articulate how they foster or stifle equality, means the continuation of systems marked by inequality. Currently, for example, few schools can afford the curricula and resources needed to make effective use of educational programs that can foster equality. Statutory recognition could help determine the significance of such programs, relative to other school curricular concerns, and increase the likelihood of obtaining funding when scarce resources are allocated among competing goals. Although the need for such assistance appears especially pronounced in the school context, other systems suffer from similar resource limitations and benefit from specific guidance. Child welfare systems, for example, have been reshaped dramatically by federal funds aimed at expediting children's permanent care (see Levesque 2008). These types of reforms have been marked by considerable variation and even resistance (see *Suter v. Artist M.*, 1992), but the power of incentives remains clear.

The need to take seriously the allocation of resources becomes particularly acute given that the distribution of economic resources remains generally outside of constitutional protection. For example, the poor have not been recognized as a protected class, and the Constitution has not been found to support a right to equal access to social resources for those who simply cannot afford them. The allocation of resources, however, can be subject to other important critical protections, such as protections against discrimination. And as we have seen, the government is free to embark on programs that would remedy discrimination, as seen in the context of juvenile justice systems and programs aimed to reduce minority youth's contact with justice systems. That context also highlights well, however, how the allocation of resources remains but one factor among several others needed to address systems' differential treatment of minority youth.

## ARTICULATING RATIONALES FOR PROGRAMS

Effective programming rests on clearly articulating and fully embracing compelling reasons for change. The effective articulation of rationales for programs serves as the touchstone upon which to determine whether the programs meet their purpose. But effective articulation accomplishes much more—it can ease implementation by detailing rights and responsibilities, and it can foster practices conducive to equality.

An effective equality jurisprudence would provide explicit guidance that could help counter impediments to the development of effective programs by decisively pinpointing the overriding legal interests and rights at stake, and thereby offering a way to deliberate those considerations in program development. Appropriate articulations of rationales address impediments to implementing initiatives by removing the need to revisit concerns. For example, engaging broad issues permits a focus on the implementation of programs in particular contexts. Illustrative of the way articulating program rationales eases reforms is the extent to which different groups have the power to reveal certain information to youth and offer social support so that they can recognize and deal with inequality. Statutory guidance could clarify who could offer support and reveal information useful in benefiting from that support. Statutes could help clarify whether teachers, public health physicians, adult volunteers, or parents are the appropriate source of certain knowledge, support, and guidance. They also should elucidate why and when individuals can support youth. Without such clarity, considerable resistance, confusion, and ambivalence surround issues of who should present certain information to youth, all of which results in the failure to provide effective services and programs.

The need to ease the implementation of programs by clearly articulating rationales for particular agendas and practices runs throughout all institutions that relate to youth development. Researchers note, for example, that the failure of many school reforms largely rests on the failure to identify explicitly the rights of parents and those of their children, other students, and schools (for a review, see Levesque 2000b). The same is true for community efforts and those relating to the media. In those sites of inculcation, reforms fail to move forward because of misperceptions of the rights of parents and fear of infringing on them when, in fact, parental rights in those contexts are reduced (Levesque 2007). As highlighted earlier, significant misunderstandings abound in visions of the government's potential role in the inculcation of values. Those misunderstandings account for much of the failure to support initiatives that would better serve public interests.

Developments in youth's rights, particularly the rebalancing of their liberties, on the one hand, and their need for protection because of their peculiar vulnerabilities, on the other, makes particularly acute the need for guidance and clear rationales. Recognizing some youth's right to protection while respecting the liberties of others can translate into potential conflicts that, heretofore, would have been either unimaginable or ignored. Illustrative are issues arising from the need to resolve clashes between youth's rights, such as the freedom to express their beliefs, on the one hand, and the freedom to be free from language deemed particularly harmful due to the recipient's age, on the other. The recent interest in protecting youth from harassment and bullying exemplifies how some protections require limitations on others' rights. For example, on the basis of political or religious beliefs, some youth have strong views about sexual orientation, sexuality, gender, nationality, race, and other religions—all of which can receive constitutional protection. But when expressed, these views can create problematic situations for those who belong to the groups that would be targeted. The status of being a minor brings many complications that confirm the need to articulate clearly the policies and overriding interests at stake. This becomes particularly important given that the resolution of conflicts can vary from one site of inculcation to the next.

Perhaps the most compelling reason for clearly articulating program rationales comes from equality jurisprudence itself. Rationales for furthering some rights and for infringing on others are critical in determining the judicial system's eventual support. Depending on the rights involved, the success of challenges to programs depends on the rationales for them. Much can ride on the interests that policies serve. Much also rides on the successful pursuit of those interests. The courts increasingly demand that programs and policies appropriately further acceptable interests, and they will give particularly close scrutiny to efforts that would involve the legal system in discrimination.

ENSURING PROGRAM EFFECTIVENESS

Effective systems supportive of equality require the implementation of effective programs and initiatives. This requirement comes not only from the need to ensure that efforts are effective but also from the current economic and political climate, which seeks to fund evidence-based, tested programming. Statutory frameworks could assist researchers in their design of robust interventions and practitioners in implementing the mandates.

An impressive body of research already reveals the determinative components of effective initiatives to reduce prejudice and discrimination. However, far less clarity exists to guide the building and operation of effective systems and to create and evaluate them. Appropriate statutory guidelines can assist in determining the needed data to isolate effective components and engage in more effective efforts. For example, administrators need evaluations to understand the strategy and chain of decisions that go into choosing a target community or model program; the selection, training, and continued support of program staff; and the selection of potential participants and services for them. Once they have been initiated, programs must gather data to evaluate the fidelity of individual program implementation and of both immediate and ongoing impacts on participants. These types of evaluations that ensure program effectiveness may be new to this area, given the pervasive failure to implement programs. But they need not proceed without guidance. A growing body of literature directly addresses the challenges of implementation, of translating research into effective practice (see Durlak & DuPre 2008; Mildon & Shlonsky 2011).

Although research now can guide the implementation of programs to ensure greater effectiveness, challenges particular to addressing inequality remain. Programs countering inequality necessarily aim to reach diverse communities, contexts, individuals, and circumstances. They do so because the programs deal with diversity and attempt to influence diverse groups, including the way they view and treat one another. Such ambitious efforts challenge the effectiveness of any program, as programs are designed for particular contexts that may not allow for generating parallel effects in others. Meeting these challenges means relying on policies and procedures within interventions for addressing changes, ensuring fidelity, evaluating program components, and committing to high-quality outcomes. Much must go into determining whether programs achieve their intended effectiveness. Again, however, it is not that current research does not support these programs and their implementation; it is that programs have yet to be implemented systematically and broadly.

Programs addressing diversity and seeking to reach diverse communities probably face even greater challenges than other programs, in that the communities most in need probably offer the most resistance. Yet even these communities can be reached. Illustrative are programs supporting sexual minority youth. Several programs have been shown to be effective in reducing bias, stigma, and discrimination, as well as increasing acceptance and enhancing positive outcomes for youth who have been discriminated against, ostracized, and victimized. To ensure effectiveness, such programs must be adjusted to fit communities. Adjustments can result in important steps toward creating supportive communities (see Szalacha 2003; Meyer & Beyer 2013). Even when dealing with controversial issues, then, interventions can achieve effectiveness through community acceptance. Such efforts reveal that policies can be enlisted to establish safer diversity environments and address potential criticisms that can stymie implementation. Simply having policies in place reduces victimization as doing so indicates that communities take the issues seriously (see Culhane 2013). Effectively implemented policies not only can result in more supportive communities for those previously targeted for negative treatment but also can benefit entire communities as they can foster a sense of equality that reverberates throughout.

## Conclusion: Capitalizing on the Law's Inculcative Powers

The legal system's lack of efficacy in charting a fuller equality jurisprudence has led us to turn to developmental science and laws relating to the inculcation of values. That turn emerged from the recognition that notions of equality inevitably rest both on individuals' beliefs about how to treat others and on individuals' actual interactions with others. Recognizing these dynamics led us to explore the social structures that could foster the inculcation of values marked by equality's ideals. A look at the legal regulation of the central systems that guide the inculcation of values in youth led to the conclusion that the legal system inevitably supports the inculcation of values, and that it does so across the multiple social systems in which youth find themselves. That finding reveals the need for our legal system to more deliberately concern itself with the inculcation of values consistent with the ideals of equality. The legal system can accomplish this by using its power to influence the social structures in which youth find themselves.

In order for the legal system to influence broad social structures that serve as sites of inculcation, we must transform vague constitutional pronouncements into actionable mandates. Supreme Court decisions may help to spur the development of those mandates but, in the end, actionable mandates achieve effectiveness only to the extent that they influence key decision makers who develop and implement policies, appropriately guide those who interact directly with youth, and shape the development of youth themselves. This chapter has shown how the legal system actually can be harnessed to attenuate discrimination. That attenuation can come from realizing the law's powerful role in shaping the values.

# Conclusion

People need encouragement to do the right thing. They need guidance and opportunities to make appropriate decisions. That is the fundamental problem with the Supreme Court's current vision of the Constitution's approach to addressing discrimination. Its vision largely does not encourage, guide, or provide opportunities for the prevention or remedying of discrimination. True, its vision may well be legally correct, as it makes sense if we follow the lines of cases supporting it. But that does not necessarily make it right.

Essentially, the Court no longer actively supports equality. It views the Constitution's equal protection mandate as requiring the legal system to remain neutral in the way it treats people who have particular group characteristics associated with discrimination. By doing so, the Court also limits what legislatures and policy makers can do to address discrimination. This makes what the legal system now addresses as discrimination quite different from what people experience as wrongful discrimination. It also means that the legal system increasingly ignores when people wrongfully discriminate against others. Much of what we view as inappropriate discrimination just does not count; it is deemed outside of the legal system's concerns.

As a result of these developments, the legal system has been viewed as unable to guide the development of values that would be more supportive of equality. The dominant value that has emerged would have the legal system treat people's group characteristics the same way by not classifying individuals according to them. This anticlassification approach seeks to ignore such important group characteristics as race, ethnicity, religion, and gender. The best way to achieve equality, it is argued, is to bar the legal system's consideration of those characteristics, to be blind to them.

The current approach to ensuring equality has multiple problems. People have difficulty ignoring others' group characteristics. Yet more problematically, people may not even be aware that they are inappropriately discriminating against individuals because of their group status. These problems are exacerbated by the legal system's not considering many forms of differential treatment as wrongful discrimination. The legal system pervasively fails to grant special protection to such group characteristics as weight, height, intelligence, sexual orientation, social class, and youth. And equality jurisprudence generally no longer supports remedies for past wrongful discrimination even when it currently contributes to differential treatment. Equality jurisprudence is turning toward the conclusion that, as long as the legal system itself does not differentiate between groups on the basis of a protected group characteristic like race, discrimination does not occur. When addressing discrimination, then, the legal system increasingly leaves people to their own devices.

If people need encouragement to treat equally individuals inappropriately deemed different, so do social institutions. That needed encouragement, which would come through an antisubordination approach, would include considering how individuals and social institutions disadvantage individuals with particular group characteristics. It even would include requiring that some people be treated differently so that they receive treatment equal to everyone else. But the legal system's current vision of equality generally does not allow for that. In fact, it increasingly seeks to do the opposite.

Fortunately, that is not the end of the story. Some members of the Court may be right in embracing the anticlassification approach as the surest and best way to have the legal system achieve equality for all. But our best evidence indicates that they only are partly right. The legal system can do better. The current vision of equality jurisprudence is not completely accurate for three reasons that commentators, researchers, and policy makers simply have not bothered to bring together. These reasons also happen to be critical to countering the limitations of current approaches to harmful discrimination and to demonstrating how the legal system actually can aggressively address it.

First, research that investigates the roots and alleviation of discrimination points to successful ways to address discrimination. Current equality jurisprudence pervasively ignores those developmental science findings. Those findings indicate that addressing discrimination requires reaching both those who hold prejudices, particularly subtle prejudices, and those who suffer inequality because of them. Accomplishing this involves recognizing the powerful role of social institutions in the inculcation of values. It is possible to shape institutions so that they do not foster harmful discrimination based on a variety of factors, particularly race and ethnicity.

Second, the legal system can support developmentally informed approaches that focus on the inculcation of preferred values. It can do so because the Supreme Court has shifted its position on how the government can shape people's values. The government increasingly is free to pass laws and fund mandates that encourage people to do the right thing. This means that the legal system can encourage institutions and individuals to develop values that would foster increased equality. The legal system especially can do so with adolescents. Multiple systems—educational, juvenile justice, criminal justice, child welfare, and especially familial—actually exist to inculcate preferred values. The legal system supports those institutions in the name of fostering effective citizenship and sometimes of protecting individuals from harm. Even religious groups—organizations aimed directly at the development of values and often incorrectly viewed as out of the government's reach—can be harnessed to support society's preferred values. The Court permits religious schools, for example, to participate in state-funded voucher programs on the condition that they will protect civil rights and not discriminate in student enrollment. These developments, coupled with the massive growth of government-supported initiatives, provide unprecedented opportunities to inculcate preferred values.

Third, we increasingly know how to shape policies so that they can reach their goals. Effective policies have clearly articulated mandates and rationales, state responsibilities and expectations; they provide adequate funding and other needed resources, develop mechanisms to ensure effective enforcement and accountability, provide for evaluating policy implementation and effectiveness, engage those who will be served and their communities, and develop values that ensure compliance and even self-maintenance. We know what makes for policies that can effectively guide behavior and even shape beliefs.

The limitations of existing mandates addressing discrimination, and the legal system's historic failure to foster broad equality, may make it seem inadvisable to involve the legal system more deliberately in efforts to address discrimination. It is true that the legal system cannot forcefully control individuals, their beliefs, or their environments because of our society's immense commitment to basic freedoms, particularly those relating to such deeply held values as individualism, individual merit, self-reliance, and human dignity. But the issue really is not only that these values contradict coercive approaches; the legal system cannot take such approaches because they remain ineffective. It is the very ineffectiveness of those approaches that leads us to focus on the development of values and to expand equality jurisprudence.

A broadening of equality jurisprudence means asking much more of those who craft policies. As we have seen, comprehensive policies addressing inequality simply do not exist. Current policies tend to use vague mandates that fail to guide appropriately. Simply stating that services provided to youth will be free of discrimination, for example, does not suffice because the legal system has adopted an exceedingly narrow view of discrimination. It is insufficient also because people do not necessarily recognize when they inappropriately discriminate. Simply telling youth to treat others equally, for example, does not result in desired behaviors, especially if they are placed in contexts that encourage the opposite. Addressing inequality requires effective guidance to make beliefs and attitudes transparent so that they can be understood and shaped. That guidance comes from appropriately structured environments. Such environments shape the contexts in which people interact with others and can help ensure that they treat others appropriately. We have seen that concrete examples of effective policies already exist to address some forms of discrimination; we just need to enact more of them and use them as models.

A broader equality jurisprudence also demands more extensive and different research. Although many fields of study already focus on discrimination and prejudice, much of the needed research actually remains to be done. For example, the study of discrimination largely has been synonymous with research on race. An effective equality jurisprudence urges investigations of other sources and consequences of inappropriately differential treatment. That includes the utility of models to reduce bias toward a broader variety of groups, including concurrent membership in multiple groups. Such investigation can reveal the markers most salient in particular contexts. For example, ethnicity, gender, and social class characteristics intersect. Depending on contexts, any one of those factors could determine the risk for differential treatment; people with several factors probably are at increased risk. And, as is often ignored, none of these factors are mutually exclusive; group characteristics shape complex identities that must be factored into efforts to address discrimination. Also needed is research addressing the effects of integration efforts, such as potential for backlash and intensification of differences, to get a better sense of efforts to treat people more equally. Provocative research demonstrates, for example, that schools with more equal percentages of students from different ethnic groups, compared to those with more uneven percentages, actually foster more ethnic tensions and fewer cross-ethnic friendships. The results of good intentions need to be investigated as much as those of intentions assumed to be harmful. Most fundamentally needed, however, is research clarifying the values that support treating people appropriately and designing ways to develop those values. We have seen that the values of neutrality and equality have become problematic; values like respect, nonviolence, and human dignity, for example, may have promise particularly since they might gain broad acceptance. We already know that some interventions focusing on respect effectively reshape the beliefs and values that contribute to gender discrimination in the form of sexual harassment and relationship violence. Existing research gives us confidence to move forward, but that is merely the first step.

A more comprehensive equality jurisprudence also necessarily means differently engaging those who work with youth and their surroundings. We already have seen that a more comprehensive equality jurisprudence would require making values more transparent and guiding interactions more deliberately. But it means much more than that. It also means that efforts must be made to respond to youth's inculcation in a variety of systems and to determine when and how best to respond to some systems that fail to foster equality effectively. Some systems now consider the influence of other systems when they respond to inequality among youth, such as efforts to address discrimination in the way schools punish youth in order to address discrimination in juvenile and criminal justice systems. This approach simply asks that issues of equality become a more salient part of institutions' missions and that social institutions also look outside themselves. Individuals directly responsible for the functioning of those institutions would need to take a stand on their values, be willing to shape the values of others, and be selected for those roles because of the values they hold and feel comfortable inculcating. Again, this may make some of us uncomfortable and may even be viewed as illegal. But it simply makes obvious and transparent what socializing institutions already do. And it does the same for what the legal system necessarily does: it shapes the development and expression of values. This broader approach to equality also makes obvious what the legal system already supports. Policy making inherently favors some values over others. It routinely does so through funding or other supportive measures, such as punishing or deterring actions and values deemed problematic. A comprehensive equality jurisprudence asks people to take a stand on difficult issues and support preferred values.

We addressed multiple criticisms of developing an equality jurisprudence focused on the development of values. Key among them was the ingrained belief that values are sacrosanct, that individuals have a right to believe as they wish, and that the government has no place in dictating those beliefs. That actually is not the case. It never has been. What people believe and value comes from their surroundings; we are the product of our communities. For example, families have long enjoyed freedom in inculcating values in their children. But many institutions now exist that can either reinforce or counter families' inculcation of values. Some of those institutions do so subtly, such as the media and schools; some can do so very forcefully, such as the child welfare and juvenile justice systems. Those institutions receive governmental support and are necessarily regulated by the government. As much as we may want to deny it, there is no escaping that some of those institutions exist for the government to impose its values. This is important because, just as no person is an island, so no institution is either. These interconnections among institutions that inculcate values are what provide hope for a more aggressive equality jurisprudence. They provide hope if for no other reason than that these very interconnections have both contributed to discrimination and failed to address it effectively. They are the places of solution.

Admittedly, and as we have emphasized, the broad tendencies toward either anticlassification or antisubordination are marked by important nuances. Notably, even the most conservative of Supreme Court justices permit some forms of remediation when the legal system has blatantly discriminated on the basis of a highly protected classification such as race. In addition, current equality jurisprudence permits differential treatment when the government has compelling reasons to enact such treatment, as long as the differential treatment is used only to the extent necessary. A recent example has been the Court's support of differential treatment based on race in order to support increased diversity in professional schools. Access requires structural support. The point we have made is that such considerations are few and far between, and the Court increasingly is hesitant to support and extend these approaches to other contexts.

In the end, this book has shown that the current state of equality jurisprudence explains its failures. Researchers can now understand why their findings have such little impact on addressing discrimination. Legal scholars can now understand why the legal system appears to have reached its limit in the way it can address discrimination. Equality jurisprudence has become too narrow. It increasingly fails to consider the root causes of discrimination, shaped by the institutions that inculcate values. Even the bulk of research on discrimination, which unquestionably demonstrates that it exists and harms, has become largely irrelevant to current equality jurisprudence. The irrelevance of key research, of what we know about discrimination, results from the unquestioned allegiance to a narrow view of the way the legal system addresses inequality. The legal system can do much more.

Addressing behaviors like discrimination that are so profoundly shaped by values requires a legal system that enlists the help of multiple institutions devoted to the inculcation of values. To address the rampant inequalities experienced by individuals, equality jurisprudence must refocus its efforts to enable the development of social structures and processes that can foster equality. Appropriate responses to discrimination require not less but more legal involvement. Scholars and researchers must realize that the legal system is not neutral in the values it supports, especially when it deals with issues of inequality. A more effective equality jurisprudence calls for the development of a legal system and policies that more aggressively support equality by shaping the institutions that influence the development of our values.

# REFERENCES

Aberson, C. L., Healy, M., & Romero, V. (2000). In-group bias and self-esteem: A meta-analysis. *Personality and Social Psychology Review*, 4, 157–73.

Aboud, F. E. (1988). *Children and prejudice*. London: Blackwell.

———(1989). Disagreement between friends. *International Journal of Behavioral Development*, 12, 495–508.

———(2003). The formation of in-group favoritism and out-group prejudice in young children: Are they distinct attitudes? *Developmental Psychology*, 39, 48–60.

———(2005). The development of prejudice in childhood and adolescence. In J. F. Dovidio, P. Glick, & L. A. Rudman (eds.), *On the nature of prejudice: Fifty years after Allport* (310–26). Malden, MA: Blackwell.

Aboud, F. E., & Doyle, A. B. (1996). Does talk of race foster prejudice or tolerance in children? *Canadian Journal of Behavioural Science/Revue Canadienne Des Sciences Du Comportement* [Special Issue: Ethnic Relations in a Multicultural Society], 28, 161–70.

Aboud, F. E., & Joong, A. (2008). Intergroup name-calling and conditions for creating assertive bystanders. In S. Levy & M. Killen (eds.), *Intergroup attitudes and relations in childhood through adulthood* (249–60). New York: Oxford University Press.

Aboud, F. E., & Levy, S. R. (1999). Introduction: Are we ready to translate research into programs? *Journal of Social Issues*, 55, 621–25.

Adarand Constructors v. Peña, 515 U.S. 200 (1995).

Adolescent Family Life Act of 1981 (AFLA). 42 U.S.C. § 300z (1982).

Adoption Assistance and Child Welfare Act of 1980 (Child Welfare Act). 42 U.S.C. (§§ 5670 et seq. 11989).

Adorno, T. W., Frenkel-Brunswik, E., Levinson, D. J., & Sanford, R. N. (1950). *The authoritarian personality*. New York: Harper.

Agostini v. Felton, 521 U.S. 203 (1997).

Alexander v. Sandoval, 532 U.S. 275 (2001).

Allport, G. W. (1954/1979). *The nature of prejudice*. Redding, MA: Addison-Wesley.

Altemeyer, R. A. (1981). *Right-wing authoritarianism*. Winnipeg, Canada: University of Manitoba Press.

American Association of University Women (AAUW). (1993). *Hostile hallways: The AAUW survey on sexual harassment in America's schools*. Washington, DC: Author.

———. (2001). *Hostile hallways: Bullying, teasing, and sexual harassment in school*. Washington, DC: Author.

Aroian, K. J. (2012). Discrimination against Muslim American adolescents. *Journal of School Nursing*, 28, 206–13.

Aronson, E., & Bridgeman, D. (1979). Jigsaw groups and the desegregated classroom: In pursuit of common goals. *Personality and Social Psychology Bulletin*, 5, 438–46.

Aronson, E., & Patnoe, S. (1997). *The jigsaw classroom*. New York: Longman.

Arthur, A. E., Bigler, R. S., Liben, L. S., Gelman, S. A., & Ruble, D. N. (2008). Gender stereotyping and prejudice in young children: A developmental intergroup perspective. In S. Levy & M. Killen (eds.), *Intergroup attitudes and relations in childhood through adulthood* (66–86). New York: Oxford University Press.

Ashcroft v. Free Speech Coalition, 535 U.S. 234 (2002).

Atzaba-Poria, N., & Pike, A. (2007). Are ethnic minority adolescents at risk for problem behavior? Acculturation and intergenerational acculturation discrepancies in early adolescence. *British Journal of Developmental Psychology*, 25, 527–41.

Baker, M. L., Sigmon, J. N., & Nugent, M. E. (2001). Truancy reduction: Keeping students in school. *Juvenile Justice Bulletin*, September. U.S. Dept. of Justice.

Balkin, J. M., & Siegel, R. B. (2003). The American civil rights tradition: Anticlassification or antisubordination. *University of Miami Law Review*, 58, 9–33.

Bandes, S. (1996). Empathy, narrative, and victim impact statements. *University of Chicago Law Review*, 63, 361–412.

Banks, J. A. (1995). Multicultural education for young children: Racial and ethnic attitudes and their modification. In W. D. Hawley & A. W. Jackson (eds.), *Toward a common destiny: Improving race and ethnic relations in America* (236–50). San Francisco: Jossey-Bass.

———— (2004). Multicultural education: Historical developments, dimensions, and practice. In J. A. Banks & C. A. M. Banks (eds.), *Handbook of research in multicultural education* (3–30). San Francisco: Jossey-Bass.

Barrett, M. (2007). *Children's knowledge, beliefs, and feelings about nations and national groups*. Hove, England: Psychology Press.

Barrett, M., & Davis, S. C. (2008). Applying social identity and self-categorization theories to children's racial, ethnic, national, and state identifications and attitudes. In S. M. Quintana & C. McKown (eds.), *Handbook of race, racism, and the developing child* (72–110). Hoboken, NJ: Wiley.

Bartholet, E. (2009). The racial disproportionality movement in child welfare: False facts and dangerous directions. *Arizona Law Review*, 51, 871–932.

Bartlett, K. T. (2009). Making good on good intentions: The critical role of motivation in reducing implicit workplace discrimination. *Virginia Law Review*, 95, 1893–1972.

Batson, C. D. (2009). Two forms of perspective taking: Imagining how another feels and imagining how you would feel. In K. D. Markman, W. M. Klein, & J. A. Suhr (eds.), *The handbook of imagination and mental simulation* (267–79). New York: Psychology Press.

Batson, C. D., Eklund, J. H., Chermok, V. L., Hoyt, J. L., & Ortiz, B. G. (2007). An additional antecedent of empathic concern: Valuing the welfare of the person in need. *Journal of Personality and Social Psychology*, 93, 65–74.

Batson, C. D., & Ventis, W. (1982). *The religious experience: A social-psychological perspective*. New York: Oxford University Press.

Bellotti v. Baird, 443 U.S. 622 (1979).

Berry, J., & Kalin, R. (1995). Multicultural and ethnic attitudes in Canada: An overview of the 1991 national survey. *Canadian Journal of Behavioural Science, 27*, 301–20.

Bethel School District No. 403 v. Fraser, 478 U.S. 675 (1986).

Bielby, W. T. (2010). Response: Accentuate the positive; Are good intentions an effective way to minimize systemic workplace bias? *Virginia Law Review* [In Brief], 95, 117–26.

Bigler, R. S. (1999). The use of multicultural curricula and materials to counter racism in children. *Journal of Social Issues, 55*, 687–705.

Bigler, R. S., Brown, C. S., & Markell, M. (2001). When groups are not created equal: Effects of group status on the formation of intergroup attitudes in children. *Child Development, 723*, 1151–62.

Bigler, R. S., & Liben, L. S. (2006). A developmental intergroup theory of social stereotypes and prejudice. In R. V. Kail (ed.), *Advances in child development and behavior* (vol. 34, pp. 39–89). San Diego, CA: Elsevier.

Black, C. (1960). The lawfulness of the segregation decisions. *Yale Law Journal, 69*, 421–30.

Black-Gutman, D., & Hickson, F. (1996). The relation between racial attitudes and social-cognitive development in children: An Australian study. *Developmental Psychology, 32*: 448–56.

Blair, I. V. (2002). The malleability of automatic stereotypes and prejudice. *Personality and Social Psychology Review, 6*, 242–61.

Blanton, H., & Jaccard, J. (2008). Unconscious racism: A concept in pursuit of a measure. *Annual Review of Sociology, 34*, 277–97.

Blau, F. D. (2012). *Gender, inequality, and wages*. Oxford: Oxford University Press.

Blöte, A. W., Bokhorst, C. L., Miers, A. C., & Westenberg, P. (2012). Why are socially anxious adolescents rejected by peers? The role of subject-group similarity characteristics. *Journal of Research on Adolescence, 22*, 123–34.

Board of Education, Island Trees v. Pico, 457 U.S. 853 (1982).

Board of Education of Independent School District No. 92 of Pottawatomie County v. Earls, 536 U.S. 822 (2002).

Board of Education of Kiryas Joel Village School v. Grumet, 512 U.S. 687 (1994).

Board of Education v. Dowell, 498 U.S. 237 (1991).

Board of Regents of University of Wisconsin System v. Southworth, 529 U.S. 217 (2000).

Bobo, L. D. (1999). Prejudice as group position: Microfoundations of a sociological approach to racism and race relations. *Journal of Social Issues, 55*, 445–72.

Bobo, L. D., & Tuan, M. (2006). *Prejudice in politics: Group position, public opinion, and the Wisconsin treaty rights dispute*. Cambridge, MA: Harvard University Press.

Bolger v. Youngs Drug Products Corp., 463 U.S. 60 (1983).

Bowen v. Kendrick, 487 U.S. 589 (1988).

Boy Scouts of America v. Dale, 530 U.S. 640 (2000).

Branch, C. W., & Newcombe, N. (1986). Racial attitude development among young black children as a function of parental attitudes: A longitudinal and cross-sectional study. *Child Development, 57,* 712–21.

Brandenburg v. Ohio, 395 U.S. 444 (1969).

Breckheimer, S. E., & Nelson, R. O. (1976). Group methods for reducing racial prejudice and discrimination. *Psychological Reports, 39,* 1259–68.

Brewer, M. B. (1999). The psychology of prejudice: Ingroup love or outgroup hate? *Journal of Social Issues, 55,* 429–44.

Bridges, G. S., & Steen, S. (1998). Racial disparities in official assessments of juvenile offenders: Attributional stereotypes as mediating mechanisms. *American Sociological Review, 63,* 554–71.

Brown, C. S., & Bigler, R. S. (2005). Children's perceptions of discrimination: A developmental model. *Child Development, 76,* 533–53.

Brown, J. M., & Sorenson, J. R. (2013). Race, ethnicity, gender, and waiver to adult court. *Journal of Ethnicity in Criminal Justice, 11,* 181–95.

Brown, R., & Hewstone, M. (2005). An integrative theory of intergroup contact. In M. P. Zanna (ed.), *Advances in experimental social psychology* (vol. 37, pp. 255–342). San Diego, CA: Elsevier.

Brown v. Board of Education (Brown I), 347 U.S. 483 (1954).

Brown v. Board of Education (Brown II), 349 U.S. 294 (1955).

Brown v. Entertainment Merchants Assoc., 131 S.Ct. 2729 (2011).

Buck, S. (2010). *Acting white: The ironic legacy of desegregation.* New Haven, CT: Yale University Press.

Buriel, R. (2012). Historical origins of the immigrant paradox for Mexican American students: The cultural integration hypothesis. In C. G. Coll & A. K. Marks (eds.), *The immigrant paradox in children and adolescents: Is becoming American a developmental risk?* (37–60). Washington, DC: American Psychological Association.

Cameron, J. A., Alvarez, J. M., Ruble, D. N., & Fuligni, A. J. (2001). Children's lay theories about ingroups and outgroups: Reconceptualizing research on "prejudice." *Personality and Social Psychology Review, 5,* 118–28.

Cameron, L., & Rutland, A. (2006). Extended contact through story reading in school: Reducing children's prejudice towards the disabled. *Journal of Social Issues, 62,* 469–88.

———(2008). An integrative approach to changing children's intergroup attitudes. In S. Levy & M. Killen (eds.), *Intergroup attitudes and relations in childhood through adulthood* (191–203). Oxford: Oxford University Press.

Cameron, L., Rutland, A., & Brown, R. (2007). Promoting children's positive intergroup attitudes towards stigmatized groups: Extended contact and multiple classification skills training. *International Journal of Behavioural Development, 31,* 454–66.

Cameron, L., Rutland, A., Brown, R. J., & Douch, R. (2006). Changing children's intergroup attitudes towards refugees: Testing different models of extended contact. *Child Development, 77,* 1208–19.

Cameron, L., Rutland, A., Hossain, R., & Petley, R. (2011). When and why does extended contact work? The role of high-quality direct contact and group norms in the development of positive ethnic intergroup attitudes amongst children. *Group Processes & Intergroup Relations*, 14, 193–206.

Cantwell v. Connecticut, 310 U.S. 296 (1940).

Carlson, J. M., & Iovini, J. (1985). The transmission of racial attitudes from fathers to sons: A study of Blacks and Whites. *Adolescence*, 20, 233–37.

Castelli, L., Zogmaister, C., & Tomelleri, S. (2009). The transmission of racial attitudes within the family. *Developmental Psychology*, 45, 586–91.

Chaplinsky v. New Hampshire, 315 U.S. 568 (1942).

Children's Internet Protection Act, 20 U.S.C. § 9134 (Supp. 2001).

Church of Lukumi Babalu Aye v. City of Hialeah, 508 U.S. 520 (1993).

Cialdini, R. B., Brown, S. L., Lewis, B. P., Luce, C., & Neuberg, S. L. (1997). Reinterpreting the empathy-altruism relationship: When one into one equals oneness. *Journal of Personality and Social Psychology*, 73, 481–94.

City of Boerne v. Flores, 521 U.S. 507 (1997).

City of Richmond v. J.A. Croson Co., 488 U.S. 469 (1989).

Civil Rights Act of 1964, 42 U.S.C.A. § 2000c-6 (West 2003).

Civil Rights Act of 1964, 42 U.S.C. § 2000d-1 (2000).

Clotfelter, C. T. (2004). *After Brown: The rise and retreat of school desegregation.* Princeton, NJ: Princeton University Press.

Colker, R. (1986). Anti-subordination above all: Sex, race, and equal protection. *New York University Law Review*, 61, 1003–66.

——— (2013). *Disabled education: A critical analysis of the Individuals with Disabilities Education Act.* New York: New York University Press.

Communications Decency Act of 1996, 47 U.S.C. § 230 (2000).

Correll, J., Park, B., & Smith, J. A. (2008). Color-blind and multicultural prejudice-reduction strategies in high-conflict situations. *Group Processes & Intergroup Relations*, 11, 471–91.

Cortina, L. M. (2008). Unseen injustice: Incivility as modern discrimination in organizations. *Academy of Management Review*, 33, 55–75.

Crawford v. Board of Education of the City of Los Angeles, 458 U.S. 527 (1982).

Crisp, R. J., & Turner, R. N. (2009). Can imagined interactions produce positive perceptions? Reducing prejudice through simulated social contact. *American Psychologist*, 64, 231–40.

Crystal, D. S., Killen, M., & Ruck, M. (2008). It is who you know that counts: Intergroup contact and judgments about race-based exclusion. *British Journal of Developmental Psychology*, 26, 51–70.

Culhane, J. G. (2013). Bullying, litigation, and populations: The limited effect of Title IX. *Western New England Law Review*, 35, 323–51.

Dasgupta, N. (2004). Implicit ingroup favoritism, outgroup favoritism, and their behavioral manifestations. *Social Justice Research*, 17, 143–69.

Davey, A. (1983). *Learning to be prejudiced.* London: Edward Arnold.

Davies, K., Tropp, L. R., Aron, A., Pettigrew, T. F., & Wright, S. C. (2011). Cross-group friendships and intergroup attitudes: A meta-analytic review. *Personality and Social Psychology Review*, 15, 332–51.

Davis, A. J. (1998). Prosecution and race: The power and privilege of discretion. *Fordham Law Review*, 67, 13–67.

Davis, S. (2003). Sex stereotypes in commercials targeted toward children: A content analysis. *Sociological Spectrum*, 23, 407–24.

Degner, J., & Jonas, D. (2013). The apple does not fall far from the tree, or does it? A meta-analysis of parent-child similarity in intergroup attitudes. *Psychological Bulletin, 139, 1270–1304.*

Derman-Sparks, L., & Phillips, C. B. (1997). *Teaching/learning anti-racism: A developmental approach.* New York: Teachers College Press.

Desforges, D. M., Lord, C. G., Ramsey, S. L., Mason, J. A., Van Leeuwen, M. D., West, S. C., & Lepper, M. R. (1991). Effects of structured cooperative contact on changing negative attitudes toward stigmatized social groups. *Journal of Personality and Social Psychology*, 60, 531–44.

DeShaney v. Winnebago County Department of Social Services, 489 U.S. 189 (1989).

Diviaio, D. (2007). The government is establishing your child's curfew. *Journal of Civil Rights and Economic Development*, 21, 797–835.

Dixon, J., Durrheim, K., & Tredoux, C. (2005). Beyond the optimal contact strategy: A reality check for the contact hypothesis. *American Psychologist*, 60, 697–711.

Dixon, J., Tropp, L. R., Durrheim, K., & Tredoux, C. (2010). "Let them eat harmony": Prejudice-reduction strategies and attitudes of historically disadvantaged groups. *Current Directions in Psychological Science*, 19, 76–80.

Dovidio, J. F., Brigham, J. C., Johnson, B. T., & Gaertner, S. L. (1996). Stereotyping, prejudice, and discrimination: Another look. In C. N. Macrae, C. Stangor, & M. Hewstone (eds.), *Stereotypes and stereotyping* (276–319). New York: Guilford.

Dovidio, J. F., Esses, V. M., Beach, K. R., & Gaertner, S. L. (2002). The role of affect in determining intergroup behavior: The case of willingness to engage in intergroup contact. In D. M. Mackie & E. R. Smith (eds.), *From prejudice to intergroup emotions: Differentiated reactions to social groups* (153–71). New York: Psychology Press.

Dovidio, J. F., & Gaertner, S. L. (1999). Reducing prejudice: Combating intergroup biases. *Current Directions in Psychological Science*, 8, 101–5.

——— (2004). Aversive racism. In M. P. Zanna (ed.), *Advances in experimental social psychology* (vol. 36, pp. 1–51). San Diego, CA: Elsevier.

Dovidio, J. F., Gaertner, S. L., & Saguy, T. (2009). Commonality and the complexity of "we": Social attitudes and social change. *Personality and Social Psychology Review*, 13, 3–20.

Dovidio, J. F., Gaertner, S. L., Stewart, T. L., Esses, V. M., Ten Vergert, M., & Hodson, G. (2004). From intervention to outcome: Processes in the reduction of bias. In W. G. Stephan & W. P. Vogt (eds.), *Education programs for improving intergroup relations: Theory, research, and practice* (243–65). New York: Teachers College Press.

Dovidio, J. F., Glick, P., & Rudman, L. A. (eds.). (2005). *On the nature of prejudice: Fifty years after Allport.* Malden, MA: Blackwell.

Dowler, K. (2004). Dual realities? Criminality, victimization, and the presentation of race on local television news. *Journal of Crime and Justice,* 27, 79–99.

Doyle, A. B., & Aboud, F. E. (1995). A longitudinal study of white children's racial prejudice as a social-cognitive development. *Merrill-Palmer Quarterly,* 41, 209–28.

Duckitt, J. (1992). *The social psychology of prejudice.* New York: Praeger.

Dunham, Y., Baron, A. S., & Banaji, M. R. (2008). The development of implicit inter-group cognition. *Trends in Cognitive Sciences,* 12, 248–53.

Durlak, J., & DuPre, E. (2008). Implementation matters: A review of research on the influence of implementation on program outcomes and the factors affecting implementation. *American Journal of Community Psychology,* 41, 327–50.

Edwards, L. M., & Romero, A. J. (2008). Coping with discrimination among Mexican-descendent adolescents. *Hispanic Journal of Behavioral Sciences,* 30, 24–39.

Eitle, D., & McNulty Eitle, T. (2003). Segregation and school violence. *Social Forces,* 82, 589–615.

Employment Division v. Smith, 494 U.S. 872 (1990).

Entman, L., & Rojecki, A. (2000). *The black image in the white mind: Media and race in America.* Chicago: University of Chicago Press.

Estrada, R., & Marksamer, J. (2006). The legal rights of LGBT youth in state custody: What child welfare and juvenile justice professionals need to know. *Child Welfare,* 85, 171–94.

Everson v. Board of Education, 330 U.S. 1 (1947).

Fazio, R. H., Jackson, J. R., Dunton, B. C., & Williams, C. J. (1995). Variability in automatic activation as an unobtrusive measure of racial attitudes: A bona fide pipeline? *Journal of Personality and Social Psychology,* 69, 1013–27.

FCC v. Pacifica Foundation, 438 U.S. 726 (1978).

Feddes, A. R., Noack, P., & Rutland, A. (2009). Direct and extended friendship effects on minority and majority children's interethnic attitudes: A longitudinal study. *Child Development,* 80, 377–90.

Fein, S., & Spencer, S. J. (1997). Prejudice as self-image maintenance: Affirming the self through derogating others. *Journal of Personality and Social Psychology,* 73, 31–44.

Fenning, P., & Rose, J. (2007). Over-representation of African American students in exclusionary discipline: The role of school policy. *Urban Education,* 42, 536–59.

Ferguson v. City of Charleston, 532 U.S. 67 (2001).

Festinger, L. (1957). *A theory of cognitive dissonance.* Evanston, IL: Row, Peterson.

Fishbein, H. D. (1996). *Peer prejudice and discrimination: Evolutionary, cultural, and developmental dynamics.* Boulder, CO: Westview.

——— (2002). *Peer prejudice and discrimination: The origins of prejudice.* Mahwah, NJ: Erlbaum.

Fisher, C., Jackson, J., & Villarruel, F. (1998). The study of African American and Latin American children and youth. In W. Damon (editor-in-chief) & R. M. Lerner (volume editor), *Handbook of child psychology.* Vol. 1, *Theoretical models of human development* (5th ed., 1145–1208). New York: Wiley.

Fisher, C. B., Wallace, S. A., & Fenton, R. E. (2000). Discrimination distress during adolescence. *Journal of Youth and Adolescence,* 29, 679–95.

Fisher v. University of Texas, 133 S. Ct. 2411 (2013).

Fiske, S. T. (2000). Stereotyping, prejudice, and discrimination at the seam between the centuries: Evolution, culture, mind, and brain. *European Journal of Social Psychology,* 29, 188–211.

Fiss, O. (1976). Groups and the Equal Protection Clause. *Philosophy & Public Affairs,* 5, 107–77.

Flores, E., Tschann, J. M., Dimas, J. M., Pasch, L. A., & de Groat, C. L. (2010). Perceived racial/ethnic discrimination, posttraumatic stress symptoms, and health risk behaviors among Mexican American adolescents. *Journal of Counseling Psychology,* 57, 264–73.

Fonts, S. A., Berger, L. M., & Slack, K. S. (2012). Examining racial disproportionality in child protective services case decisions. *Children and Youth Services Review,* 34, 2188–2200.

Frankenberg, E., Lee, C., & Orfield, G. (2003). *A multiracial society with segregated schools: Are we losing the dream?* Cambridge, MA: Civil Rights Project, Harvard University.

Freeman v. Pitts, 503 U.S. 467 (1992).

Fuller-Rowell, T. E., Evans, G. W., & Ong, A. D. (2012). Poverty and health: The mediating role of perceived discrimination. *Psychological Science,* 23, 734–39.

Furnham, A., & Paltzer, S. (2010). The portrayal of men and women in television advertisements: An updated review of 30 studies published since 2000. *Scandinavian Journal of Psychology,* 51, 216–36.

Gaertner, S. L., & Dovidio, J. F. (1986).The aversive form of racism. In J. F. Dovidio & S. L. Gaertner (eds.), *Prejudice, discrimination, and racism* (61–89). Orlando, FL: Academic Press.

——— (2000). *Reducing intergroup bias: The common in-group identity model.* Philadelphia: Psychology Press.

Galinsky, A. D., & Moskowitz, G. B. (2000). Perspective-taking: Decreasing stereotype expression, stereotype accessibility, and in-group favoritism. *Journal of Personality and Social Psychology,* 78, 708–24.

Gant, J., Parry, Y., & Guerin, P. (2013). An investigation of culturally competent terminology in healthcare policy finds ambiguity and lack of definition. *Australian and New Zealand Journal of Public Health,* 37, 250–56.

Garcetti v. Ceballos, 547 U.S. 410 (2006).

Gersen, J. E., & Posner, E. A. (2008). Soft law: Lessons from congressional practice. *Stanford Law Review,* 61, 573–627.

Gibbons, F. X., Gerrard, M., Cleveland, M. J., Wills, T. A., & Brody, G. (2004). Perceived discrimination and substance use in African American parents and their children: A panel study. *Journal of Personality and Social Psychology,* 86, 517–29.

Gillen-O'Neel, C., Ruble, D., & Fuligni, A. (2011). Ethnic stigma, academic anxiety, and intrinsic motivation in middle childhood. *Child Development*, 82, 1470–85.

Gilliam, F. D., Jr., & Bales, S. N. (2001). Strategic frame analysis: Reframing America's youth. *Social Policy Report*, 15, 2–24.

Ginsberg v. New York, 390 U.S. 629 (1968).

Glasman, L. R., & Albarracin, D. (2006). Forming attitudes that predict future behavior: A meta-analysis of the attitude-behavior relation. *Psychological Bulletin*, 132, 778–822.

Gogtay, N., Giedd, J. N., Lusk, L., Hayashi, K. M., Greenstein, D., Vaituzis, A. C., Nugent, T. F., III, Herman, D. H., Clasen, L. S., Toga, A. W., Rapoport, J. L., & Thompson, P. M. (2004). Dynamic mapping of human cortical development during childhood through early adulthood. *Proceedings of the National Academy of Sciences of the United States of America*, 101, 8174–79.

Gonzales v. O Centro Espirita Beneficiente Uniao Do Vegetal (UDV), 546 U.S. 418 (2006).

Gonzales, N. A., Knight, G. P., Morgan-Lopez, A., Saenz, D., & Sirolli, A. A. (2002). Acculturation and the mental health of Latino youths: An integration and critique of the literature. In J. M. Contreras, K. A. Kerns, & A. M. Neal-Barnett (eds.), *Latino children and families in the United States: Current research and future directions* (45–74). Westport, CT: Praeger.

Good News Club v. Milford Central School, 533 U.S. 98 (2001).

Gorski, P. C., Davis, S. N., & Reiter, A. (2013). An examination of the (in)visibility of sexual orientation, heterosexism, homophobia, and other LGBTQ concerns in U.S. multicultural teacher education coursework. *Journal of LGBT Youth*, 10, 224–48

Goss v. Board of Education of the City of Knoxville, 373 U.S. 683 (1963).

Graber, M. A. (2008). The price of fame: *Brown* as celebrity. *Ohio State Law Journal*, 69, 939–1015.

Graham, S. (2006). Peer victimization in school: Exploring the ethnic context. *Current Directions in Psychological Science*, 15, 317–21.

Graham, S., & Lowery, B. S. (2004). Priming unconscious racial stereotypes about adolescent offenders. *Law and Human Behavior*, 483–504.

Graham v. Florida, 560 U.S. 825 (2010).

Green v. County School Board of New Kent County, 391 U.S. 430 (1968).

Greene, M. L., Way, N., & Pahl, K. (2006). Trajectories of perceived adult and peer discrimination among Black, Latino, and Asian American adolescents: Patterns and psychological correlates. *Developmental Psychology*, 42, 218–38.

Griffin v. County School Board of Prince Edward County, 377 U.S. 218 (1964).

Grutter v. Bollinger, 539 U.S. 306 (2003).

Guardians Association v. Civil Service Commission of New York City, 463 U.S. 582 (1983).

Gurin, P., Peng, T., Lopez, G., & Nagada, B. R. (1999). Context, identity, and intergroup relations. In D. Prentice & D. T. Miller (eds.), *Cultural divides: The social psychology of intergroup contact* (133–70). New York: Russell Sage Foundation.

Hand, J., & Sanchez, L. (2000). Badgering or bantering? Gender differences in experience of, and reactions to, sexual harassment among U.S. high school students. *Gender & Society*, 14, 718–46.

Harris v. McRae, 448 U.S. 297 (1980).

Hazelwood School District v. Kuhlmeier, 484 U.S. 260 (1988).

Hebl, M., Foster, J. B., Mannix, L. M., & Dovidio, J. F. (2002). Formal and interpersonal discrimination: A field study of bias toward homosexual applications. *Personality and Social Psychology Bulletin*, 28, 815–25.

Henning, K. (2013). Criminalizing normal adolescent behavior in communities of color: The role of prosecutors in juvenile justice. *Cornell Law Review*, 98, 383–461.

Hewstone, M. (1996). Contact and categorization: Social psychological interventions to change intergroup relations. In C. N. Macrae, C. Stangor, & M. Hewstone (eds.), *Stereotypes and stereotyping* (323–68). New York: Guilford.

Hoover, R., & Fishbein, H. D. (1999). The development of prejudice and sex role stereotyping in White adolescents and White young adults. *Journal of Applied Developmental Psychology*, 20, 431–48.

Horn, S. S. (2006). Group status, group bias, and adolescents' reasoning about the treatment of others in school contexts. *International Journal of Behavioral Development*, 30, 208–18.

Hughes, J. M., Bigler, R. S., & Levy, S. R. (2007). Consequences of learning about historical racism among European American and African American children. *Child Development*, 78, 1689–1705.

Hurley v. Irish-American Gay, Lesbian, and Bisexual Group of Boston, 515 U.S. 557 (1995).

Huynh, V. W. (2012). Ethnic microaggressions and the depressive and somatic symptoms of Latino and Asian American adolescents. *Journal of Youth and Adolescence*, 41, 831–46.

Huynh, V. W., & Fuligni, A. J. (2010). Discrimination hurts: The academic, psychological, and physical well-being of adolescents. *Journal of Research on Adolescence*, 20, 916–41.

Ingraham v. Wright, 430 U.S. 651 (1977).

In re Gault, 387 U.S. 1 (1967).

Johanns v. Livestock Marketing Association, 544 U.S. 550 (2005).

Jones, E. N. (2012). Disproportionate representation of minority youth in the juvenile justice system: A lack of clarity and too much disparity among states "addressing" the issue. *Journal of Juvenile Law & Policy*, 16, 155–201.

Jordan, C. H., Spencer, S. J., & Zanna, M. (2005). Types of high self-esteem and prejudice: How implicit self-esteem relates to ethnic discrimination among high explicit self-esteem individuals. *Personality and Social Psychology Bulletin*, 31, 693–702.

Judd, C. M., Park, B., & Wolsko, C. (2001). Measurement of subtyping in stereotype change. *Journal of Experimental Social Psychology*, 37, 325–32.

Juvenile Justice and Delinquency Prevention Act, 42 U.S.C. §§ 5601–5785 (2006).

Kahlenberg, S. G., & Hein, M. M. (2010). Progression on Nickelodeon? Gender-role stereotypes in toy commercials. *Sex Roles*, 62, 830–47.

Kahne, J. E., & Sporte, S. E. (2008). Developing citizens: The impact of civic learning opportunities on students' commitment to civic participation. *American Educational Research Journal, 45*, 738–66.

Kalev, A., Dobbin, F., & Kelly, E. (2008). Best practices or best guesses? Assessing the efficacy of corporate affirmative action and diversity policies. *American Sociological Review, 71*, 589–617.

Kao, G., & Joyner, K. (2004). Do race and ethnicity matter among friends? Activities among interracial, interethnic, and intraethnic adolescent friends. *Sociological Quarterly, 45*, 557–73.

Katz, I. (1981). *Stigma: A social-psychological perspective*. Hillsdale, NJ: Erlbaum.

Kent v. United States, 383 U.S. 541 (1966).

Keyes v. School District No. 1, Denver, Colorado, 418 U.S. 717 (1973).

Killen, M., Lee-Kim, J., McGlothlin, J., & Stangor, C. (2002). How children and adolescents evaluate gender and racial exclusion. *Monographs of the Society for Research in Child Development, 67*, 1–119.

Killen, M., & Rutland, A. (2011). *Children and social exclusion: Morality, prejudice, and group identity*. New York: Wiley-Blackwell.

Killen, M., Rutland, A., & Ruck, M. D. (2011). Promoting equity, tolerance, and justice in childhood. *Social Policy Report, 25*, 1–25.

Killen, M., Sinno, S., & Margie, N. G. (2007). Children's experiences and judgments about group exclusion and inclusion. In R. Kail (ed.), *Advances in child psychology* (vol. 35, pp. 173–218). New York: Elsevier.

Kosciw, J. G. (2004). *The 2003 National School Climate Survey: The school-related experiences of our nation's lesbian, gay, bisexual, and transgender youth*. New York: Gay, Lesbian, and Straight Education Network (GLSEN).

Kosciw, J. G., & Diaz, E. M. (2006). *The 2005 National School Climate Survey: The experiences of lesbian, gay, bisexual, and transgender youth in our nation's schools*. New York: Gay, Lesbian, and Straight Education Network (GLSEN).

Kosciw, J. G., Greytak, E. A., Diaz, E. M., & Bartkiewicz, M. J. (2010). *The 2009 National School Climate Survey: The experiences of lesbian, gay, bisexual, and transgender youth in our nation's schools*. New York: Gay, Lesbian, and Straight Education Network (GLSEN).

Kovel, J. (1970). *White racism: A psychohistory*. New York: Pantheon.

Kressin, N. R., Raymond, K. L., & Manze, M. (2008). Perceptions of race/ethnicity-based discrimination: A review of measures and evaluation of their usefulness for the health care setting. *Journal of Health Care for the Poor and Underserved, 19*, 697–730.

LaFree, G., & Arum, R. (2006). The impact of racially inclusive schooling on adult incarceration rates among U.S. cohorts of African Americans and Whites since 1930. *Criminology, 44*, 73–104.

Lassiter v. Department of Social Services, 452 U.S. 18 (1981).

Lawson, T. J., McDonough, T. A., & Bodle, J. H. (2010). Confronting prejudiced comments: Effectiveness of a role-playing exercise. *Teaching of Psychology, 37*, 257–61.

Lebowitz, M. S. (2013). Stigmatization of ADHD: A developmental review. *Journal of Attention Disorders*. Advance online publication, February 13, 2013. doi: 10.1177/1087054712475211.

Lee v. Weisman, 505 U.S. 577 (1992).

Legal Services Corp. v. Velazquez, 531 U.S. 533 (2001).

Leiber, M. (2003). *The contexts of juvenile justice decision making: When race matters.* Albany: State University of New York.

Leiber, M., Bishop, D., & Chamlin, M. B. (2010). Juvenile justice decision-making before and after the implementation of the Disproportionate Minority Contract (DMC) Mandate. *Justice Quarterly*, 28, 460–92.

Leiber, M., & Johnson, J. (2008). Being young and Black: What are their effects on juvenile justice decision making? *Crime & Delinquency*, 54, 560–81.

Leippe, M. R., & Eisenstadt, D. (1994). Generalization of dissonance reduction: Decreasing prejudice through induced compliance. *Journal of Personality and Social Psychology*, 67, 395–413.

Lemon v. Kurtzman, 403 U.S. 602 (1971).

Levesque, R. J. R. (2000a). *Adolescents, sex, and the law: Preparing adolescents for responsible citizenship.* Washington, DC: American Psychological Association.

———— (2000b). Sexuality education: What adolescents' educational rights require. *Psychology, Public Policy, and Law*, 6, 953–88.

———— (2002). *Not by faith alone: Religion, adolescence, and the law.* New York: New York University Press.

———— (ed.) (2003). *Sexuality education: What adolescents' rights require.* Hauppauge, NY: Nova Science Publishers.

———— (2006). *The psychology and law of criminal justice processes.* Hauppauge, NY: Nova Science Publishers.

———— (2007). *Adolescents, media, and the law: What developmental science reveals and free speech requires.* New York: Oxford University Press.

———— (2008). *Rethinking child maltreatment law: Returning to first principles.* New York: Springer.

———— (2014a). Discrimination, developmental science, and the law: Addressing dramatic shifts in civil rights jurisprudence. *American Journal of Orthopsychiatry*, 84, 2014, 25–34.

———— (2014b). The law's promise of religious freedom to support emerging adults' religious development and experiences. In C. N. Barry & M. M. Abo-Zena (eds.), *Emerging adults' religiousness and spirituality: Meaning-making in an age of transition* (109–32). New York: Oxford University Press.

Levy, S. R., & Dweck, C. S. (1999). The impact of children's static versus dynamic conceptions of people on stereotype formation. *Child Development*, 70, 1163–80.

Linville, P. W. (1998). The heterogeneity of homogeneity. In J. M. Darley & J. Cooper (eds.), *Attribution processes, person perception, and social interactions: The legacy of Edward E. Jones* (423–87). Washington, DC: American Psychological Association.

Little, R. K. (2011). The ABA's project to revise the criminal justice standards for the prosecution and defense functions. *Hastings Law Journal, 62*, 1111–57.

Lopez, G. E. (2004). Interethnic contact, curriculum, and attitudes in the first year of college. *Journal of Social Issues, 60*, 75–94.

Martin, C. L., Ruble, D. N., & Szkrybalo, J. (2002). Cognitive theories of early gender role development. *Psychological Bulletin, 128*, 903–33.

Massey, D. S. (2006). Social background and academic performance differentials: White and minority students at selective colleges. *American Law and Economics Review, 8*, 390–409.

Mastro, D. (2009). Effects of racial and ethnic stereotyping. In J. Bryant & M. B. Oliver (eds.), *Media effects: Advances in theory and research* (3rd ed., 325–41). New York: Routledge.

McConahay, J., Hardee, B., & Batts, V. (1981). Has racism declined in America? It depends on who is asking and what is asked. *Journal of Conflict Resolution, 25*, 563–79.

McGlothlin, H., & Killen, M. (2010). How social experience is related to children's intergroup attitudes. *European Journal of Social Psychology, 40*, 625–34.

McKown, C. (2004). Age and ethnic variation in children's thinking about the nature of racism. *Journal of Applied Developmental Psychology, 25*, 597–617.

McLoyd, V. C. (2006). The legacy of *Child Development*'s 1990 special issue on minority children: An editorial retrospective. *Child Development, 77*, 1142–48.

McNeese v. Board of Education, Community Unit School District 187, 373 U.S. 668 (1963).

Merrell, K. W., Gueldner, B. A., Ross, S. W., & Isava, D. M. (2008). How effective are school bullying intervention programs? A meta-analysis of intervention research. *School Psychology Quarterly, 23*, 26–42.

Meyer, I. H., & Beyer, R. (2013). School-based gay-affirmative interventions: First Amendment and ethical concerns. *American Journal of Public Health, 103*, 1764–71.

Meyer v. Nebraska, 262 U.S. 390 (1923).

Mickelson, R. A., Bottia, M. C., & Lambert, R. (2013). Effects of school racial composition on K–12 mathematics outcomes: A metaregression analysis. *Review of Educational Research, 83*, 121–58.

Mildon, R., & Shlonsky, A. (2011). Bridge over troubled water: Using implementation science to facilitate effective services in child welfare. *Child Abuse & Neglect, 35*, 753–56.

Miller v. Alabama, 132 S.Ct. 2455 (2012).

Milliken v. Bradley (Milliken I), 418 U.S. 717 (1974).

Milliken v. Bradley (Milliken II), 433 U.S. 267 (1977).

Minow, M. (2010). *In Brown's wake: Legacies of America's educational landmark*. New York: Oxford University Press.

Missouri v. Jenkins, 515 U.S. 70 (1995).

Mitchell v. Helms, 530 U.S. 793 (2000).

M.L.B. v. S.L.J., 519 U.S. 102 (1996).

Monroe v. Board of Commissioners of the City of Jackson, 391 U.S. 450 (1968).

Monteith, M. J. (1993). Self-regulation of prejudiced responses: Implications for progress in prejudice-reduction efforts. *Journal of Personality and Social Psychology, 65,* 469–85.

Monteith, M. J., Arthur, S. A., & Flynn, S. M. (2010). Self-regulation and bias. In J. F. Dovidio, M. Hewstone, P. Glick, & V. M. Esses (eds.), *The Sage handbook of prejudice, stereotyping, and discrimination* (493–507). Los Angeles: Sage.

Montgomery, E., & Foldspang, A. (2008). Discrimination, mental problems, and social adaptation in young refugees. *European Journal of Public Health, 18,* 156–61.

Moore, L. D., & Padavic, I. (2010). Racial and ethnic disparities in girls' sentencing in the juvenile justice system. *Feminist Criminology, 5,* 263–85.

Morrill Anti-Bigamy Act, Ch. 126, 12 Stat. 501 (1862) (codified as amended at U.S. Rev. Stat. § 5352) (repealed prior to codification in the U.S.C.).

Morrongiello, B. A., Midgett, C., & Stanton, K. (2000). Gender biases in children's appraisals of injury risk and other children's risk-taking behaviors. *Journal of Experimental Child Psychology, 77,* 317–36.

Morse v. Frederick, 551 U.S. 393 (2007).

Nagda, B. A., Kim, C., & Truelove, Y. (2004). Learning about difference, learning with others, learning to transgress. *Journal of Social Issues, 60,* 195–214.

Nagda, B. A., & Zuñiga, X. (2003). Fostering meaningful racial engagement through intergroup dialogues. *Group Processes & Intergroup Relations, 6,* 111–28.

National Endowment for the Arts v. Finley, 524 U.S. 569 (1998).

Nelson, T. D. (2009). *Handbook of prejudice, stereotyping, and discrimination.* New York: Psychology Press.

Nesdale, D. (2001). Development of prejudice in children. In M. Augoustinos & K. J. Reynolds (eds.), *Understanding prejudice, racism, and social conflict* (57–72). London: Sage.

——— (2008). Peer group rejection and children's intergroup prejudice. In D. H. Bayley, S. R. Levy, & M. Killen (eds.), *Intergroup attitudes and relations in childhood through adulthood* (32–46). New York: Oxford University Press.

Nesdale, D., Maass, A., Durkin, K., & Griffiths, J. (2005). Group norms, threat, and children's racial prejudice. *Child Development, 76,* 652–63.

New York v. Ferber, 458 U.S. 747 (1982).

Nucci, L. P. (2001). *Education in the moral domain.* Cambridge: Cambridge University Press.

Ortiz, M., & Harwood, J. (2007). A social cognitive approach to intergroup relationships on television. *Journal of Broadcasting & Electronic Media, 51,* 615–31.

Pager, D., & Shepherd, H. (2008). The sociology of discrimination: Racial discrimination in employment, housing, credit, and consumer markets. *Annual Review of Sociology, 34,* 181–209.

Paolini, S., Hewstone, M., & Cairns, E. (2007). Direct and indirect intergroup friendship effects: Testing the moderating role of the affective-cognitive bases of prejudice. *Personality and Social Psychology Bulletin, 33,* 1406–20.

Paolini, S., Hewstone, M., Cairns, E., & Voci, A. (2004). Effects of direct and indirect cross-group friendships on judgments of Catholics and Protestants in Northern

Ireland: The mediating role of an anxiety-reduction mechanism. *Personality and Social Psychology Bulletin*, 30, 770–86

Parents Involved in Community Schools v. Seattle School District No. 1, 551 U.S. 701 (2007).

Parham v. J.R., 442 U.S. 584 (1979).

Parker, W. (1999). The future of school desegregation. *Northwestern University Law Review*, 94, 1157–1227.

Pasadena City Board of Education v. Spangler, 427 U.S. 424 (1976).

Pascoe, C. J. (2007). *Dude, you're a fag: Masculinity and sexuality in high school.* Los Angeles: University of California Press.

Pearson, A. R., Dovidio, J. F., & Gaertner, S. L. (2009). The nature of contemporary prejudice: Insights from aversive racism. *Social & Personality Psychology Compass*, 3, 314–38.

Perry, R., & Sibley, C. G. (2011). Social dominance orientation: Mapping a baseline individual difference component across self-categorization. *Journal of Individual Differences*, 32, 110–16.

Pettigrew, T. F., & Tropp, L. R. (2000). Does intergroup contact reduce prejudice? Recent meta-analytic findings. In S. Oskamp (ed.), *Reducing prejudice and discrimination: Social psychological perspectives* (93–114). Mahwah, NJ: Erlbaum.

——— (2006). A meta-analytic test of intergroup contact theory. *Journal of Personality and Social Psychology*, 90, 751–83.

——— (2008). How does intergroup contact reduce prejudice? Meta-analytic tests of three mediators. *European Journal of Social Psychology*, 38, 922–34.

Pfeifer, J. H., Ruble, D. N., Bachman, M. A., Alvarez, J. M., Cameron, J. A., & Fuligni, A. J. (2007). Social identities and intergroup bias in immigrant and nonimmigrant children. *Developmental Psychology*, 43, 496–507.

Pfeifer, J. H., Spears Brown, C., & Juvonen, J. (2007). Prejudice reduction in schools. *Social Policy Report*, 21, 3–24.

Pierce v. Society of Sisters, 268 U.S. 510 (1925).

Pinard, M. (2010). Collateral consequences of criminal convictions: Confronting issues of race and dignity. *New York University Law Review*, 85, 457–534.

Pleasant Grove City v. Summum, 555 U.S. 460 (2009).

Plessy v. Ferguson, 163 U.S. 537 (1896).

Plous, S. (2000). Responding to overt displays of prejudice: A role-playing exercise. *Teaching of Psychology*, 27, 198–200.

Plous, S., & Neptune, D. (1997). Racial and gender biases in magazine advertising: A content analytic study. *Psychology of Women Quarterly*, 21, 627–44.

Poteat, V. P. (2007). Peer group socialization of homophobic attitudes and behavior during adolescence. *Child Development*, 78, 1830–42.

Poteat, V. P., Espelage, D. L., & Green, H. D., Jr. (2007). The socialization of dominance: Peer group contextual effects on homophobic and dominance attitudes. *Journal of Personality and Social Psychology*, 92, 1040–50.

Poteat, V. P., Mereish, E. H., DiGiovanni, C. D., & Koenig, B. W. (2011). The effects of general and homophobic victimization on adolescents' psychosocial and educational concerns: The importance of intersecting identities and parental support. *Journal of Counseling Psychology*, 58, 597–609.

Pratto, F., Sidanius, J., Stallworth, L. M., & Malle, B. F. (1994). Social dominance orientation: A personality variable predicting social and political attitudes. *Journal of Personality and Social Psychology*, 67, 741–63.

Prelow, H. M., Danoff-Burg, S., Swenson, R. R., & Pulgiano, D. (2004). The impact of ecological risk and perceived discrimination on the psychological adjustment of African American and European American youth. *Journal of Community Psychology*, 32, 375–89.

Prince v. Massachusetts, 321 U.S. 158 (1944).

Puhl, R. M., & King, K. M. (2013). Weight discrimination and bullying. *Best Practice & Research Clinical Endocrinology & Metabolism*, 27, 117–27.

Puhl, R. M., & Luedicke, J. (2012). Weight-based victimization among adolescents in the school setting: Emotional reactions and coping behaviors. *Journal of Youth and Adolescence*, 41, 27–40.

Raabe, T., & Beelman, A. (2011). Development of ethnic, racial, and national prejudice in childhood and adolescence: A multinational meta-analysis of age differences. *Child Development*, 82, 1715–37.

Raney v. Board of Education of the Gould School District, 391 U.S. 443 (1968).

R.A.V. v. City of St. Paul, 505 U.S. 377 (1992).

Reardon, S. F., Grwal, E. T., Kalogrides, D., & Greenberg, E. (2012). *Brown* fades: The end of court-ordered school desegregation and the resegregation of American public schools. *Journal of Policy Analysis and Management*, 31, 876–904.

Regents of University of California v. Bakke, 438 U.S. 265 (1978).

Religious Freedom Restoration Act (RFLA), 42 U.S.C. § 2000bb to 2000bb-1 (Supp. V 1993).

Reno v. American Civil Liberties Union (ACLU), 521 U.S. 844 (1997).

Renzaho, A. M. N., Pomios, P., Crock, C., & Sønderlund, A. L. (2013). The effectiveness of cultural competence programs in ethnic-minority patient-centered health care: A systematic review of the literature. *International Journal for Quality in Health Care*, 25, 261–69.

Reynolds, K. J., & Turner, J. C. (2006). Individuality and the prejudiced personality. *European Review of Social Psychology*, 17, 233–70.

Reynolds v. United States, 98 U.S. 145 (1878).

Richards, Z., & Hewstone, M. (2001). Subtyping and subgrouping: Processes for the prevention and promotion of stereotype change. *Personality and Social Psychology Review*, 5, 52–73.

Roberts v. United States Jaycees, 468 U.S. 609 (1984).

Robinson, R. K. (2008). Perceptual segregation. *Columbia Law Review*, 108, 1093–1180.

Rogers v. Paul, 382 U.S. 198 (1965).

Rokeach, M. (1971). Long-range experimental modification of values, attitudes, and behavior. *American Psychologist*, 26, 453–59.

Romero, A. J., & Roberts, R. E. (2003). Stress within a bicultural context for adolescents of Mexican descent. *Cultural Diversity & Ethnic Minority Psychology*, 9, 171–84.

Rooth, D. (2010). Automatic associations and discrimination in hiring: Real-world evidence. *Labour Economics*, 17, 523–34.

Roper v. Simmons, 543 U.S. 551 (2005).

Rosenberg, G. N. (2008). *The hollow hope: Can courts bring about social change?* Chicago: University of Chicago Press.

Rosenbloom, S. R., & Way, N. (2004). Experiences of discrimination among African American, Asian American, and Latino adolescents in an urban high school. *Youth & Society*, 35, 420–51.

Roth v. United States, 354 U.S. 476 (1957).

Ruck, M. D., & Wortley, S. (2002). Racial and ethnic minority high school students' perceptions of school disciplinary practices: A look at some Canadian findings. *Journal of Youth and Adolescence*, 31, 185–95.

Rudman, L. A., & Borgida, E. (1995). The afterglow of construct accessibility: The behavioral consequences of priming men to view women as sexual objects. *Journal of Experimental Social Psychology*, 31, 493–517.

Ruggiero, K. M., & Taylor, D. M. (1997). Why minority group members perceive or do not perceive the discrimination that confronts them: The role of self-esteem and perceived control. *Journal of Personality and Social Psychology*, 72, 373–89.

Runyon v. McCrary, 427 U.S. 160 (1976).

Russell, S. T., Kosciw, J., Horn, S. S., & Saewyc, E. (2010). Safe schools policy for LGBTQ students. *Social Policy Report*, 24, 1–24.

Russell, S. T., Sinclair, K. O., Poteat, V. P., & Koenig, B. W. (2012). Adolescent health and harassment based on discriminatory bias. *American Journal of Public Health*, 102, 493–95.

Rust v. Sullivan, 500 U.S. 173 (1991).

Rutland, A., Cameron, L., Bennett, L., & Ferrell, J. M. (2005). Interracial contact and racial constancy: A multi-site study of racial intergroup bias in 3–5-year-old Anglo-British children. *Journal of Applied Developmental Psychology*, 26, 699–713.

Ryan, C. S., Casas, J. F., & Thompson, B. K. (2010). Interethnic ideology, intergroup perceptions, and cultural orientation. *Journal of Social Issues*, 66, 29–44.

Ryan, C. S., Hunt, J. S., Weible, J. A., Peterson, C. R., & Casas, J. F. (2007). Multicultural and color-blind ideology, stereotypes, and ethnocentrism among Black and White Americans. *Group Processes & Intergroup Relations*, 10, 617–37.

Ryana, J. P., Herzb, P. M., Hernandeza, J. M., & Marshalla, J. M. (2007). Maltreatment and delinquency: Investigating child welfare bias in juvenile justice processing. *Children and Youth Services Review*, 29, 1035–50.

Sable Communications of California v. FCC, 492 U.S. 115 (1989).

Safford Unified School District No. 1 v. Redding, 557 U.S. 364 (2009).

Salzman, M., & D'Andrea, M. (2001). Assessing the impact of a prejudice-prevention project. *Journal of Counseling & Development*, 79: 341–47.

San Antonio Independent School District v. Rodriguez, 411 U.S. 1 (1973).

Santa Fe Independent School District v. Doe, 530 U.S. 290 (2000).

Santosky v. Kramer, 455 U.S. 745 (1982).

Sarine, L. E. (2012). Regulating the social pollution of systemic discrimination caused by implicit bias. *California Law Review*, 100, 1359–99.

Schiappa, E., Gregg, P. B., & Hewes, D. E. (2005). The parasocial contact hypothesis. *Communication Monographs*, 72, 92–115.

Schneider, B. H., Dixon, K., & Udvari, S. (2007). Closeness and competition in the inter-ethnic and co-ethnic friendships of early adolescents in Toronto and Montreal. *Journal of Early Adolescence*, 27, 115–38.

Schofield, J. (1982). *Black and White in school: Trust, tension, or tolerance?* New York: Praeger.

Schulze, C. (2012). The masculine yardstick of physical competence: U.S. police academy fitness tests. *Women & Criminal Justice*, 22, 89–107.

Schuman, H., Steeh, C., Bobo, L., & Krysan, M. (1997). *Racial attitudes in America: Trends and interpretations.* Cambridge, MA: Harvard University Press.

Schwartz, S. J., Montgomery, M. J., & Briones, E. (2006). The role of identity in acculturation among immigrant people: Theoretical propositions, empirical questions, and applied recommendations. *Human Development*, 49, 1–30.

Schwartz, S. J., Unger, J. B., Zamboanga, B. L., & Szapocznik, J. (2010). Rethinking the concept of acculturation: Implications for theory and research. *American Psychologist*, 65, 237–51.

Sears, D. O., & Henry, P. J. (2005). Over thirty years later: A contemporary look at symbolic racism. *Advances in Experimental Social Psychology*, 37, 95–150.

Seaton, E. K., Caldwell, C. H., Sellers, R. M., & Jackson, J. S. (2008). The prevalence of perceived discrimination among African American and Caribbean Black youth. *Developmental Psychology*, 44, 1288–97.

Sellers, R. M., Caldwell, C. H., Schmeelk-Cone, K. H., & Zimmerman, M. A. (2003). Racial identity, racial discrimination, perceived stress, and psychological distress among African American young adults. *Journal of Health and Social Behavior*, 44, 302–17.

Sellers, R. M., & Shelton, J. (2003). The role of racial identity in perceived racial discrimination. *Journal of Personality and Social Psychology*, 84, 1079–92.

Shavers, V. L., Fagan, P., Jones, D., Klein, W. M. P., Boyington, J., Moten, C., & Rorie, E. (2012). The state of research on racial/ethnic discrimination in the receipt of health care. *American Journal of Public Health*, 102, 953–66.

Shaw v. Reno, 509 U.S. 639 (1993).

Shelton, J. N., & Richeson, J. A. (2005). Pluralistic ignorance and intergroup contact. *Journal of Personality and Social Psychology*, 88, 91–107.

Sherbert v. Verner, 374 U.S. 398 (1963).

Sibley, Chris G., & Duckitt, J. (2008). Personality and prejudice: A meta-analysis and theoretical review. *Personality and Social Psychology Review*, 12, 248–79.

Sidanius, J., & Pratto, F. (1999). *Social dominance: An intergroup theory of social hierarchy and oppression.* New York: Cambridge University Press.

Sidanius, J., Pratto, F., van Laar, C., & Levin, S. (2004). Social dominance theory: Its agenda and method. *Political Psychology*, 25, 845–80.

Simons, R. L., Murry, V., McLoyd, V., Lin, K. H., Cutrona, C., & Conger, R. D. (2002). Discrimination, crime, ethnic identity, and parenting as correlates of depressive symptoms among African American children: A multilevel analysis. *Development and Psychopathology*, 14, 371–93.

Sinclair, L., & Kunda, Z. (1999). Reactions to a black professional: Motivated inhibition and activation of conflicting stereotypes. *Journal of Personality and Social Psychology*, 77, 885–904.

Skiba, R. J., Michael, R. S., Nardo, A. C., & Peterson, R. (2002). The color of discipline: Sources of racial and gender disproportionality in school punishment. *Urban Review*, 34, 317–42.

Sleeter, C. E., & Grant, C. A. (1987). An analysis of multicultural education in the United States. *Harvard Educational Review*, 57, 421–44.

Smetana, J. G. (2006). Social-cognitive domain theory: Consistencies and variations in children's moral and social judgments. In M. Killen & J. G. Smetana (eds.), *Handbook of moral development* (119–54). Mahwah, NJ: Erlbaum.

Smith, R. J., & Levinson, J. D. (2012). The impact of implicit racial bias on the exercise of prosecutorial discretion. *Seattle University Law Review*, 35, 795–826.

Snyder v. Phelps, 131 S.Ct. 1207 (2011).

Sommers, S. R., & Norton, M. I. (2007). Race-based judgments, race-neutral justifications: Experimental examination of peremptory use and the Batson challenge procedure. *Law and Human Behavior*, 31, 261–73.

Son Hing, L. S., Li, W., & Zanna, M. P. (2002). Inducing hypocrisy to reduce prejudicial responses among aversive racists. *Journal of Experimental Social Psychology*, 38, 71–78.

Spencer, S. J., Fein, S., Wolfe, C. T., Fong, C., & Dunn, M. A. (1998). Automatic activation of stereotypes: The role of self-image threat. *Personality and Social Psychology Bulletin*, 24, 1139–52.

Steele, C. (1997). A threat in the air: How stereotypes shape the intellectual identities and performance of women and African Americans. *American Psychologist*, 52, 613–29.

Stephan, C. W., Renfro, L., & Stephan, W. G. (2004). The evaluation of multicultural education programs: Techniques and a meta-analysis. In W. G. Stephan & W. P. Vogt (eds.), *Education programs for improving intergroup relations: Theory, research, and practice* (227–42). New York: Teachers College Press.

Stephan, W. G. (1986). Effects of school desegregation: An evaluation 30 years after *Brown*. In M. Saks & L. Saxe (eds.), *Advances in applied social psychology* (181–206). New York: Academic Press.

Stephan, W. G., & Finlay, K. (1999). The role of empathy in improving intergroup relations. *Journal of Social Issues*, 55, 729–43.

Stewart, T. L., LaDuke, J. R., Bracht, C., Sweet, B. A. M., & Gamarel, K. E. (2003). Do the "Eyes" have it? A program evaluation of Jane Elliott's "Blue-Eyes/Brown-Eyes" diversity training exercise. *Journal of Applied Social Psychology*, 33, 1898–1921.

Sue, D. W., Capodilupo, C. M., Torino, G. C., Bucceri, J. M., Holder, A. M. B., Nadal, K. L., & Esquilin, M. (2007). Racial microaggressions in everyday life: Implications for clinical practice. *American Psychologist*, 62, 271–86.

Suter v. Artist M., 503 U.S. 347 (1992).

Swaim, R. C., & Kelly, K. (2008). Efficacy of a randomized trial of a community- and school-based anti-violence media intervention among small-town middle school youth. *Prevention Science*, 9, 202–14.

Swann v. Charlotte-Mecklenburg Board of Education, 402 U.S. 1 (1971).

Szalacha, L. A. (2003). Safer sexual diversity climates: Lessons learned from an evaluation of Massachusetts safe schools program for gay and lesbian students. *American Journal of Education*, 110, 58–88.

Szalacha, L. A., Erkut, S., Coll, C. G., Alarcon, O., Fields, J. P., & Ceder, I. (2003). Discrimination and Puerto Rican children's and adolescents' mental health. *Cultural Diversity & Ethnic Minority Psychology*, 9, 141–55.

Szapocznik, J., & Kurtines, W. M. (1993). Family psychology and cultural diversity: Opportunities for theory, research, and application. *American Psychologist*, 48, 400–407.

Talaska, C. A., Fiske, S. T., & Chaiken, S. (2008). Legitimating racial discrimination: Emotions, not beliefs, best predict discrimination in a meta-analysis. *Social Justice Research*, 21, 263–96.

Taylor, D. M., Wright, S. C., & Porter, L. E. (1994). Dimensions of perceived discrimination: The personal/group discrimination discrepancy. In M. P. Zanna & J. M. Olson (eds.), *The psychology of prejudice: The Ontario symposium* (vol. 7, pp. 233–55). Hillsdale, NJ: Erlbaum.

Telecommunications Act of 1996, 47 U.S.C. § 151 (2012).

Tenenbaum, H. R., & Leaper, C. (2002). Are parents' gender schemas related to their children's gender-related cognitions? A meta-analysis. *Developmental Psychology*, 38, 615–30.

Tillfors, M., Persson, S., Willén, M., & Burk, W. J. (2012). Prospective links between social anxiety and adolescent peer relations. *Journal of Adolescence*, 35, 1255–63.

Tinker v. Des Moines Independent Community School District, 393 U.S. 503 (1969).

Tinkler, J. E., Li, Y. E., & Mollborn, S. (2007). Can legal interventions change beliefs? The effect of exposure to sexual harassment policy on men's gender beliefs. *Social Psychology Quarterly*, 70, 480–94.

Todd, A. R., Bodenhausen, G. V., Richeson, J. A., & Galinsky, A. D. (2011). Perspective taking combats automatic expressions of racial bias. *Journal of Personality and Social Psychology*, 100, 1027–42.

Todd, A. R., Galinsky, A. D., & Bodenhausen, G. V. (2012). Perspective taking undermines stereotype maintenance processes: Evidence from social memory, behavior explanation, and information solicitation. *Social Cognition*, 30, 94–108.

Tropp, L. R., & Prenovost, M. A. (2008). The role of intergroup contact in predicting children's inter-ethnic attitudes: Evidence from meta-analytic and field studies. In

S. Levy & M. Killen (eds.), *Intergroup attitudes and relations in childhood through adulthood* (236–48). New York: Oxford University Press.

Ttofi, M. M., & Farrington, D. P. (2011). Effectiveness of school-based programs to reduce bullying: A systematic and meta-analytic review. *Journal of Experimental Criminology, 7,* 27–56.

Turiel, E. (2002). *The culture of morality: Social development, context, and conflict.* Cambridge: Cambridge University Press.

Turner, R. N., & Brown, R. (2008). Improving children's attitudes toward refugees: An evaluation of a school-based multicultural curriculum and an anti-racist intervention. *Journal of Applied Social Psychology, 38,* 1295–1328.

Turner, R. N., Crisp, R. J., & Lambert, E. (2007). Imagining intergroup contact can improve intergroup attitudes. *Group Processes & Intergroup Relations, 10,* 427–41.

Tynes, B. M., Umana-Taylor, A. J., Rose, C. A., Lin, J., & Anderson, C. J. (2012). Online racial discrimination and the protective function of ethnic identity and self-esteem for African American adolescents. *Developmental Psychology, 48,* 343–55.

United States v. American Library Association, 539 U.S. 194 (2003).

United States v. Carolene Products Co., 304 U.S. 144 (1938).

United States v. Playboy Entertainment Group, Inc., 529 U.S. 803 (2000).

United States v. Scotland Neck City Board of Education, 407 U.S. 484 (1972).

United States v. Stevens, 130 S.Ct. 1577 (2010).

Verkuyten, M. (2008). Multiculturalism and group evaluations among minority and majority groups. In S. Levy & M. Killen (eds.), *Intergroup attitudes and relations in childhood through adulthood* (157–72). Oxford: Oxford University Press.

Verkuyten, M., & Thijs, J. (2001). Ethnic and gender bias among Dutch and Turkish children in late childhood: The role of social context. *Infant and Child Development, 10,* 203–17.

——— (2002). Racist victimization among children in the Netherlands: The effect of ethnic group and school. *Ethnic and Racial Studies, 25,* 310–31.

Vernonia School District 47J v. Acton, 515 U.S. 646 (1995).

Vervoort, M. H. M., Scholte, R. H. J., & Overbeek, G. (2010). Bullying and victimization among adolescents: The role of ethnicity and ethnic composition of school class. *Journal of Youth and Adolescence, 39,* 1–11.

Vescio, T. K., Sechrist, G. B., & Paolucci, M. P. (2003). Perspective taking and prejudice reduction: The mediational role of empathy arousal and situational attributions. *European Journal of Social Psychology, 33,* 455–72.

Wagner, U., Tropp, L. R., Finchilescu, G., & Tredoux, C. (eds.) (2008). *Improving intergroup relations.* Malden, MA: Blackwell.

Walsemann, K. M., & Bell, B. A. (2010). Integrated schools, segregated curriculum: Effects of within-school segregation on adolescent health behaviors and educational aspirations. *American Journal of Public Health, 100,* 1687–95.

Walz v. Tax Commission, 397 U.S. 664 (1970).

Wechsler, H. (1959). Toward neutral principles of constitutional law. *Harvard Law Review, 73,* 1–35.

Weiner, M. J., & Wright, F. E. (1973). Effects of undergoing arbitrary discrimination upon subsequent attitudes toward a minority group. *Journal of Applied Social Psychology*, 3, 94–102.

Wells, S. J., Merritt, L. M., & Briggs, H. E. (2009). Bias, racism, and evidence-based practice: The case for more focused development of the child welfare evidence base. *Children and Youth Services Review*, 31, 1160–71.

West Virginia State Board of Education v. Barnette, 319 U.S. 624 (1943).

Wheeler, S. C., & Petty, R. E. (2001). The effects of stereotype activation on behavior: A review of possible mechanisms. *Psychological Bulletin*, 127, 797–826.

Williams, J. E., & Moreland, J. K. (1976). *Race, color, and the young child.* Chapel Hill: University of North Carolina Press

Williams, R. M., Jr. (1947). *The reduction of intergroup tensions.* New York: Social Science Research Council.

Wilmot, K. A., & Spohn, C. (2004). Prosecutorial discretion and real-offense sentencing: An analysis of relevant conduct under the Federal Sentencing Guidelines. *Criminal Justice Policy Review*, 15, 324–43.

Wilson, T. D., Lindsey, S., & Schooler, T. Y. (2000). A model of dual attitudes. *Psychological Review*, 107, 101–26.

Wisconsin v. Yoder, 406 U.S. 205 (1972).

Wittig, M. A., & Molina, L. E. (2000). Moderators and mediators of prejudice reduction in multicultural education. In S. Oskamp (ed.), *Reducing prejudice and discrimination* (295–318). Mahweh, NJ: Erlbaum.

Wolsko, C., Park, B., & Judd, C. M. (2006). Considering the Tower of Babel: Correlates of assimilation and multiculturalism among ethnic minority and majority groups in the United States. *Social Justice Research*, 19, 277–306.

Wolsko, C., Park, B., Judd, C. M., & Wittenbrink, B. (2000). Framing interethnic ideology: Effects of multicultural and color-blind perspectives on judgments of groups and individuals. *Journal of Personality and Social Psychology*, 78, 536–654.

Wright, S. C., Aron, A., McLaughlin-Volpe, T., & Ropp, S. A. (1997). The extended contact effect: Knowledge of cross-group friendships and prejudice. *Journal of Personality and Social Psychology*, 73, 73–90.

Wright v. Council of the City of Emporia, 407 U.S. 451 (1972).

Wygant v. Jackson Board of Education, 476 U.S. 267 (1986).

Youngberg v. Romeo, 457 U.S. 307 (1982).

Zelman v. Simmons-Harris, 536 U.S. 639 (2002).

Zirkel, S. (2008). The influence of multicultural educational practice on student outcomes and intergroup relations. *Teachers College Record*, 110, 1147–81.

# INDEX

## ABOUT THE AUTHOR

Roger J. R. Levesque is Professor of Criminal Justice, Indiana University. He writes on topics mainly addressing the nature of adolescence, family life, and the laws that shape our intimate lives. He teaches courses on adolescence and children's rights and serves as Editor-in-Chief of the *Journal of Youth and Adolescence* and the *New Criminal Law Review*.

Lightning Source UK Ltd.
Milton Keynes UK
UKOW04n1320210415

250043UK00002B/7/P